D1038588

Introduction to Middle School Teaching

Introduction to Middle School Teaching

Larry L. Sale

Gardner-Webb College

CHARLES E. MERRILL PUBLISHING CO.
A Bell & Howell Company
Columbus Toronto London Sydney

Published by
Charles E. Merrill Publishing Company
A Bell and Howell Company
Columbus, Ohio 43216

This book was set in Optima and Windsor.

The production editor was Dawna Ramage Ayers.

The cover was prepared by Will Chenoweth.

Library of Congress Catalog Card Number: 78-71167
International Standard Book Number: 0-675-08279-X
1 2 3 4 5 6 7 8 9 10/ 85 84 83 82 81 80 79
Printed in the United States of America

Foreword

The education of the early adolescent in American society has long contained a significant paradox. On the one hand, educators have recognized the crucial importance of these years in shaping the values, social skills, and broad competencies which to a large extent determine the individual student's educational and vocational future. On the other hand, school programs for early adolescents have been staffed chiefly by persons trained for roles in other segments of the school, i.e., for teaching in the elementary or the senior high school.

I once surveyed over 1000 secondary school teachers-in-training to discover that 80 percent of them were planning and preparing to teach in senior high schools. Subsequent follow-up revealed that 800 of these teachers, following graduation, accepted teaching positions not in high schools, but rather in middle schools. I also recall clearly, while serving as a public school administrator, transferring many effective elementary teachers to the early adolescent grades in the hope that they would adapt to these older and different pre- and early teenagers. Experience clearly shows that the successes of school programs for early adolescents have been, most often, the result of the dedication and the trial and error learning of experienced teachers. We have not prepared teachers at the preservice level who are equipped to teach and understand early adolescents from the outset of their professional careers. Dr. Sale in this book carries us a giant step forward in the campaign to prepare successful middle school teachers.

This is a propitious time for *Introduction to Middle School Teaching* to appear. It is now clear that the middle school movement is firmly established. The demand for teachers who are knowledgeable about its mission and skilled in techniques of working with middle school students will be as great as any in our field.

Readers are urged to immerse themselves in the numerous beyond-the-book activities suggested by Dr. Sale. There are many persons who are successful high school or elementary school teachers who would not be equally effective as middle school instructors. The reason for this lies in their inability to understand both students and subject matter, and especially in the insecurities they feel in dealing with students who behave as children one minute and as adults the next. There are teachers, however, who find that the multiplicity of challenges and unpredictability of student responses are both rewarding and exciting. One must become part of the action of middle school education to ascertain if one's intellectual understanding can be matched by one's visceral response to the participants.

As you learn about successful middle school teaching, you may find it helpful to keep the following frame of reference in mind. Remember that in any educational setting there are three kinds of variables or factors which the teacher must consider. The first of these variables might be labeled as *irrelevant* since they do not affect how much a student learns. The organization of the school and the location of classrooms are examples. A second set of variables are *relevant,* that is, they do affect how much a student learns, but they are also *nonmanipulatable,* that is, the teacher cannot change them. An illustration is that intelligent students consistently learn more than less intelligent pupils. A third set of factors is *both relevant* and *manipulatable.* For example, research shows a close relationship between amount of time spent in studying a topic and how much is learned about that topic. Your task as a teacher-learner, then, is to attempt to identify variables in middle school education; to ignore the irrelevant factors; to recognize and accept those factors which are relevant but unchangeable; and to concentrate your attention on those variables which both make a difference in how much middle school students learn and which you can modify and control. Mastery of this process will assist you to learn to become an effective middle school teacher.

Frederick R. Cyphert

Preface

Historically, we have had the problem in American education of having to select elementary teachers and move them up to teach the emerging adolescent, or we have had to select high school teachers and move them down.

Recently, we have come to the realization that we need teachers specifically trained to teach the emerging adolescent learner. I am currently serving as a middle school teacher trainer, and my students have motivated me to write *Introduction to Middle School Teaching*. I desire to share these concepts and strategies with anyone concerned with providing better education for middle school learners.

Introduction to Middle School Teaching is primarily designed to help the prospective middle school teacher develop an understanding of middle school philosophy and curriculum and to develop competence in teaching methods appropriate for the emerging adolescent learner. A secondary intent of the book is to provide information for anyone who desires to learn about teaching the middle school learner.

Introduction to Middle School Teaching is a product of my sixteen years of teaching experience in middle school education. I have served as a middle school classroom teacher, supervisor of middle school student teachers, professor of middle school education in both private and public institutions of higher education, and consultant for development of model middle school programs in several states. The text is a practical how-to-do-it book that interrelates middle school research and practical classroom application. It is most appropriate for preservice or in-service courses in middle school methods, middle school curriculum, teaching emerging adolescent learners, junior high curriculum/methods or elementary school curriculum/methods, and student teaching/internship.

To engage you as an inquirer, open-ended questions, self-evaluation instruments, and related inquiry processes are used extensively throughout the book. Additional significant features of the book are:

1. The book treats relevant concerns of the middle school teacher, including program development, characteristics of the emerging adolescent learner, classroom management and discipline, personalizing instructional strategies, assessing learner progress, teaching exceptional learners, career education, and guidance.
2. Each chapter contains the most current research in middle school

education. A bibliography of reference materials is included at the end of each chapter.

3. A special feature of this book involves the use of learning modules. To facilitate flexible use of the text and to reinforce learnings, a self-instructional learning module is included at the end of each chapter. Modules may be used with or without the chapter material. This feature allows you to design a personalized program of study based upon your specific needs.
4. A great variety of "real-world" activities are provided throughout the book to enable you to internalize and reinforce learnings.

I should like to express a special note of appreciation to my wife, Jan, who has played a key role in the development of this book, providing support and patience, editorial advice, research assistance, and typing the manuscript. Her practical classroom experience as a middle school teacher has served as a constant reference to keep my ideas relevant and workable. I would also like to give special thanks to our daughter and son, Kelly and Lowell, who have provided daily models of life during the middle school years. I sincerely appreciate the contributions of the many other individuals who have contributed to the development of the text, including Linda Donahey, Gilbert File, and Joyce Summers. Finally, thanks to all the students at Gardner-Webb College who have given me the opportunity to serve as their teacher.

L. L. S.

Contents

Part 1 The Middle School Arrives

Part 2 Teaching the Middle School Learner

Part 1

The Middle School Arrives

Chapter 1

The Middle School: An Overview

Educators and parents are becoming increasingly concerned about the quality of the educational program currently being provided for the child who is in the emerging adolescent period of growth and development. Research indicates that this period of transition from childhood to adolescence, or the in-between ages of approximately ten to fourteen, is characterized by very significant physical, emotional, and social change processes. Because of these growth characteristics, the emerging adolescent requires an educational program that is significantly different from that provided for the elementary or secondary school student.

Widespread dissatisfaction with the traditional junior high among both American educators and the public has led to the emergence of a new type of school for the emerging adolescent, the middle school. What are the major purposes, the underlying rationale for the existence of the American middle school? How is the middle school different from the traditional junior high school in philosophy, curriculum, instruction, and administration? What competencies are needed to become a successful teacher of middle school learners? Let's begin to find some answers to these and other significant questions.

The middle school is designed to provide custom-tailored educational experiences for the student who is making the transition from childhood to adolescence. Eichhorn (1966) has referred to this period as "transescence," the stage of development that begins prior to the onset of puberty and extends through the early stages of adolescence. For most students, this period ranges from age nine through age fourteen. A middle school's success is based on the degree to which it meets the developmental needs of the emerging adolescents who are going through this transitional stage of development.

Let's look briefly at some of the problems associated with traditional programs for the emerging adolescent. Many educators have charged that the curriculum of the traditional junior high school is a watered-down version of senior high curriculum and is not specifically designed to meet the needs of the emerging adolescent. In other words, it follows the old concept of "getting them ready for high school." The focal point of the curriculum, however, should not be the student's career in later years. Instead, the emphasis should be on meeting the student's current and emerging needs. We cannot get students ready for tomorrow by neglecting their needs today. Intellectually stimulating experiences that build on academic learning acquired during the elementary school years should be emphasized and used toward helping each student to become a more self-dependent learner.

A second major criticism of past programs is that upon entering junior high the student often finds himself thrust into a rigidly organized, departmentalized program that presents too abrupt a change from his relatively secure, self-contained elementary school background. What is needed in terms of instructional organization is a cooperative planning-teaching unit that incorporates the security of the elementary school program with the flexibility and strength that comes through students' identifying with several teacher models.

An excessive emphasis on interscholastic sports for the few students who excel rather than on appropriate health and physical fitness programs for all pupils has been a problem in the past. A greater emphasis should be placed upon helping each individual student develop a healthy body through personal hygiene, physical fitness, and carry-over sports such as tennis, golf, and swimming. Team sports should be provided, but there should be less emphasis on mimicking secondary school athletics.

Another problem found in the traditional junior high is the separation of students into two groups or tracks consisting of vocational education and academics. This problem dates back to 1905 when approximately two-thirds of the pupils enrolled in the public school dropped out before they reached grade nine. In order to provide an educational program relevant to this phenomenon, the junior high was created with two types of programs: (1) a terminal vocational education program for those who planned to enter the labor market and (2) an introduction to high school academics for the small number that were going on to secondary or postsecondary studies. Over the years, this program division has resulted in vocational education being viewed as primarily for the lower academic achievers, thus causing a stigma to be placed on vocational education as a separate program. The modern middle school program should emphasize career education for all students, helping each student to interrelate vocational and academic concepts and skills. It should focus on exploration of varied occupational roles in society and avoid specific job training. Specialization can better be achieved in later years.

Historically, we have not had teachers who were specifically trained to teach the emerging adolescent learner. We have had the problem of having to select elementary school teachers and move them up the school ladder or select high school teachers and move them down the school ladder. In both cases, both the student and the teacher suffer. Neither elementary nor secondary teachers are trained to understand the growth and developmental characteristics of the emerging adolescent. The emerging adolescent requires a teacher specifically and competently prepared in middle school psychology, curriculum, instructional organization, and teaching methods. The transitional nature of adolescence demands a transition in the role of the teacher from being primarily a dispenser of knowledge to being a coordinator of many sources of knowledge, with significant emphasis upon the functions of diagnosis, prescription, planning, decision making, utilization of human and material resources, and evaluation.

Too many "in-between-agers" have not received sufficient assistance in the development of a personal values system. Teaching efforts in this area have often been shoddy or neglected. We need to help the student analyze various value orientations in society and internalize a personal set of values in which he can truly believe. The teacher need not preach, but rather teach value analysis strategies; a better treatment of valuing should result in the removal or reduction of tension that often erupts during the emerging adolescent period.

Another problem associated with traditional programs for the emerging adolescent has been the excessive emphasis on evaluation in terms of the group norm, or normative evaluation. Since the student is progressing through a transitional period of growth and development, he may vary significantly from his peers in intellectual, physical, and social competence. Greater emphasis should be placed on criterion-referencing than on normative or group-comparison evaluation. Each student should know where he stands in regard to group, school, local, and national norms; it is much more important, however, for the student to be evaluated on the basis of his progress in relation to his own ability.

Some school divisions have attempted to develop a middle school program by simply juggling the grades around in such combinations as 6-2-4, 6-3-3, 5-3-4, or 4-4-4. Others are merely changing the sign on the front entrance of the school from "Junior" to "Middle." Juggling grades and changing labels will have little, if any, positive effect on learners. The central question is: How can we provide a better educational program designed to meet the needs, interests, and abilities of our local population of emerging adolescent learners? Any changes made in existing programs must be based upon needs assessment, valid research, and proven alternatives related to educating the emerging adolescent learner.

Major Characteristics of the Middle School

The middle school should provide:

1. A custom-tailored program attuned to the growth and development characteristics of an emerging adolescent learner. The environment should emphasize that the learner, not the program, is important.
2. An intellectually stimulating curriculum that is rich in options and exploratory experiences and that builds on learning acquired during the elementary school years rather than mimicking the secondary school program.
3. Instructional organization patterns that provide students with a smooth transition from elementary to secondary school, incorporating the security features of the self-contained classroom with the benefits of interaction with varied teachers.
4. A personalized health and physical education program that emphasizes physical fitness, personal hygiene, and carry-over sports for all as opposed to secondary school-type team sports aimed at a few students.
5. Career-based curricular experiences for all students that interrelate career exploration with all academic areas.
6. Competent teachers, administrators, guidance staff, and related school personnel specifically prepared to help the emerging adolescent learner.
7. Assistance to students in developing a personal values system based on careful assessment of various value positions in society. Assistance in developing positive self-concepts should also be provided to all students.
8. A school evaluation program that places primary emphasis on assessment based on the progress a student makes in relation to his own ability and secondary emphasis on assessment in terms of the norm.
9. Facilities and material resources adaptable to the current needs of the emerging adolescent.
10. A school-community relations program that provides for positive citizen involvement in and support of school activities.

In recent years, the American public has come to the realization that what is needed is a program that is based on meeting the educational needs of the emerging adolescent learner through the application of the best research-based practices in psychology, curriculum, instruction, and administration. The middle school has firmly established itself as a legitimate and acceptable model for educating the emerging adolescent in America.

Leadership Implications for Effective Programs

The new middle school, being less hampered by tradition and standardization than the traditional junior high, provides educators and local citizens with an excellent opportunity to create educational structures and processes that are flexible and adaptive to the changing and transitional nature of emerging adolescents. Unfortunately, because of reasons such as overcrowding, finances, or busing, some school systems have expediently created so-called middle schools with little or no planning. Although such schools are labeled "middle schools," they often do not incorporate the program ingredients of a real middle school. The establishment of a new middle school or a reorganized middle school must involve a comprehensive planning process that includes input from educators, students, and citizens. Since the middle school serves as a critical link or bridge between elementary and secondary education, planning groups should include individuals representing both these important areas. Planning processes should emphasize the correlation and interrelationships among elementary, middle, and secondary education.

A wide range of individual differences will generally be found in a representative population of incoming middle school students. Because of this fact and the nature of the emerging adolescent, curriculum programs must be custom-tailored to provide students at widely varying entry points the opportunity to move forward successfully. Effective instructional programs increase, not decrease, the differences among learners. Too often we make the mistake of attempting to group students into "alike" instructional modes that are intended to decrease differences in the student population. The middle school has a unique opportunity to provide programs and services to serve the personalized needs of a variable and transitional school population. A renamed administrative unit without the internal changes in philosophy, purposes, and programs necessary to meet these needs will be unsuccessful.

Rosenau (1975) conducted a research study to identify practices recommended for middle schools by authors of current literature on the subject and to determine how the practices described in the literature compared with actual practices of middle schools. The characteristics derived from the literature were verified by a jury of six nationally recognized middle school educators. A questionnaire was developed and submitted to 200 randomly selected middle schools to determine the relationship between characteristics identified in the literature and practices identified in the schools. Rosenau reached two major conclusions:

1. The middle school curriculum should be a blend of general education and a variety of exploratory activities.
2. In the development of a middle school curriculum, greater emphasis should be placed on the philosophy of an individual school district than on space and building conditions.

At long last, teacher education programs are changing to provide specially trained middle school personnel. This is a wholesome and exciting change process that is long overdue. Across the nation, we are experiencing a significant movement toward making better educational provisions for both the preservice and in-service middle school teacher. Several states have recently changed their teacher certification procedures and have developed a middle school certificate. North Carolina was one of the early leaders in this area with the adoption of a 4–9 certificate for middle school teachers.

A survey conducted in January 1978 showed that fourteen states now issue a middle school certificate and that thirteen others have a proposed middle school certificate.[1] Processes should be developed in every state to create a middle school certificate for school personnel, establish guidelines for development of middle schools, and disseminate information concerning middle school developments throughout the state. Each state department of education should have a middle school coordination committee and a middle school coordinator.

Greater attention must be given to the retraining and reorientation of teachers and related school personnel in middle school philosophy and processes. School districts should avoid "hit or miss" in-service programs that claim to retrain an elementary or secondary school teacher for successful middle school teaching by simply adding one or two brief workshops or courses to the usual training activities. Formal training in the district or on a college campus may be essential, but it must be accompanied by carefully planned, continuous on-the-job assistance over an extended period of time. The best model combines formal and informal training that is relevant to the individual teacher's own classroom.

Suggestions for providing in-service education experiences for middle school personnel include:

---

1. This information was obtained from Robert M. Malinka, Project Director, National Middle School Resource Center, SCIPS Building, 901 North Carrollton Avenue, Indianapolis, Indiana 46202.

1. Conduct a needs assessment of school personnel.
2. Develop a well-planned in-service program based on priority needs.
3. Read and discuss middle school publications.
4. Survey middle school research studies.
5. Visit model middle schools in your state or region. If funds permit, visit selected nationally recognized middle schools. Plan your visits. Limit the number of people in your visitation team and program each team member to collect specific information regarding the physical plant, the guidance program, exploratory programs, pupil assessment, teaching methods, and the administration. Each visitation team should include representatives from faculty, administration, school board, and lay public.

   During one visitation team's plane trip from one state to another, one teacher was overheard to remark, "I hope I learn a lot about the middle school, but this is fantastic. I've never flown before! When I get back home I'm going to have so much to tell my students." Like that teacher, you may have an unexpected learning experience during a school visitation. When you return home, you should therefore collate and synthesize all the information you have collected, including the "bonus" information, and apply it to your local situation.
6. Hold faculty workshops with guest consultants. When possible, arrange to hold them in settings away from the school. A lodge or camp setting is especially good for weekend workshops, allowing faculty to combine business with pleasure. Maintaining faculty involvement and morale is an important consideration in planning these workshops.
7. Always follow up workshops with practical application, support, and supervision in the regular classroom setting.
8. Arrange for small groups of teachers to be released from their regular teaching responsibilities in order to participate in selected in-service experiences.
9. Select consultants very carefully in terms of expertise and specific personnel needs. Require consultants to demonstrate the material they are covering rather than only talk about it.
10. Involve emerging adolescents and faculty members in joint in-service ventures that focus on the kind of school they need and desire.

Leadership of National Organizations

The educator who is interested in providing leadership in the development of a middle school can obtain invaluable assistance from the resources of two major national organizations: the National Middle School Association and the Association for Supervision and Curriculum Development. The National Middle School Association is an organization of middle school teachers and administrators, educators of middle school personnel at the college level, and lay community leaders who possess an interest in middle school education. The Association has three major purposes:

1. To promote the development and growth of the middle school as a distinct and necessary entity in the structure of American education
2. To disseminate information about the middle school movement
3. To promote forums for the sharing of ideas and innovations relevant to contemporary middle school programs

The first conference of the National Middle School Association was held at Columbus, Ohio, November 7–8, 1974. The Association publishes the quarterly *Middle School Journal* featuring articles by middle school practitioners. Information on membership and subscriptions to the *Middle School Journal* may be obtained by writing the National Middle School Association, P. O. Box 968, Fairborn, Ohio 45324.

The internationally recognized Association for Supervision and Curriculum Development provides valuable assistance to middle school development through working groups, publications, institutes, and related leadership activities that focus on the emerging adolescent learner. Two very valuable documents produced by ASCD include a book of readings edited by Robert R. Leeper, *Middle School in the Making* (1974), and a booklet prepared by Thomas E. Gatewood and Charles A. Dilg, *The Middle School We Need* (1975).

Self-Instruction: A Personal Note

We have explored several dimensions of the purpose and rationale for a middle school. As a prospective middle school educator, you will also want to explore some of the following questions in greater depth: What are the characteristics and needs of the emerging adolescent learner? What competencies are essential for becoming a successful middle school teacher? What specialized competencies are required to successfully teach exceptional learners? How do I establish an effective, personalized middle school instructional program? The pages that follow are designed to help you find some answers to these and related questions.

Each chapter is followed by a learning module to help you internalize concepts and skills and practice self-instructional behaviors you will later want to employ in middle school teaching. In too many cases, prospective teachers have been asked to read, listen to a lecture, and take a test.

This represents a very narrow, sterile type of instruction. What is even worse, prospective teachers are often told in the lectures they are asked to listen to that they should not lecture too much to students! A well-presented, stimulating lecture could be a very effective mode of instruction for some learners. Do all students, however, learn the same way? Are all students ready to pursue the same objectives? Obviously, the answer to these questions is no. Some students learn best by viewing television, while others learn best by viewing a film, listening to a recording, performing a concrete experiment, listening to a lecture, participating in a group discussion, working independently, or in a combination of ways. We need to give specific attention to the learning act as well as the teaching act.

In attempting to personalize instruction, we need to let students know what they need to learn, how they can learn it, and how they can evaluate their progress. The learning module is a delivery system, a practical instructional tool that helps us communicate this information to students. It is a set of learning activities intended to facilitate the student's achievement of a specific objective or objectives. Although a learning module may be referred to by different terms including *mini-pack, modular instruction, Learning Activity Package* (LAP), or *contract,* each should contain the following basic ingredients:

1. *Title*—the name of the module
2. *Overview*—a brief prospectus of what will be found in the module
3. *Pretest*—an index to what the learner already knows about the subject to be treated in the module
4. *Behavioral objective(s)*[2]—statements of what behavior(s) the learner must demonstrate upon completion of the module
5. *Required/optional activities*—experiences designed to enable the learner to reach the objective(s)
6. *Posttest*—a measurement of the degree to which the learner has demonstrated competency in reaching the objective(s)

Each module should be designed to lead the learner through a series of programmed educational experiences relevant to his interests and goals at a particular time. In addition to the essential ingredients stated above, a module may include additional elements such as teacher checkpoints and varied opportunities for learner self-evaluation. One major goal of most teachers is to help learners to assume greater responsibility for their own learning. A learning module offers learners several opportunities to become decisionmakers; it allows them to make decisions about the content they will study, the activities in which they will engage, and the

2. For a detailed treatment of behavioral objectives, see Chapter 9.

modes of instruction that they will employ. The teacher assumes the roles of diagnostician, programmer, facilitator of learning, but not that of a "crutch." Each module should be based upon learners' self-pacing and self-assessment in addition to evaluation by the teacher. "Teacher-made" or "tailor-made" modules are highly desirable. Commercially prepared modules, on the other hand, will require modification to be appropriate to the learner. The teacher who understands the philosophy and procedures involved in the design and use of a learning module is in a much better position to select from commercially prepared materials than one who is not. The wholesale adoption of commercially prepared modules could be disastrous! That is why it is important to remember that the advantages of the module lie in its emphasis upon sound principles of personalized instruction.

The module is not a panacea. It is, however, one of our best attempts to date to reach the goal of providing for individual learner differences. Also, the module does not negate the need for other modes of instruction. It should be used selectively and effectively in conjunction with large and small group instruction, pupil-team learning, simulation, and a great variety of other modes of instruction. An entire instructional program that uses only learning modules to the exclusion of all other modes of instruction could be as ineffective as a program that excluded learning modules. In other words, any instructional tool can lose its effectiveness through misuse or overuse.

At the end of each chapter in this book, you will have the opportunity to engage in a learning module experience. Through this experience, you shall have the opportunity to develop competencies relating to the subject matter treated within the module, to become a more confident, self-reliant learner, and to develop skills that will aid you in utilizing learning modules with middle school learners.

Summary

Educators and citizens have become increasingly concerned about the quality of educational programs provided for emerging adolescent learners. The special needs of the emerging adolescent require an educational program that is significantly different from that provided for the elementary or secondary school student.

Traditional programs have included characteristics identified by educators as ineffective and undesirable in educating the emerging adolescent. The middle school is designed to incorporate philosophy, programs, and teaching strategies that are in tune with the transitional growth and development needs of the emerging adolescent. At this time, significant changes are occurring in program development, preservice and in-service teacher preparation, and teacher certification processes designed to provide personalized, successful learning experiences for middle school students. As a prospective middle school teacher, your challenge is to become the most competent teacher possible. Future middle school learners will profit from your efforts.

REFERENCES

Eichorn, Donald. *The Middle School.* New York: The Center for Applied Research in Education, 1966.

Gatewood, Thomas E., and Dilg, Charles A. *The Middle School We Need.* Washington, D.C.: Association for Supervision and Curriculum Development, 1975.

Leeper, Robert, ed. *Middle School in the Making.* Washington, D.C.: Association for Supervision and Curriculum Development, 1974.

Rosenau, Alan Edgar. "A Comparative Study of Middle School Practices Recommended in Current Literature and Practices of Selected Middle Schools." *Middle School Journal* 6 (1975): 53–54.

Learning Module

The Middle School: Purpose and Rationale

Directions

This module is designed to help you develop a basic understanding of the purposes and characteristics of a middle school. Begin by taking the pretest. Review your pretest with your instructor who will assist you in selecting appropriate objectives. Complete the activities that will assist you in reaching your objectives. Then take the posttest to see what you have accomplished.

Pretest

1. Present the major purposes of the middle school.
2. Contrast the objectives and program characteristics of a modern middle school and a traditional junior high school.
3. Discuss some of the major problems or criticisms associated with traditional programs for emerging adolescents.
4. Discuss the role and functions of the National Middle School Association.
5. Present some specific guidelines for the development of a model middle school.

Check

Review your pretest performance with your instructor.

Objectives

Select those that are appropriate for you:
1. Discuss recent research findings relative to planning successful programs for the emerging adolescent learner.
2. Construct a curricular model of the middle school we need.
3. Discuss the major components of the historical development of the American junior high school.
4. Contrast the philosophy and programs of a junior high school and a middle school.

5. Compare the results of your visits to middle schools in two different school districts.

Activities

(Numbers in parentheses correlate with corresponding objectives.)

1. Read the booklet *The Middle School We Need* by Thomas E. Gatewood and Charles A. Dilg (Washington, D.C.: Association for Supervision and Curriculum Development, 1975). (2) (4)
2. Interview two middle school principals concerning their schools' purposes and programs. (4) (5)
3. Read selected readings from *Middle School in the Making,* a book of readings edited by Robert R. Leeper (Washington, D.C.: Association for Supervision and Curriculum Development, 1974). (1) (2)
4. Read Chapters 1 and 2 of *The Emergent Middle School* by William M. Alexander and others (New York: Holt, Rinehart, and Winston, 1969). (3) (4)
5. Invite a middle school curriculum specialist to class to discuss the topic, "The Rationale for Development of a Middle School." (1) (2) (3) (4)
6. Review four current periodical references concerning the middle school. Report your findings in class. (1) (2) (3) (4)
7. Interview a school psychologist concerning the intellectual development of an emerging adolescent. (1)
8. Read Chapter 2, "What Level of Teaching?" in William Van Til's *Education: A Beginning,* Second Edition (Boston: Houghton Mifflin Co., 1974) with specific attention to pp. 35–47. (3)
9. Contrast the ideas presented in the following references: Gordon F. Vars, "Change—and the Junior High School," *Educational Leadership* 23(1965):189 and Thomas E. Curtis, "The Middle School in Theory and Practice," *National Association of Secondary Principals Bulletin* 52(1968):135-40. (4)
10. Interview a random sample of local citizens concerning the type of educational program they think should be provided for emerging adolescents in the local community. (1) (2)
11. Attend local or regional workshops or conferences that focus on middle school program development. (1) (2)
12. Write a brief position paper expressing your views concerning a viable educational program for emerging adolescent learners. (1) (2) (4)
13. View the multimedia presentation *The Emerging Adolescent Learner in the Middle Grades* developed by the Association for Supervision and Curriculum Development. Inquiries concerning this program

should be directed to Educational Leadership Institute, Inc., P.O. Box 863, Springfield, Massachusetts 01101. (1) (2) (3) (4)

14. Interview a random sample of current high school students who have completed a middle school program to ascertain their views concerning the strengths and weaknesses of local middle school programs. (1) (2) (3) (4) (5)
15. Write to the Executive Secretary, National Middle School Association, requesting information and materials concerning current middle school development. The Association mailing address is National Middle School Association, P.O. Box 968, Fairborn, Ohio 45324. (1) (2) (4)
16. Prepare a questionnaire and conduct a random sampling interview of current middle school students to obtain their views on current school programs. (5)

Posttest

Based on the objective(s) that you selected, prepare a written report of your findings to be presented to your instructor for evaluation. (Your report should not exceed five typewritten pages.)

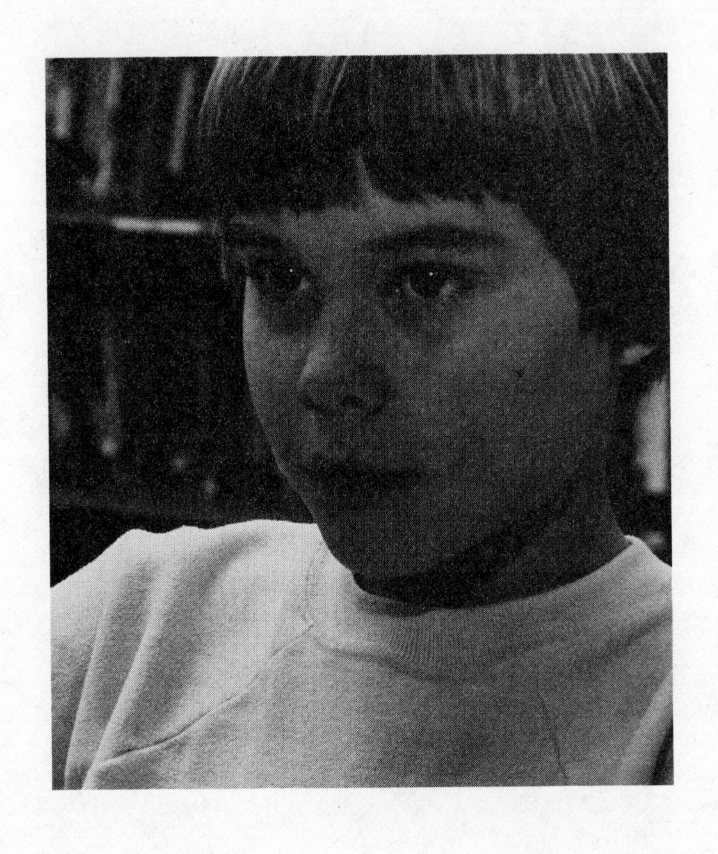

Chapter 2

The Middle Schooler: An Emerging Adolescent

As a middle school teacher, you shall encounter a most interesting and challenging learner—the emerging adolescent. In order for you to experience successful teaching, you need to understand the characteristics and needs of the learner. The emerging adolescent is progressing through a distinct period of growth and development. As we noted in Chapter 1, Eichhorn (1966) has referred to this stage of development as *transescence,* a period of growth and development that begins prior to the onset of puberty and extends through the early stages of adolescence. This period of transition from childhood to adulthood is characterized by significant physical, social, emotional, and intellectual changes. What are some of these changes? What does the prospective teacher need to know and understand in order to successfully teach the emerging adolescent? What are the characteristics and needs of a middle schooler? Let's pursue some answers to these and related questions.

The Emerging Adolescent Speaks

What is it like to be an emerging adolescent? Let's listen to what the learners are saying. The following excerpts are taken from written responses given by eleven-year-old students in a middle school classroom to the question, "What is it like to be eleven years old?"

> Being an eleven year old is very interesting. Wondering what your occupation will be, where you will go to college or if you will. It is full of concern also. Worrying about if the energy crisis will be where it is now and if maybe we in our classroom will be taking care of it.

I have fears of getting a whipping when I do something wrong. I have fears of my big brother when he gets mad at me. I'm concerned about making bad grades on my test.

I am interested in reading and I am afraid of snakes. I don't like lizzards and I don't like liver. My favorite food is dumplings.

I like girls. Some girls are pretty. Some are ugly. I have a lot of girlfriends. I like luscious legs Lynn and luscious lips Kesha.

School is okay. I'm not wild about it but its alright. Sometimes I worry though, about the teacher's attitude. She can be in a mood where she gets her paddle and slams it on a desk to get your attention or she will just say a word real loud.

I like to have my life run with happiness and joy but I guess everyone has sad and unhappy moments in their lives. To my little sister I'm probably big and not scared of anything, but I am sure scared of snakes, bees, lions, tigers, and especially the Oakland Raiders.

Sometimes I worry about the fuel crisis, because I wonder what it will be like when I'm grown up. And about Charles Manson and the "Manson family," so to speak. Thousands and thousands of Americans have been sentenced for 25, 50, 75 years of prison, and Charles Manson is eligible for parole in 1978! I wonder why that is so. Because the murders he is accused of are a disgrace to America!

I think any kind of dress is okay if it is the right length and not too far down at the top.

I'm the oldest girl and I have to do all the work.

It is hard to be eleven.

I have to make up my bed and wash dishes everyday and sweep up the floor. I don't like to wear dresses except on picture day.

Portrait of Kelly: An Emerging Adolescent

Kelly is a thirteen-year-old emerging adolescent with a promising future. She is an A student with varied interests and a zest for life. She is vocal and energetic—an instant "adult" at thirteen! Kelly is suffering from symptoms of a "disease" called adolescence. The symptoms are as follows:

— emotional highs and lows
— fear of being away from her closest friend or having to attend a public function in the company of only her parents
— splotched complexion
— strong emphasis on privacy at home
— selfishness, "hands-off-my-property" attitude

— renewed interest in fashionable clothing
— demanding and impulsive behavior
— "anything you can do I can do better" attitude
— belief that parents have the intelligence of apes and should be kept out of sight
— attitude that household responsibilities impose a deprivation of freedom
— habit of writing notes to parents regarding feelings rather than discussing them openly
— excessive appetite, may be compared to a human garbage disposal!

One of Kelly's favorite activities is spending enormous amounts of time talking on the telephone. No matter what time of day or night, the phone rings, rings, and rings. Answer—"Kelly, it is for you!" And the cycle is repeated day after day. Conversations are characterized by discussions on almost anything and are flavored by "teenese"—the dialect of teenagers.

Another favorite activity involves spending long periods of time in the bathroom. Kelly may announce, "I need to spend just fifteen more minutes drying my hair." Then fifteen minutes later she yells, "Don't rush me! I have not finished combing my hair!" She spends literally hours primping, plucking, combing, looking in the mirror, combing her hair, battling acne, and the list goes on and on!

Recently Kelly has begun to really show her drive for independence. She talks about *my* room, *my* clothes, *my* chair, *my* rights, and on rare occasions, *my* responsibilities. One of her favorite strategies is to quickly jump into her father's favorite green recliner chair just prior to his arrival on the scene and exclaim, "This is not *your* chair. It is *my* chair because I got here first!"

A very interesting phenomenon called "downgrading your parents" has recently appeared. This is evidenced in Kelly's vocal expressions of disagreement with her own parents' positions or views on issues. It is particularly interesting to note, however, that the views of another teenager's parents are often held in high esteem. In contrast, one of Kelly's friends may express strong agreement with Kelly's parents' point of view. This tendency to oppose one's parents' point of view and authority is a rather typical characteristic of the emerging adolescent.

Another interesting development is the real discovery of sex. Recent physiological changes have caused Kelly to become increasingly more sexually aware. One of her tendencies at present is to be "in love" with a "star" college basketball player. This is not known by the ball player, but the evidence appears in many forms—Kelly's moving his picture to a favored position on the wall of her room, eagerness to invite members of the college basketball team, including the "star," over for dinner, and a strong, new desire to attend all the local college basketball games. It is

also interesting to note that Kelly pays very little attention to boys of her own age and class in school.

Clothes have recently become extremely important, too. Everybody has one of these! I need a new dress; I have only two! I need two more pairs of shoes! Mercy, I never have anything to wear! (Kelly always insists on making her own selection. If her parents like it, forget it!)

Observing Kelly's behavior fluctuate from very adultlike to very childlike is fascinating. One moment she may be discussing a significant world issue on a highly intelligent level, and a few minutes later she may regress to playing with a doll or skating on a skateboard. For a parent, this can be an exciting and sometimes frustrating experience. Kelly's regression to childlike behavior is an effort to retain some of the positive, secure feelings of childhood. The emerging adolescent is searching for a new adult identity but at the same time desires to retain these feelings.

Some of the very positive and encouraging behaviors demonstrated by Kelly recently include:

How does Kelly reflect your concept of an emerging adolescent?

— a stated awareness of the need to carefully examine one's strengths and weaknesses in choosing a vocation
— an outward, sincere expression of concern for people who are less fortunate in life
— a better understanding of the roles that parents and children must play in order to build a wholesome family relationship
— a better understanding of the value of money and its relationship to other material possessions
— an understanding of the need for maintaining high academic and social standards in order to advance in school and society
— little things that communicate that deep in her heart she really loves her parents

Like other emerging adolescents, Kelly is making a transition from childhood to adulthood. She needs parents, teachers, and friends who are patient, understanding, supportive, and who really care about her as a person. There is only one "treatment" for adolescence, and it is painstakingly difficult for patient, parents, and teachers. The treatment is TIME: *T*olerance, *I*nsight, *M*oderation, *E*ndearment.

Self-Perceptions at Age Fourteen

In order to obtain insight into how a fourteen-year-old emerging adolescent perceives the world, I asked a local middle school English teacher to have her fourteen-year-old students write a brief essay, "What Is It Like To Be Fourteen Years Old?" The following excerpts should provide some interesting perceptions:

> The age of fourteen is a hard one to conquer. It is full of hardships, undecided opinions, family battles, and heartbreaks. These all add up to tears.
>
> At this age I'm concerned with people. I try to respect other persons' opinions and feelings, because there is no way you can survive in this world if you can't relay your thoughts with others and be able to accept their opinions in return. I'm also concerned about boys; they are constantly on my mind since I'm now allowed to date.
>
> I want to hurry up and become an adult, but then again, I want to stay a teenager as long as possible.
>
> Most people regard a fourteen-year-old's thoughts and views as of little importance and fail to realize that our opinions to us are as important as theirs are to them. I feel this is where a lot of parent and children relationships fall apart, the failure to listen and discuss. And being a fourteen-year-old, I ought to know.

> Probably the hardest thing about being a teen is parents. They inform the teen that he or she is too young to date, stay up too late, or see a particular movie. But yet, the next moment, that same teen is too old to play with the younger children ("You might hurt one of them!"), watch something silly on T.V., or fight for the biggest apple. A fourteen-year-old is so much older than the little kids, but also so much younger than the older kids, both at the same time! It's really difficult to be in the middle like that.

> A fourteen-year-old is full of questions and my main one is—What will I do with my life? Someday soon maybe I'll figure it out. Maybe when I'm sixteen!

> No one else could do it! Swallow fourteen pieces of pizza, a twin pack of potato chips, and three milkshakes! No one else could do it! But it was fun, and that is what is really important! Sure, we knew that pizza, potato chips, and milkshakes from 2 a.m. until 7 a.m. weren't exactly what doctors would call a good, balanced diet, but tomorrow is Saturday, and we can sleep all day and don't have to eat anything—we're finally teenagers and we're making the most of it!

Physical Characteristics

The emerging adolescence years are characterized by pronounced and accelerated physical development. Both boys and girls experience increasing height, body breadth and depth, lung capacity, heart size, and muscular strength. Boys tend to lag a year or two behind girls in height, but they usually have more physical energy and endurance. Skin disorders, especially acne, are a major concern to both.

The acceleration and unevenness of physical development may cause selected problems for individuals. For example, the emerging adolescent may be concerned about changes in body contour, weight, and muscle development. Menstruation and the development of breasts and hips may cause anxiety and emotional disturbances in girls, while boys may be concerned about growth of the genitals. Shortness or tallness, awkwardness, crooked teeth, obesity, and many other physical characteristics may also cause concern. Masturbation is practically universal.

Bone growth usually is faster than muscle development, and bones may lack the protective covering and support that is needed for rigorous sports competition. This uneven bone-muscle growth pattern may result in emerging adolescents' having poor body mechanics and coordination. Specific adult guidance is needed to help emerging adolescents avoid overextending or damaging bone-muscle structure. They need to be taught, for example, to avoid the "throwing their arm away" syndrome that often causes severe damage to muscle fibers within the arm.

Who is an emerging adolescent? What is an emerging adolescent *really* like? Garner and Suggs (1976) provide a closer look in "Losing All Your Dimples."[1]

I'm ten years old.
I've never understood my environment much,
But from what I've been told,
My environment understands me
And will let me know what it wants me to do.
School district fourteen is where I reside.
Add and subtract. Multiply and divide.
Over and over.
And why do I have to write about how I spent my summer vacation?
I never get to go anywhere, so I always lie:
"Summer vacation was fun. We went to Florida and saw Disney World,
and boy it was fun, and boy it was crowded, and boy it was hot, but
we went anyway cause everybody does it, and if I don't write good,
remember I been out of school all summer."
And rewrites tomorrow, over and over.
My teacher says that she's doing reviews,
But I've already done this before and it bores me.
I've got the reviews blues.

Reading groups? Again?
Sometimes I think that I'll be a redbird all my life:
Not good enough to be a vulture.
Just average.
Part of the majority
They teach you that majority means powerful,
But when you're average, you're not worth much:
Not good enough to get some praise,
Not bad enough to get some help.
I wish I could sail with the current.
I'd let it take me anywhere.
Anywhere but here.
Now here,
You see,
It takes all the running you can do,
To keep in the same place.
If you want to get somewhere else,
You must run at least twice as fast as that.
"You were under the impression
That when you were walking forwards
You would end up further onward,
But things ain't quite that simple.
You got altered information.

1. Reprinted by permission from *Middle School Journal,* December 1976, p. 24.

You were told to not take chances.
You missed out on new dances.
Now you're losing all your dimples."

Having just been placed in grade number six,
I've been put to the task of picking up sticks.
All the students are forming new cliques,
But I'd rather be a loner with individual tricks.
The fellow on the corner tries to sell me a fix,
But what does he know about sixth grade kicks?
An interesting process is sixth grade.
We review what was done in the fifth grade.
Since the fifth held no news,
We're reviewing reviews!
And those who are cool have it made.

Why is it I can't keep still? Why?
I'm energetic, not cybernetic.
I want to be with girls and yet I don't.
And I would join school clubs, but I won't.
Because my grades aren't high enough for me to qualify.

My teachers have told me that I don't use my talents,
And I agree that I could do with a balance,
But my talents are to be applied to the same old stuff.
To conform to the norm.

I am moved to the junior high to develop my gifts.
Why couldn't the seventh grade develop my "ifs"?
"If I could just . . .
"If I had my wish . . .
"If only . . ."

"Hi there, Freddy! I'm your advisor,
Here to make you all the wiser
With arithmetic, English, spelling, and writing.
I'm sure that you will find this exciting!
History, science, health and phys. ed.
You shouldn't expect to have much trouble, Fred.
You have grades that are average, but a better I.Q.
So this isn't drudgery; it's simply review.
And now comes the fun part! Your choice young man:
Which would you prefer? Football or band?"

Clarinet players don't wear shoulder pads.
But clarinet players can be under five feet tall.
It's not so bad to get your second choice,
Unless, of course, there are only two choices.
And I'm third clarinet in a section of three. I play:
"The Star Spangled Banner" and "God Bless America" and "Stars and
Stripes Forever."

Three tunes for every football game.
At first it was fun, but the three same
Tunes get older after a while, no matter how stirring.
Bus fee: Twenty dollars; uniform: forty dollars; clarinet: eighty dollars.
But I get into every junior high football game free.

I sit next to Gloria, the girl in my spelling class.
She sure is pretty even though she can't spell,
And she plays first oboe with braces on her teeth and big blue eyes.
She's a whole foot taller than me,
And she's in love with the ninth grade quarterback who's more her size.
His voice doesn't squeak like mine.
He doesn't pay much attention to her, though, "cause she didn't make cheerleader."
If I was that quarterback, I'd say, "Gloria, so what if you're not a cheerleader."
But I'm short and squeaky and play third clarinet.

I'm in the ninth grade—fifteen years old now.
But things in our school are not different somehow.
The same old math problems, the same old band tunes.
All I've accomplished that I can tell
Is that now I'm first clarinet.
But next year, in tenth grade, I'll go back to third!
And if all of high school is like that I'm leaving!
Why, junior high school is just like elementary!
I feel as if I'm being buried in sedimentary
Dirt on the bottom of a river
That flows by me constantly
Leaving me stuck in the mud.
But this stick in the mud will finally erode loose
Or break away.
And when I start moving,
I'll never, ever, ever come back again.

Diversity and rapid change are two characteristics of middle school students that must receive careful consideration. Researchers agree that what the early adolescent experiences from ages ten to fifteen is critical to his healthy and productive functioning throughout life. Lipsitz (1977) conducted a two-year study of programs and services for young adolescents in the United States under a Ford Foundation grant and published *Growing Up Forgotten*. The report emphasizes some critical facts that show the results of the "lack of fit" between young adolescents and the social institutions that serve them. They include the following:

1. Suicide is now the fourth leading cause of death among adolescents, drug abuse peaks during seventh and eighth grades, and

children under fifteen are the only age group that has recently shown an increase in first-time admission rates to mental hospitals.

2. It is forecast that one out of nine young people (one out of six males) will be referred to the juvenile courts before their eighteenth birthdays.
3. Youth-serving agencies, particularly those with long-standing traditional programs like Boy Scouts and Girl Scouts, are losing about half their young members by the time they reach age twelve. According to one research study, major reasons given by members for dropping out were childish activities, domineering adult leaders, and lack of opportunity to share in decision making.

The report concludes that these facts are signs of an underlying social confusion about how we want our children to grow up in America.

Personality Growth Characteristics

Personality development is a significant part of the emerging adolescent's transition from childhood to adolescence. Gatewood and Dilg (1975) identified four major domains of social-emotional development: self-concept, sex role identification, peer influence, and emotional control.

During this time of life, the learner begins to find the "me" as opposed to the "not me." The conflict between dependence and independence in the family structure intensifies. "How do I look in the eyes of others?" and "Who am I becoming?" are common questions. Students' feelings of adequacy in human relations may be somewhat strained during this period by their attempt to gain adult status and privileges without being ready for the concomitant responsibilities.

Sex role identification is a major concern of the emerging adolescent. Adolescence is a period generally characterized by a growing sensitivity to the opposite sex. Adolescents express an increased desire for information about sex and a keen interest in human reproduction. Puberty is accompanied by increasing sexual impulses.

Peer group acceptance is critical to the emerging adolescent, and peer pressures are at peak levels. Adolescents generally tend toward conformity in their appearance, possessions, and activities. The desire for attention and association is often expressed through close friendships with age-mates, "crushes" on adults, and such forms of behavior as poking, teasing, and kidding. Hero worship is a common phenomenon, and the "heroes" are usually playground supervisors, camp counselors, and older friends.

The emerging adolescent learner's emotional behavior fluctuates rapidly; sometimes it is cheerful, while at other times it is affectionate, timid, worried, hurt, sad, jealous, or competitive. These emotional "peaks and valleys" are characteristic of this stage of growth and development.

In this stage, average preadolescents come to view themselves and each other as autonomous actors reciprocating respect and adherence to a code governing peer relationships. Violation of the code, such as that found in a "white lie" that is intended to deceive, is a denial of respect and consequently is the worst crime of this age. Bantel (1968) illustrates this point by sharing the Irish folk tale of the rural young man who during a dispute clouts his father with a shovel and flees to town claiming to have killed the old man, thereby becoming something of an audacious hero. When the furious father appears, very much alive, the indignant villagers run the son out of town as a *liar,* ignoring the fact that if his story had been true, he would have been a murderer.

Mental and Intellectual Growth Characteristics

Most emerging adolescents are moving through Piaget's stage of concrete operations to the stage of formal operations. They are becoming increasingly more adultlike intellectually, which is characterized by the ability to hypothesize and solve abstract problems. They are intellectually curious and display a wide range of exploratory interests, skills, and abilities.

Also, emerging adolescents frequently set goals they cannot reach. They have a tendency to overgeneralize when making judgments based on examination of data.

Theories of Development: Implications for Emerging Adolescents

There are many theories of development that have implications for the education of emerging adolescents. Van Slooten (1974) has categorized these theories under three distinct conceptual viewpoints. The first involves the developmental task concept of growth and development advocated by Robert Havighurst. A *developmental task* is a significant accomplishment that an individual must achieve by a certain time if he is going to meet the demands placed upon him by society. Havighurst (1967) presents the following as developmental tasks of adolescence.

Developmental Tasks of Adolescence

1. Achieving new and more mature relations with age-mates of both sexes.
2. Achieving a masculine or feminine social role.
3. Accepting one's physique and using the body effectively.
4. Achieving emotional independence from parents and other adults.
5. Achieving assurance of economic independence.
6. Selecting and preparing for an occupation.

7. Preparing for marriage and family life.
8. Developing intellectual skills and concepts necessary for civic competence. Concepts of laws, government, economics, politics, human nature, and social institutions are the important ones.
9. Desiring and achieving socially responsible behavior.
10. Acquiring a set of values and an ethical system as a guide to behavior.

Havighurst (1968) has outlined these three major developmental tasks of preadolescence:

1. *Organizing one's knowledge of social and physical reality.* During the preadolescence period, the learner develops an interest in ordering, organizing, and systematizing knowledge. As the learner moves through this period, he becomes increasingly selective in what he studies. One youngster may like sports, another local history, and a third space travel. All may want to explore subjects in greater depth than they have previously, and they may experience a need to organize concepts more systematically.
2. *Learning to work well in the peer group.* During this stage of growth and development, boys and girls are very much concerned with their ability to get along with their age-mates in the peer group. They like to form teams, committees, and clubs. This is an excellent time for them to get involved in democratic social relationships and practice learning to live, work, and play with their equals.
3. *Becoming an independent person.* Preadolescents are expected to become physically independent, but they may not be able to become emotionally independent. Many youngsters of ten or twelve years do not have enough self-control to cope with societal pressures on their own. Patience, understanding, and support from teachers, parents, and friends are critical toward helping the preadolescent develop a valid self-concept.

The second viewpoint is that of *age and stage* periods of development. This concept refers to periods of development that are characterized by certain types of behavior. The age-stage theory of human development is best demonstrated by the writings of Erik Erikson (1968). He has presented the following eight stages of development:[2]

1. Trust vs. mistrust: The child learns to trust himself and the permanency of his environment.

---

2. The author wishes to thank Dr. Anita Aldrich, Chairperson, Department of Physical Education, Indiana University, for permission to use her summary of Erickson's Eight Stages of Development, which was presented as part of a class lecture.

2. Autonomy vs. shame and doubt (early childhood): The child's autonomy is developed by realizing that he can control his environment as well as himself.
3. Initiative vs. guilt (middle childhood): Curiosity, guilt, and anxiety are developed. The conscience is established.
4. Industry vs. inferiority (7 years–puberty): Skills necessary for life and family are developed.
5. Identity vs. role confusion (adolescence):
   a) Rapid body growth and sexual maturity take place.
   b) Identification with sex roles is developed.
   c) Feelings of acceptance or rejection by peer groups are important.
   d) Conflict arises between what is said by society and what is said by the peer group.
   e) The child seeks competency.
   f) He strives for success, accomplishment, and competition.
   g) He feels ready to face the challenges of the adult world.
   h) Trust in the body is shaken; it must be regained gradually.
   i) The child wants to be heard and looked upon as part of society.
   j) He selects certain adults with whom to identify.
   k) The child's peer group is more important to him than parents and other adults.
   l) Play is not as important to the child as it once was since it pertains to role playing.
   m) Developmental crises of adolescence occur.
6. Intimacy vs. isolation (late teens and early twenties): In this stage, the individual accepts himself and goes on to accept others.
7. Generactivity vs. stagnation: The individual becomes interested in the next generation rather than being caught up in his own problems.
8. Integrity vs. despair: The individual realizes that he has been able to have a good life, and he feels an integrity in his own existence.

Understanding Erikson's fourth stage, industry vs. inferiority, and his fifth stage, identity vs. role confusion, should be most helpful toward working with the emerging adolescent in a classroom setting.

A third conceptual viewpoint of human development encompasses developmental milestones. This viewpoint is best expressed by the work of Jean Piaget. His theory is primarily descriptive and does not attempt to explain behavior. He believes that intellectual development follows a predictable pattern consisting of these five phases or milestones:[3]

---

3. Adapted from H. Maier, *Three Theories of Child Development* (New York: Harper and Row, 1965). Used with permission.

1. Sensory-Motor Phase (0–2 years): Actions, or motor activities, are coordinated into a tenuous whole.
2. Pre-Conceptual Phase (2–4 years): This is a period of transition from self-satisfying behavior to rudimentary socialized behavior.
3. Intuitive Thought Phase (4–7 years): First real beginnings of cognitive thought appear. The child becomes aware of relationships and may begin to generalize.
4. Concrete Operations Phase (7–11 years): The child is aware of alternative solutions to problems. He also has the capacity to relate an event or thought to a total system of interrelated parts and to conceive of it from beginning to end.
5. Formal Operations Phase (11–15 years):
   a) Cognitive development has a bearing on concept formation and the learning of many subjects.
   b) Concept formation is great during this period.
   c) The child enters into the world of ideas.
   d) The child takes a systematic approach to problems.
   e) Logical deduction takes place by implication.
   f) The child does not grasp reality, but he can dream.
   g) Deduction by hypothesis and judgment by implication enable the child to reason beyond cause and effect.
   h) Logical deduction helps the child to understand the physical and social world.
   i) The acquisition of many new values occurs.
      (1) The social world becomes an organic unit with laws and regulations and a division of roles and social functions.
      (2) Moral solidarity is cultivated.
      (3) Personality is developed by social communications.
      (4) The child's sense of equality supersedes submission to adult authority.
      (5) The realization of a deity takes place.

As a prospective middle school teacher, you may want to study each of these theories of human growth and development in greater depth. You may also want to develop your own theoretical viewpoint for working with the emerging adolescent learner.

Summary

The emerging adolescent is indeed a unique learner. The period of transescence is characterized by significant physical, social, emotional, and intellectual changes. During this period of transition from childhood to adulthood, the emerging adolescent experiences a great variety of needs, fears, concerns, and pressures. As a prospective middle school teacher, it is imperative that you thoroughly understand emerging adolescents so that you may provide them with optimum learning experiences.

What does the prospective teacher need to know and understand about growth and development in order to successfully teach the emerging adolescent? What are the characteristics and needs of a middle schooler? Mastery of the content presented in this chapter and the accompanying learning module should assist you toward providing appropriate responses to these and related questions.

REFERENCES

Bantel, Edward. "Pre-Adolescent: Misunderstood." In *Transitional Years.* Washington, D.C.: Association for Childhood Education International, 1968.

Eichhorn, Donald H. *The Middle School.* New York: The Center for Applied Research in Education, 1966.

Erikson, E. H. *Youth and Crisis.* New York: Norton, 1968.

Garner, Art, and Suggs, Keith. "Losing All Your Dimples." *Middle School Journal* 7(1976):24.

Gatewood, Thomas, and Dilg, Charles. *The Middle School We Need.* Washington, D.C.: Association for Supervision and Curriculum Development, 1975.

Havighurst, Robert J. *Developmental Tasks and Education.* New York: Longmans, Green Publishers, 1967.

———. "The Middle School Child in Contemporary Society." *Theory Into Practice,* June 1968, pp. 120–22.

Lipsitz, Joan. *Growing Up Forgotten.* Lexington, Mass.: Lexington Books, 1977.

Maier, H. *Three Theories of Child Development.* New York: Harper and Row, 1965.

Van Slooten, Philip H. "Four Theories of Development and Their Implications for the Physical Education of Adolescents." *Physical Educator* 31(1974):181–86.

Learning Module

The Emerging Adolescent: Your Pupil

Directions

This module is designed to help you understand the emerging adolescent learner. Begin by taking the pretest. Review your pretest results with your instructor. He will assist you in selecting the objectives you need to work on. Complete the required activities that will help you in reaching your objectives. (In order to broaden your understanding, you may also choose activities that are not required.) Then take the posttest to see what you have learned.

Pretest

1. Define adolescence. Name some problems facing adolescents today.
2. What distinguishes the thinking of an adolescent from that of a child?
3. According to Guy Manaster, what are life tasks?
4. According to Ginzberg, what are the three principal psychological periods that individuals move through as a part of the process of making vocational choices?
5. How can training in creativity help adolescents?
6. According to research studies on motivation of learners, what are the ultimate goals of motivation?

Check

Review your pretest performance with your instructor.

Behavioral Objectives

Select the appropriate objectives: You should be able to:
1. Name problems that face adolescents and discuss the educational implications of these problems.
2. Name and describe the stages of cognitive development according to Piaget.
3. Distinguish between concrete and formal stages in cognitive development.

4. Define life tasks and compare them to developmental tasks.
5. State reasons to include career development programs in the middle school.
6. Discuss the nature of creative ideas and note guidelines for stimulating creativity in the classroom.
7. Explain the value of using motivation in the middle school.

Required Activities

Numbers in parentheses correlate with corresponding objectives. Do only those that you and your instructor agree would be beneficial for you.

1. Read Chapter 1, "Adolescents in an Age of Crisis," in James F. Adams' *Understanding Adolescence* (Boston: Allyn and Bacon, 1973). (1)
2. Interview adolescents in a middle school. What are the problems they face? (1)
3. Read Chapter 3 in Donald H. Eichhorn's *The Middle School* (New York: The Center for Applied Research in Education, 1966). (2) (3)
4. Read Chapter 7, "Cognitive Development and Learning in the Adolescent" by Jeannette McCarthy Gallagher in *Understanding Adolescence* (Adams 1973). (2) (3)
5. Read "Adolescent Thinking a la Piaget" by Everett Dulit in Robert E. Grinder's *Studies in Adolescence* (New York: Macmillan Co., 1975). (2) (3)
6. Read Chapter 3 in *Adolescent Development and the Life Tasks* by Guy J. Manaster (Boston: Allyn and Bacon, 1977). (2) (3)
7. Obtain materials needed for the experiment discussed in pp. 167–69 of *Understanding Adolescence* (Adams 1973). Test several adolescents and several preadolescents. Record your observations and compare them to the observations in the book. (3)
8. Read Chapter 1 in *Adolescent Development and the Life Tasks* (Manaster 1977). (4)
9. Read Chapter 17, "Career Development in Adolescence," by Henry Borow in *Understanding Adolescence* (Adams 1973). (5)
10. Visit a middle school and survey its career development program. (5)
11. Survey a class of third graders, a class of eighth graders, and a class of twelfth graders. In which period of vocational choice does each group of children fall? Does Ginzberg's theory hold true? (5)
12. Read "Care and Feeding of Creative Adolescents" by Gary A. Davis in *Studies in Adolescence* (Grinder 1975). (6)
13. Interview a middle school teacher. Discuss his or her students and compare his or her views to your own and those of Gary Davis. (6)
14. Read "Varieties of Adolescent Creativity and the High School Envi-

ronment" by Herbert J. Walberg in Rolf E. Meuss' *Adolescent Behavior and Society* (New York: Random House, 1975). (6)

15. Read Don Reggins' "Motivation and Teaching" in *Learning to Teach in the Elementary School,* edited by Hal D. Funk and Robert T. Olberg (New York: Dodd, Mead, & Co., 1971). (7)
16. Read Edward F. DeRoche's "Motivation: An Instructional Technique" in *Learning to Teach in the Elementary School* (Funk and Olberg 1971). (7)
17. List ideas for middle school motivational techniques relating to the area of your concentration. (7)

Optional Activities

Select activities from the Required Activities list that you have not already completed.

Posttest

Prepare for your instructor's evaluation a written report presenting what you have learned from this unit of study. You should thoroughly cover the objectives you have completed, summarizing your readings and stating your research findings, your research conclusions, and their educational implications. The report should be typed and double-spaced, using approximately one to one and one-half pages per objective.

Early Adolescence (Ages 11-14)

I. Maintaining Personal Health and Promoting Healthful Living

A. Meeting Needs of Rest, Diet, and Freedom from Infection

1. Rest needs are approaching the rest needs of adults—8 to 8½ hours of sleep each day.
2. These children are likely to feel that they have unlimited resistance and unlimited sources of energy. In many instances, they are unwilling to get as much sleep as they need and tend to go beyond the normal fatigue point, especially in strenuous play.
3. Boys usually have more physical energy and endurance than girls. Girls tend to tire easily and do not have the physical endurance to play as strenuously as boys, even though they are interested in many of the same activities.
4. Childhood diseases have usually run their course prior to this period. But since resistance to infection may be low in many of these children, frequent health examinations are extremely important. This is a period of many minor illnesses (with many but short absences from school) but a period of few deaths.
5. Rapid growth is likely to cause either a tremendous increase in appetite or sometimes, particularly in girls, a finickiness with loss of appetite. Both diet and eating habits are involved.
6. Boys usually have a more adequate supply of nutrients than do girls of the same age because they consume more food. Teenage girls do least well of all children in the adequacy of their food intake. Both boys and girls must be urged to keep in mind that an adequate diet is one that provides all the known essential nutrients in sufficient quantities to meet the needs of the body.
7. Knowledge of food values helps to eliminate the unwise

From Mary Jane Loomis, ed., *How Children Develop* (Columbus, Ohio: The Ohio State University, 1964), pp. 41–53. Used with permission.

choices of food that children tend to make at this age. They need to know that eating the necessary foods to supply the nutrients in an adequate diet satisfies the appetite to some extent and helps to curtail the consumption of nonessential foods.

8. Most of these children can be taught to take complete responsibility for treating minor cuts, wounds, and sprains, and to realize why it is important to care for them.

B. Achieving Optimal Physical and Organic Development

1. This is a period of rapid growth, especially of the long bones of the body, with great differences apparent among individuals.
2. Most girls of these ages are taller and proportionately heavier than the boys. Differences tend to decrease by the age of 14.
3. Most boys are growing broad-shouldered, deep-chested, and heavier. Voice changes occur more noticeably among boys.
4. Children with rapidly growing bodies may have difficulty in learning how to carry themselves, or they may feel tired and inclined to slump. Self-consciousness accompanying rapid growth causes some adolescents, especially girls, to assume unhealthy postures in an attempt to look small or less ungainly. Special attention to posture is advisable at this time.
5. Skin disorders, especially acne, are a major concern. Acne is caused by the discrepancy in growth between the small ducts which carry oil to the skin and increased activity of the glands secreting the oil.
6. During this age period, vision and hearing are often altered by the child's rapid physical development. To help ensure the child's maximum response and comfort in the classroom, he should be given the prescribed number of medically recommended vision and hearing tests.
7. Some girls at this age level are physically mature, menstruation begins, and the development of breasts and hips is becoming noticeable. Many young girls are bewildered and frightened by the first menses. The girl who is ill-informed often mistakes the menarche for a mysterious illness or injury. Even girls who have been well prepared may pass through a period of considerable emotional disturbance and of exaggerated concern over health.
8. Most investigators agree that masturbation is practically universal in the male adolescent for varying periods of time, and also that quite a few girls masturbate. It is usually at puberty that the child first becomes aware of the genital organs as

sources of pleasure. From now on the sex activities of the child, which have been infantile in their expressions, tend to become adult. Sexual tension will find release in playing games, romping, walking, dancing, skating, and engaging in baseball or other sports. Straightforward discussions of sex also are helpful.

C. Engaging in Suitable Recreational Activities and Promoting Healthful Living

1. Games popular with these children are team games that involve increasing organization—baseball, volleyball, football, and softball. However, children are still unable to choose recreational activities wisely in terms of strength and need for development. Also, they still need adult supervision in this area.
2. Sometimes there is self-consciousness about undertaking new physical activities in which an individual is unskilled. Children who are skilled are usually more inclined to try new physical activities than those who are awkward.
3. This age group prefers active types of social recreation and exhibits a willingness to practice in order to become adept in physical skills and games.
4. The child of this age begins to broaden his understanding of group health problems, such as contagious diseases, and of the importance of preventive measures.
5. These children are becoming aware of the theoretical need for proper eating habits and the need for rest, but they do not always apply this awareness to their own behavior.
6. This is a period of relatively poor physical coordination. Growth is often rapid; and since some parts of his body grow more rapidly than others, the child may have difficulty becoming accustomed to his increased size and coordinating his movement.
7. Children of this age show a decided preference for group games and individual activities of a self-testing nature.
8. Some of these children may feel frustrated as a result of physical inadequacies; others may be stimulated to improve. Physical superiority may lead to "showing off" and exhibitionism. Withdrawal from group activities or exhibitionism may imply the existence of a more basic problem.
9. Differences in interests often cause difficulties in social adjustment. Girls dance earlier than boys. Dancing with girls is rejected by some boys.

II. Achieving and Maintaining a Sense of Security

A. Gaining and Holding Affection, Confidence, Esteem, and Status

1. These children often achieve status in the family and feel happy in it if the responsibilities they are given are within their capacities to perform; however, the main concern of children of these ages is their standing with their peers. They feel it necessary to conform in their appearance, possessions, and activities.
2. An attempt to gain adult status may be made by trying to imitate adult behavior in language, dress, and use of cosmetics.
3. However a 13- or 14-year-old wants to retain child status in some areas where the family wants him to grow up—for example, in assuming some home responsibilities and in acquiring more adult manners.
4. These children experiment with various roles in an attempt to find status. One day a boy will be the suave diplomat; the next, the "tough guy." On one occasion, the girl is the demure and petite maiden; on another, the sophisticated young lady.
5. There is a tendency for children to refer to the privileges of their age-mates to exert pressure to gain similar privileges for themselves. This is especially significant to parents and teachers.
6. The amount of freedom allowed children of this age differs greatly between lower- and middle-class families as well as among families in each class.
7. The desire for group approval increases the child's participation in clubs and groups. He also expects his family to recognize the importance of his friends, clubs, and group interests.
8. This desire for attention and association is frequently expressed through close friendships with age-mates, "crushes" on adults, and such forms of behavior as poking, teasing, and kidding.
9. Preadolescent children are capricious in their friendships and their enmities in that they do not understand other children and do not know why they associate with them or dislike them. In contrast, hero worship is a usual accompaniment of the "emotional" friendships of 13-to-14-year-olds. The hero or heroes are usually playground supervisors, camp counselors, and older friends.
10. "Dates" are beginning to be a factor in a girl's achieving group status, but boys at this level often lose status with other boys if they show an interest in girls or dating.

11. Children who are slow to grow, especially boys, worry about losing status because of their small size.

B. Becoming A Social Personality

1. Most of these children are congenial in their relations with others. They are rapidly learning the "niceties" of social relations where personality comes into play, but are most likely to display these traits when dealing with adults (other than parents.)
2. These boys and girls are well aware of and respond to the pressure of the group concerning acceptable behavior; however, rivalries and conflicts do arise between individuals and groups who are maturing at different rates.
3. Children with similar intellectual abilities, social skills, or physical skills quite frequently group together at this level. Isolation results from the inability of children to solve their personality problems or from their having little to contribute to group activities rather than from any desire to display social independence.
4. Adolescents who are not accepted by an already established group tend to drift into a group of their own. The group may either conform to social codes or become antisocial.

III. Developing and Maintaining a Sense of Achievement

A. Gaining a Sense of Personal Adequacy and Control Over the Environment

1. Insecurities and feelings of inferiority may develop in both rapidly and slowly maturing individuals. The person who is either too far behind or too far ahead of his age group is likely to have problems in connection with such things as participation in sports, dancing, and activities requiring physical strength and endurance.
2. These children generally enjoy doing things that yield the satisfaction of achievement and of self-improvement, especially in some activity valued by their group.
3. The child's feelings of adequacy in family relations may be somewhat strained during this period by his attempt to gain adult status and privileges without being ready for full responsibility.
4. These children frequently ask for help in learning effective means of group participation—for example, parliamentary procedure, committee organization, and discussion techniques.
5. Adolescents begin to grope for means of community participation, but it remains on an elementary level—for example,

carrying papers, caring for children, doing odd jobs, joining dancing clubs, and taking part in interschool sports.

6. In his desire to achieve and to "shine," a child may choose an activity that is neither constructive nor wholesome. Likewise, he may put his energy into achieving, with his group, a code of behavior in direct conflict with adult codes.
7. Children of these ages should be able to handle money and budget allowances to the extent of buying some of their own clothes and paying for some of their own recreation.
8. Most boys and girls at this age are able to care for their personal grooming in terms of their own standards. These standards may be far from acceptable to adults. Lack of grooming is a characteristic of most boys; good grooming usually coincides with an interest in girls. The desire to be attractive on the part of both boys and girls may not include cleanliness, however, unless adults have managed to establish it as part of the group pattern.
9. The child has already acquired many of the mechanics for meeting simple needs and understanding his environment better.
10. Thirteen- and 14-year-olds are interested in learning to do almost anything useful that they see adults doing, but they frequently conceal this interest because of the adult tendency to pass routine responsibilities over to them.
11. These boys and girls also do not want to "carry through" if adult activities are too difficult or devoid of sensory experience.
12. Young people of these ages frequently are able to plan on a higher level than they can execute.
13. They have a short attention span in group discussion; it is still difficult for them to concentrate for a long period of time. Girls tend to have a greater capacity for concentration than boys.
14. The 12-to-14 year old youths tend to be concerned with the activities of the moment and rarely plan for the future.
15. These children are beginning to understand the relationship between their material wants and the size of the family income.
16. They become increasingly able to distinguish between necessities and luxuries in terms of their allowances or the family income, and they begin to judge values.
17. There is a great interest in moneymaking activities. Some of these children are learning to supplement an allowance with

other earnings; however, a child's "need" for money to satisfy his new desires frequently outruns his earning ability.

18. Most early adolescents are still dependent upon the family for their major financial needs, and many of their opportunities to make money still come from doing chores at home and in the neighborhood—for example, carrying papers, cutting grass, washing cars, and minding small children.
19. The child's growing but limited understanding of his environment leads to overgeneralizing.

B. Developing Sensitivity to the Opposite Sex

1. In the early part of this age range, there is a tendency to prefer one's own sex. This is more marked in boys than girls.
2. Boys and girls at this age frequently have "crushes" on agemates and adults.
3. The girl of this level who tends to be a tomboy retains status with both sexes. The boy who tends to be feminine is labeled "sissy" and hence loses status in his group.
4. Interest in the opposite sex sometimes shows itself in action that is contrary to the expected, such as teasing, pulling hair, and poking. Affectionate girl-boy relationships may be expressed in such forms as "swiping" or hiding notebooks and other possessions and untying shoes.
5. Boys go through a short period of roughness and rudeness to all females, even older ones. This is followed by a period of overt interest in the other sex.
6. Girls show social awareness earlier than boys and take the initiative in their relations with boys. They prefer parties attended by both boys and girls.
7. Children of these ages develop a keen interest in their own bodies and in sex and in sex processes, including human reproduction. There is a continued interest in other living organisms.
8. Most children of these ages desire associations with the opposite sex. Some of the least mature children still respond without reference to sex. This tendency is more marked in boys than in girls.
9. Less mature youngsters tend to shy away from the opposite sex, and most youngsters are somewhat insecure in their relationships with the opposite sex.
10. Puberty is accompanied by increasing sexual impulses. Nearly all normally growing personalities feel a desire to express sincere, idealistic affection by some physical means. Holding hands, walking with arms around one's companion,

even fairly intense kissing remain for most young people expressions of friendship rather than erotic excitations. Overly suspicious adults may by the wrong attitude create a sexual consciousness in the young person that does not naturally exist.

11. At this age level, there is an increased desire for information about sex. The amount of information possessed differs greatly among individuals and between children of different social groups.
12. Some adolescents experiment with sexual intimacies in order to allay unconscious self-doubt of their sexual adequacy. Sometimes, in a desire to assure himself and others of his adequacy, the adolescent may boast of sexual intimacies that he never experienced. Sometimes, an adolescent's mixed feelings about the ethical implications of his sexual impulses may lead him to find gratification in an eroticism that is devoid of companionship.
13. Masturbation may become a source of future personality difficulties if the matter is not properly handled.

IV. Developing and Deepening Interests and Appreciations

A. Achieving Intellectual and Aesthetic Interests and Appreciations

1. Imaginative play virtually disappears at this age level.
2. Children of this level enjoy the manipulation of concrete things. Their understanding of abstract concepts continues to grow but is still very weak.
3. Children of this age level choose art experiences that broaden and deepen past experiences.
4. They have an interest in experimenting with color and media and derive a sense of satisfaction from developing new skills.
5. If children of this age level are given enough freedom of expression, they find enjoyment both in a process for its own sake and in the resulting product.
6. During this age period, children begin to take more responsibility in planning and evaluating their work. They also derive enjoyment from individual problem-solving experiences rather than from teacher-directed experiences.
7. At this age, they are ready to study art on a comparative basis and to develop generalizations concerning specific works of art or types of art. Like the 6-to-11-year-olds, this age group maintains a spontaneous enthusiasm for recognized works of art, but 11-to-14-year-olds are much more responsive to new experiences.

8. A child of this age may be able to read and grasp as many words per minute as a mature person, but this does not mean that he will enjoy adult reading material.
9. At this age, children will try almost anything for experience, but they tend to lack confidence if their results are to be made public.
10. The child's ability to memorize tempts teachers and other adults to teach him a multitude of facts rather than to challenge him to think.
11. Toward the end of this age range, children are able to read and think for long periods without becoming restless. It is a great age for reading and exploring. Girls prefer to explore vicariously through books; boys prefer first hand experiences.
12. At these ages, sensory impressions are sharpened and emotional responses become more diversified by the onset of adolescence.
13. It is also a time for learning the skills of problem solving and for practicing the skill of finding "Third alternatives," which are new and more creative solutions.
14. Children of this age range are more capable of intellectualizing their experiences than at earlier levels, and for some individuals intellectual activity is a satisfying end in itself. However, other individuals will attempt these activities because they are trying to imitate the intellectual group.

B. Developing Social Values and Respect for the Cultural Heritage
   1. After passing through a negative phase in which adult opinions are considered a hindrance, these children may seek adult companionship and guidance.
   2. At this time, there is growing recognition of the possibilities of cooperative endeavor. Under proper guidance, these children can become increasingly conscious of the value of group service. They also learn to do things for others when no immediate and tangible rewards are involved.
   3. Most children of these ages show an awareness of the codes of moral conduct and are usually willing to exhibit behaviors that are implied by these codes. Some children adopt the codes of such organizations as the Scouts and Camp Fire Girls and try to live by them.
   4. Small groups of adolescents often develop codes of acceptable group behavior that are in direct conflict with adult codes. Such codes are frequently a challenge to, or actually a defiance of, adult codes.

5. Undemocratic organizations are very common at this age. However, most individuals have begun to recognize the need for cooperative endeavors, and the drive towards group activity makes it possible for teachers and group leaders to develop principles of democratic living.
6. Children of this level show a continued interest in factual information concerning the building of culture. They are particularly curious and interested in specific dramatic aspects of the present culture—for example, space travel and automation.
7. There is also an intense interest in the scientific aspects of the culture and its imaginative derivation, science fiction.
8. In beginning to understand the contributions of past achievements to present living, these children show a continued interest in the dramatic episodes of the past, especially the colorful opening of the West, historic battles, and the World Wars.
9. Some hobbies are carried over from earlier age levels. Other interests develop during this period and often continue into adult life.
10. Solitary hobbies practiced in moderation are normal for these children. Absorption in a hobby to the exclusion of all other interests may, however, sometimes by symptomatic of a poor personal adjustment, and it may in turn make the child's withdrawal and isolation more pronounced.

Part 2

Teaching the Middle School Learner

Chapter 3

Developing a Personal Teaching Style

Historically, prospective teachers have been admonished to consider the individual differences of learners in the learning process. Yet, too many teacher preparation programs continue to function in large lecture hall settings, giving little attention to either students' own individuality or to practical application of theory. Obviously, many college professors have not *modeled* the kind of behavior they *advocate* but have operated using the "do as I say not as I do" philosophy.

Each teacher has her own teaching style—her own unique, personal characteristics, philosophic principles, subject matter strengths, and effective methods of working with students. How do you develop a personalized teaching style? What do *you* value as being desirable characteristics of an effective teaching style? What kind of teacher are you becoming? How can you become an effective facilitator of personalized education (individualized instruction based on personal needs as well as subject matter needs)? As a prospective teacher, you will need to find answers to these questions. More specifically, you will want to develop competence and confidence in the different areas of facilitating personalized learning experiences for middle school learners. Let's begin the competency development process together.

Major Concepts of Teaching

What is teaching? What competencies does a teacher need to teach effectively? Some of the major concepts of teaching are:

1. *Teaching is talking or "telling."* This concept emphasizes that teaching primarily a process of imparting knowledge through verbal communication. A simplistic concept of teaching/learning would be "teaching is talking," and "learning is listening." Research studies have indicated that teacher talk dominates classrooms from kindergarten through graduate school and too much of this talk does not result in effective learning on the part of students. There is nothing wrong with talking as a method of teaching; but learning is incomplete when the teacher does nothing more than talk.
2. *Teaching is imparting knowledge or "dishing out the subject matter."* This concept places prime emphasis upon teaching as a process of transmitting the cognitive, or facts and concepts, to the learner. It seems that no one could be opposed to knowledge. This concept of teaching, however, fails to give proper attention to variables related to the learning process, including child growth and development principles, matching methodology to the learner and subject matter, and the readiness and interest of the learner. How many times have you heard a teacher say, "Boy, I really laid a good history lecture on them today," and thought to yourself, "did the students learn anything?"
3. *Teaching should be creative.* This concept involves the teacher's ability to invent or improvise new roles or alternative lines of action in helping learners change their behavior. It involves providing learners with opportunities to explore and experiment with new ideas, materials, and human and material resources. In essence, it is flexible, receptive guidance of learners.
4. *Teaching is changing the behavior of the learner.* This concept involves diagnosing learners' needs, determining what learning experiences would be appropriate for them, and helping them to assess their progress toward reaching objectives or behavioral changes. Teaching involves the application of principles essential to changing the cognitive (intellectual), affective (emotional), or psychomotor (physical) behavior of the learner.

These are some of the more prevalent societal views of a teacher. Now let's look briefly at three current conceptions of an *effective* teacher: the teacher as dispenser of knowledge, the competencies approach to teaching, and the self as instrument concept.

The Teacher as Dispenser of Knowledge

One of the earliest conceptions of being a good teacher was that of being a scholar and sharing that scholarship with others. As a result of the contributions of Herbart, Dewey, and related educators, however, serious questions were raised about this very narrow concept of teaching. Many of us can recall a teacher who had a very enriched academic background and knew her subject matter in depth, yet had great difficulty teaching that subject matter to others. In contrast, you can probably identify an effective teacher who did not possess a great depth of knowledge on any one subject but had a general knowledge of several subjects and was an effective teacher.

Certainly it is imperative that today's middle school teacher possess accurate, current, reliable knowledge of several subjects. The rapid development of the fields of instructional technology and communication, however, have provided today's student with many sources of knowledge in addition to the teacher. In essence, it may be more important for the teacher to help students use knowledge sources and to clarify knowledge they obtain from her than to merely transmit knowledge.

The Competencies Approach to Teaching

A second way of looking at good teaching involves defining and assessing teaching in terms of teacher "competencies." This approach emphasizes identifying what expert teachers do and helping the prospective teacher master similar competencies. *Webster's New Collegiate Dictionary* (1973) defines *competent* as "fitted, suitable, or sufficient for the purpose. . . ." Therefore, when we speak of teacher competencies, we are referring to competencies needed to accomplish goals. Having identified instructional objectives, we need to identify those competencies needed to reach the objectives. Bowles (1973) states that the rationale for competency-based teacher education requires educators to take a thorough look at what their teaching is designed to accomplish and to review carefully the way they go about accomplishing it; then, it compels educators to modify their programs on the basis of the response of teacher trainees in order to elicit more efficient learning.

The following statements describe some competencies considered desirable for a middle school teacher. The middle school teacher should be able to:

1. Guide pupils in using systematic approaches to solving problems that they have identified.
2. Implement a variety of informal and formal diagnostic procedures in the classroom setting.
3. Utilize a variety of teaching methods including simulation, role playing, small group interaction, expository teaching, demonstration, and discovery approach.
4. Create a supportive learning environment that provides human and material resources relating to selected instructional objectives.

5. Determine meaningful instructional objectives for learners based on valid diagnostic data.
6. Possess sufficient knowledge of various academic disciplines to guide learners in a productive exploration of them in terms of concepts and processes.

The above statements are examples of competencies and are not designed to be an all-encompassing list. These examples, however, direct attention to the fact that a set of competencies can provide guidance for the prospective teacher who desires to become an effective teacher.

Cooper, Jones, and Weber (1973) have identified these four different bases for generating teacher competencies: philosophical, empirical, subject matter, and practitioner. If you use a philosophical base from which to draw statements of needed teacher competencies, you should emphasize assumptions and values regarding the nature of human beings, the purpose of education, and the nature of learning and instruction. This base encompasses statements that have little or no empirical basis. In essence, to generate competencies from it, you must develop a set of philosophical assumptions concerning the role of the teacher. Here are some examples of such assumptions:

1. Education should help the individual establish her self-identity.
2. The teacher should be a guide to discovery.
3. The teacher should be concerned with all of the student's needs, not just subject matter needs.
4. A teacher should be a figure worthy of emulation.
5. A teacher should be a promoter of self-discipline.

You could then state specific competencies relating to each of these general assumptions. For example, for the assumption "education should help the individual establish her self-identity" you could develop the following teacher competencies:

1. Implement a variety of self-appraisal processes and instruments in a middle school setting.
2. Establish a variety of supportive learning environments that provide for the student's exploration of self in relation to others.

If you use an empirical base for generating competencies, the competencies must be linked to knowledge derived from experience or experiment, not to philosophical assumptions. Stated differently, empirically based competencies rely heavily on data derived from the behavioral and social sciences. For example, specific attention is given to such empirically derived concepts as self-concept, reinforcement theory, and behavior modification techniques. A teacher competency relating to self-concept could be stated as follows: Having diagnosed a student who has a poor self-concept, the teacher will implement procedures designed to increase the student's self-concept level.

Another base for deriving competencies consists of the various subject matter areas or disciplines the teacher is expected to teach. The competencies developed from this base range across the spectrum of disciplines treated within the middle school curriculum. For example, the teacher should be able to:

1. Describe the major factors contributing to the American Civil War.
2. Apply set theory to fundamental mathematical operations.
3. Differentiate between helpful and harmful bacteria.
4. Contrast the various instruments in a symphony orchestra.

One problem encountered when deriving competencies from subject matter areas is whether to use as a guide current school curriculum or what is regarded as general education in the arts and sciences. Actually, it is best to use a combination of these two standards in order to develop a relevant guide.

A fourth base for deriving competencies involves a job analysis of what effective practitioners do when working with learners. What competencies should a teacher possess in order to teach effectively? The answer would include competencies involving such daily functions as asking questions, planning lessons, evaluating papers, and organizing physical features of the classroom.

An effective teacher preparation model should include competencies derived from all four bases: philosophical, empirical, subject matter, and practitioner. All competencies should be screened through a conceptualized role of the teacher and should be tested empirically in a middle school setting. Through a continuous process of testing and validation, specific competencies may be modified and refined.

The Self as Instrument Concept

Combs (1964) presents the "self as instrument" concept of teaching that involves a shift in thinking from a mechanistic to a personal view of teaching. Instead of functioning as a "methods robot," the teacher functions as an intelligent human being who uses herself, her knowledge, and the resources at hand to solve problems and meet the learners' needs, for which she is responsible. The teacher who has learned to use "self as instrument" will change her behavior from moment to moment, from situation to situation, in order to meet the needs of students. In subscribing to this concept, Combs identifies the effective teacher as one who has learned to use self to personalize instruction for students.

This concept emphasizes teacher preparation that concerns itself with persons rather than "how to do" or "what to do if." The thrust of this kind of preparation would be directed toward helping the prospective teacher change her own behavior and see herself and the world around her differently. According to perceptual psychologists, whether an individual can behave effectively and efficiently in a given situation will depend upon how she is perceiving at that moment. In essence, we need to know how effective teachers perceive and to help prospective teachers perceive themselves and their tasks in the same way. This will require more in-depth treatment of perceptual psychology (nature of self), research findings on successful practitioners in related professions, and the research and classroom experiences of thousands of teachers (action research).

In order for the prospective teacher to develop the "self as instrument" concept, preservice experiences will have to be closely related to the personal concerns of the prospective teacher. Too often in the past, preservice education experiences have been perceived by the participant as irrelevant and sterile, failing to "hit her where she lives." As a result, many preservice education experiences have proved to be of little or questionable value. In contrast, the "self as instrument" concept requires greater personalization of preservice education.

Characteristics of Effective Teachers

Based on an extensive review of several research studies, Hamachek (1969) concluded that good teachers differ from poor teachers in how they perceive others in five ways:

1. In general, they seem to have more positive perceptions of others.
2. They do not seem to be as prone to view others as critical, attacking people with ulterior motives; rather, they see them as potential friends.
3. They tend to use more democratic classroom procedures.
4. They seem to have the capacity to see things from another's point of view.
5. They do not appear to see students as persons "you do things to" but rather as self-dependent individuals to be valued and respected.

Combs (1965) in *The Professional Education of Teachers,* cites several studies that reached similar conclusions about the way good teachers perceive themselves:

1. Good teachers see themselves as being identified with others rather than alienated from them.
2. Good teachers feel trustworthy rather than untrustworthy.
3. Good teachers feel basically adequate and able to cope with problems and events as they happen.
4. Good teachers see themselves as wanted and likable as opposed to feeling ignored and rejected.
5. Good teachers see themselves as people of consequence, dignity, and integrity.

Matching Student, Teacher, and Method

Rubin (1973) expresses concern about teacher-pupil mistakes that cause child and teacher untold aggravation. When the behavioral styles of the student and teacher blend, the student can be herself and progress. When there is a sharp contrast in behavioral styles between teacher and student, however, one must either adapt to the other, or the two must separate. Rubin and associates conducted an experiment among selected teachers in California in an attempt to find answers to the following questions: Is there some way that children and teachers can be matched on variables of compatibility? Can a formula be devised for a successful school marriage between a teacher and a child so that the relationship is mutually rewarding? The results of the experiment revealed the following points:

1. Classroom interests of children and their teachers conflict sharply.
2. Children are interested less in knowledge than in emotional success. Children want to be "psychological winners"—to experience a positive self-concept, peer acceptance, successful relationships with teacher and students, and a feeling of accomplishment with little frustration and confusion.
3. In contrast, teachers are most often valued by their administrators according to the amount of information their students learn. Therefore, teachers tend to place heavy stress upon cognitive learning as opposed to affective learning.
4. There is an urgent need to provide a better balance between cognitive and affective emphasis within schooling.
5. When behavioral styles of teacher and student are more closely matched, learners progress at a more productive rate, and interpersonal relationships are more positive.

Patterson (1973) states that the teacher is the most important factor in teaching and learning. Teacher education should focus on the feelings, attitudes, and beliefs of the teacher, including her attitudes toward herself, or her self-concept. Students teach like they have been taught rather than the way they are taught to teach. Teacher educators, therefore, should be personalized teaching models—models of humanistic education.

Self-Concept Development

Self-concept, as used in professional literature, is a term that refers to a group of feelings and cognitive processes that are inferred from observed, or manifest, behavior. LaBenne (1969) provides the following formal definition, "Self-concept is the person's total appraisal of his appearance, background and origins, abilities and resources, attitudes and feelings which culminate as a directing force in behavior" (p. 10). In other words, it is primarily what a person thinks and feels about herself that guides, controls, and regulates her actions. Self-concept is a psychological construct, an imaginary mechanism, that helps the psychologist think about and explain human behavior.

Self-concept development is greatly affected by the influence of "significant others." At an early age, the most significant others in the life of a child are her parents. Later, the child begins to recognize an increasing number of significant others, including friends, teachers, and other adults. An individual's self-concept is developed as a result of varied experiences with these significant persons.

People tend to behave in terms of how they see themselves, or students become what they are thought to be. If a person experiences failure after failure, she will sooner or later begin to believe she is a failure and will act like one. In the same way, success tends to breed success.

As a prospective teacher, you need to carefully examine the relative status of your self-concept through the use of one or more of the following techniques (LaBenne 1969):

1. Introspective self-reflections in personal, family, social, and school or work settings
2. Comparison of your descriptions of current self-concept and ideal self-concept
3. Comparison of subjective self-reports and the objective reports of clinically trained observers
4. Examination of nonintrospective inferences derived from projective techniques and clinical interview (p. 11)

Some of the most important lessons that children obtain from teachers are often the ones teachers do not consciously teach at all—lessons in human relations that teachers give to their children simply by just being themselves. What is your H.R.Q. (Human Relations Quotient)? What "messages of self" are you conveying? The following H.R.Q. test may help you find out.[1]

Human Relations—How Do You Rate?

1. I help my students accept each other on the basis of individual worth regardless of sex or race or religion or socioeconomic background.
   Rating (rate yourself on a low-high scale of 1–10):______

2. I help my students recognize clearly the basic similarities among all members of the human race and the uniqueness of every individual.
   Rating: ______

3. I help my students value the multicultural character of our society and reject stereotypes or caricatures or any derogatory reference to any segment of our community.
   Rating: ______

4. I help my students recognize prejudice as a wall which blocks communication, interaction, and mutual understanding and respect.
   Rating: ______

5. I help my students understand the influences and pressures—historical and contemporary, environmental, social, political and economic—that have been instrumental in developing group differences, progress and antagonism.
   Rating: ______

6. I help my students analyze intergroup tension and conflict with honesty and objectivity and with a will to resolve them and to seek resolution on the basis of fairness and cooperation and affirmative action.
   Rating: ______

7. I help my students appreciate the contributions of all groups—sexual, racial, religious, social class, nationality.
   Rating: ______

8. I help my students become motivated to their responsibilities as good citizens by working and striving to achieve a true democratic society with injustice for none and with equal rights and opportunities for all.
   Rating: ______

9. I help my students by carefully evaluating all curriculum materials—books, pamphlets, films, filmstrips, bulletin board pictures, charts, etc.—to insure fair and balanced treatment of all groups.
   Rating: ______

10. I help my students to learn the art of good human relations by providing a living model in my own treatment of people—each and every child, all

---

1. "Test Your H.R.Q." is reprinted from the March issue of *Teacher Magazine* with permission of the publisher.

members of the staff, from custodian to administrator, every parent and other members of the community, without exception.
Rating: ______

Scoring Yourself

Add up your ratings for the statements above. If you score 70 or more you're doing a good job. Keep it up. A score between 50 and 70 indicates you're on the right track, but can always strive harder. If you rate below 50, you need to take a good hard look at yourself and the ever-changing world around you.

Self-Knowledge Questionnaire

No one can ultimately know self, but the better you understand yourself the better you will be able to understand others. The beginning teacher should therefore engage in a great variety of self-analysis and self-awareness experiences designed to provide her with a better understanding of her personality, basic behavioral traits and characteristics, philosophy of education, attitudes toward children and adults, and degrees of sensitivity to needs of others.

This process should enable the beginning teacher to develop confidence in her becoming a humane facilitator of learning. Respond to the following self-knowledge questionnaire.[2] After reviewing your responses, you may want to discuss your responses with your instructor or fellow students.

Self-Knowledge Questionnaire

1. When I enter a new group I feel ______________.
2. When a group starts I ______________.
3. When people first meet me they ______________.
4. When I'm in a new group I feel most comfortable when ______________.
5. When people remain silent I feel ______________.
6. When someone does all the talking I ______________.
7. I feel most productive when a leader ______________.
8. I feel annoyed when a leader ______________.
9. I feel withdrawn when ______________.
10. In a group, I am most afraid of ______________.
11. When someone feels hurt I ______________.
12. I am hurt most easily when ______________.
13. I feel loneliest in a group when ______________.

2. Adapted from Atkins-Katcher Associates, Consultants to Management, Los Angeles, California.

14. Those who really know me think I am ________.
15. I trust those who ________.
16. I am saddest when ________.
17. I feel closest to others when ________.
18. People like me when I ________.
19. Love is ________.
20. I feel loved most when ________.
21. If I could do it all over again ________.
22. My greatest strength is ________.
23. I could be ________.
24. I am ________.

The Changing Role of the Middle School Teacher

Teachers were once regarded simply as a major source of information and instiller of the three "Rs." Significant changes, however, are developing in the role expectations of the middle school teacher. Tomorrow's teacher will be expected to fulfill roles as:

1. A diagnostician, who carefully analyzes students' aptitudes and achievements before guiding them into new learning experiences.
2. One among many sources of information.
3. A human-development specialist, who plans learning experiences according to sound principles of growth, development, and learning.
4. A programmer of behavioral change, who helps each student to develop desirable behavior within the affective, cognitive, and psychomotor domains.
5. An executive, who makes significant decisions about the appropriate involvement of the learner with human and material resources (particularly media and paraprofessionals) within the learning environment.
6. A team member, who cooperates with other professionals in planning and teaching.
7. An evaluator of student programs, who assesses and reports each student's progress in terms of his own capabilities.
8. An identity model, who facilitates the positive development of the student's personality and self-concept.
9. A curriculum and instruction strategist, who tests the effectiveness of instructional materials and is expert in planning individualized experiences for students.
10. An inquiry agent, a master teacher, who helps the student to clarify, internalize and apply facts, concepts, and processes.
11. A specialist in particular subject matter.

12. A source of guidance, who assists children to solve individual problems.
13. A public-relations and communications specialist, who can interpret the school program to all segments of the larger society.
14. A clerk and custodian.
15. A friend, a source of help and inspiration when the child feels forsaken.[3]

Personalized Teacher Preparation Models

If a significant change in teacher performance is going to occur, significant changes must occur in teacher preparation programs. The following selected models illustrate some of the emerging changes in teacher preparation.

Identifying Personal Concerns Model

Fuller (1969) has identified a developmental sequence of preservice teachers' concerns about teaching. Many educators agree that the reason many education courses are judged to be irrelevant by preservice teachers is that there is little if any relationship between their experiences in the courses and their concerns. The University of Texas Research and Development Center has developed a conceptual model for personalizing teacher education that is based upon Fuller's research. Figure 3.1 presents the model in simplified form.

The basic components of the model involve *assessing* the concerns and needs of preservice teachers, making them *aware* of these needs, *arousing* them to the point of wanting to take action to resolve these needs, and providing *accomplishing* activities that would enable them to meet their needs. This approach is designed to provide a sequence of experiences and processes that interrelates professional and subject matter development with teacher concerns.

The following guide, "Overview of Concerns Codes," should help you to evaluate teacher concern statements.[4]

I. Concerns About Self
Code 0. *Non-teaching Concerns*
Statement contains information or concerns which are unrelated to teaching: Codes 1 through 6 are always concerns with teaching. All other statements are coded 0.

---

3. From Larry L. Sale and Ernest W. Lee, *Environmental Education in the Elementary School* (New York: Holt, Rinehart and Winston, 1972). Reprinted with permission.
4. From Gene E. Hall, *Strategies for Personalized Teacher Education* (Minneapolis, Minn.: Association for Supervision and Curriculum Development, 1973), p. 3–5.

Figure 3.1

Teacher Concerns as a Basis for Personalizing Teacher Education

PROCESSES

		Assessment	Awareness	Arousal	Accomplishing
Impact	6				
	5				
Concerns of Task	4				
	3				
Teacher's Self	2				
	1				
Correlated	0				

SOURCE: From Gene E. Hall, *Strategies for Personalized Teacher Education* (Minneapolis, Minnesota: Association for Supervision and Curriculum Development, 1973), p. 2.

II. Concerns About Self as Teacher

Code 1. *Where Do I Stand?*
Concerns with orienting oneself to teaching situation, i.e., psychological, social, and physical environment of the classroom, school, and/or community. Concerns about supervisors, cooperating teachers, principal, parents. Concerns about evaluation, rules, or administrative policy, i.e., concern about authority figures and/or acceptance by them.

Code 2. *How Adequate Am I?*
Concern about one's adequacy as a person and as a teacher. Concern about discipline and subject matter adequacy.

Code 3. *How Do Pupils Feel About Me? What Are Pupils Like?*
Concern about personal, social, and emotional relationships with pupils. Concern about one's own feelings toward pupils and about pupils' feelings toward the teacher.

III. Concerns About Pupils

Code 4. *Are Pupils Learning What I'm Teaching?*
Concern about whether pupils are learning material selected by the teacher. Concern about teaching methods which help pupils learn what is planned for them. Concern about evaluating pupil learning.

Code 5. *Are Pupils Learning What They Need?*
Concern about pupils' learning what they *need* as per-

sons. Concern about teaching methods (and other factors) which influence that kind of learning.

Code 6. *How Can I Improve Myself as a Teacher?* (And improve all that influences pupils?)
Concern with anything and everything which can contribute to the development not only of the pupils in the class, but of children generally. Concern with personal and professional development, ethics, educational issues, resources, community problems, and other events in or outside the classroom which influence pupil gain.

Practice coding the following teacher concern statements:

a. Concern about how I can get more sleep.
b. I am concerned about the way I respond to the children. I think it is important that they never feel they are totally wrong, and I certainly don't want them to feel that I think they are wrong.
c. I am also concerned about moving to San Antonio where I will be teaching—what will my new school be like?
d. I'm concerned with the great individual differences in children—how to approach them and how to challenge the faster students without losing the slower ones.

Your answers should be as follows: a—0, b—3, c—1, d—5.

Read the following paragraphs and code the statements according to the Concerns Code.
I am concerned about being an effective teacher. I hope I'll hold a mutual respect for and from my students. I hope I can present the material in an exciting and interesting way. Since the typical students of today are drastically changing, I am deeply concerned about helping them in a way they will accept and understand. I hope I get to know each of my students personally. I doubt that I would ever degrade my students or stop trying to help and understand them, however, I am concerned in thinking I may get frustrated with some students and act on emotions. I am also concerned about relationships with the school administration. I think I could fit into almost any school and be equally excited about them all.

When I think about teaching, I am concerned about the students *really* learning about life. I believe there is a need to relate subject taught with the student's life. Also, it is important to sharpen the student's intelligence and teach him how to think for himself; to teach him how to evaluate clearly and maturely things told him, those things he reads, etc. Also, I would *de*-emphasize the importance of grades. Too many students are grade hungry for they have been brought up to believe that making grades is the only reason one goes to school. I am concerned about understanding my students. A *real* communication and mutual respect is important.

Competency-Based Teaching Models

The competencies approach to teaching has been presented previously in this chapter. Several programs have emerged across the United States that emphasize the competency-based teaching approach. One promising example is the Auburn Training Teacher Trainers (TTT) Project, Auburn University (Cadenhead and Newell 1973). The program, funded by the U.S. Office of Education, has concentrated on the improvement of teacher education through the involvement of professors from the schools of Education, Arts and Sciences, and Engineering as well as public school teachers and administrators, community representatives, and thirty-three prospective elementary school teachers. The program was structured around mastery of performance criteria, relating to four roles: diagnostician, facilitator, interactor, and innovator.

The major instrument that was used for organizing learning experiences was a competency-based learning module. Each module contained a general objective, rationale, specific performance objectives, pretest, required and optional activities, and posttest.

The following list from Cadenhead and Newell (1973) includes examples of modules relating to the various teacher roles:

> DIAGNOSTICIAN—(1) Learning Theory, (2) Technology of Evaluation, (3) Diagnostic and Prescriptive Procedures, (4) Self-Concept; FACILITATOR—(1) Operation of Equipment, (2) Instructional Design, (3) Curriculum Resources, (4) Teaching-Learning Strategies (Demonstration, Presentation, Simulation, Questioning, Discussion), (5) Classroom Organization (Team Organization, Grouping, Record Keeping), (6) Independent Study; INTERACTOR—(1) Non-Verbal Communication, (2) Facilitative Interaction, (3) Group Problem Solving; INNOVATOR—(1) Teacher as Change Agent. (p. 52)

In addition to working on modules, prospective teachers engage in laboratory experiences in area public schools, work in the TTT Learning Center, and complete a ten-week professional internship in a public school setting.

As we noted earlier, the rationale for competency-based teacher education requires educators to take a thorough look at what their teaching is designed to accomplish and to carefully review the way they go about accomplishing it. It also compels educators to modify their programs on the basis of the response of teacher trainees in order to elicit more efficient learning.

Bowles (1973) has presented the major characteristics of the University of Houston Competency-Based Teacher Education (CBTE) model. One of the major instructional tools used in the program is the learning module. The rationale of the Houston program is based primarily on three criteria—knowledge, performance, and product—that are used to assess students' cognitive understanding and their teaching behavior and effectiveness. The major thrust of the program involves the preassessment of the prospective teacher, which includes setting relevant instructional objectives, designing related learning activities, and posttesting to ascertain if the objectives have been reached.

Based on a careful review of these and similar emerging teacher preparation programs across the United States, it would appear that effective programs in the future will possess some of the following characteristics:

1. Greater attention to the personal concerns and needs of the prospective teacher in planning, implementing, and evaluating preservice experiences
2. More attention to helping prospective teachers develop a personal teaching style commensurate with both their academic and professional competencies
3. A better balance and interrelationship between liberal arts and professional preparation
4. More carefully defined entrance and exit criteria within the teacher preparation program
5. Increased effort on the part of teacher trainers to model effective teaching behaviors and themselves become learners in partnership with prospective teachers
6. Greater use of learning modules and related instructional modes designed to help the prospective teacher assume a greater voice in and responsibility for teacher preparatory experiences
7. Better quality empirical analysis of the teaching act, leading to the determination of the skills, attitudes, and knowledge that are necessary for effective teaching
8. A self-identification and analysis process earlier in the collegiate program, enabling the prospective teacher to make an earlier decision and commitment to become a teacher

Summary

Historically, prospective teachers have been admonished to consider individual differences of the learner in the learning process. Yet, in too many teacher preparation programs, behaviors are advocated or talked about but not modeled or experienced by either instructor or student.

Each learner has her own learning style, and each teacher has her own teaching style.

In order for you to develop a personal teaching style, you will need to accomplish some or all of the following:

1. Carefully assess your own personal concerns, strengths and weaknesses, and personal objectives relating to becoming an effective teacher.
2. Become knowledgeable regarding concepts of teaching, research on teaching, and characteristics of effective teaching.
3. Experiment with varied approaches to teaching under the supervision of a qualified professional.
4. Carefully analyze the varied teaching styles of several teachers.
5. Become competent in the utilization of various materials and processes designed to help you assess your effectiveness in teaching.
6. Develop competence in the development and utilization of learning modules to personalize instruction.

Competence breeds confidence. Confidence breeds success. The chapters and experiences that follow are designed to help you develop competence in the varied elements of facilitating personalized learning experiences for middle school learners.

REFERENCES

Bowles, F. Douglas. "Competency-Based Teacher Education? The Houston Story." *Educational Leadership* 30(1973):510–12.

Cadenhead, A. Kenneth, and Newell, Laura. "Personalizing Teacher Education." *Educational Technology* 13(1973):51–55.

Combs, Arthur W. "The Personal Approach to Good Teaching." *Educational Leadership* 21(1964):360–77.

Combs, Arthur W. *The Professional Education of Teachers.* Boston: Allyn and Bacon, 1965.

Cooper, James M.; Jones, Howard L.; and Weber, Wilford A. "Specifying Teacher Competencies." *The Journal of Teacher Education* 24(1973):17–23.

Fuller, Francis F. "Concerns of Teachers: A Developmental Conceptualization." *American Educational Research Journal* 6(1969):207–26.

Hall, Gene E. "Teacher Concerns as a Basis for Personalizing Teacher Education." *Strategies for Personalized Teacher Education.* Mimeographed. Minneapolis, Minn.: The Association for Supervision and Curriculum Development, 1973.

Hamachek, Don. "Characteristics of Good Teachers and Implications for Teacher Education." *Phi Delta Kappan* 50(1969):341-45.

LaBenne, Wallace D., and Greene, Bert I. *Educational Implications of Self-Concept Theory*. Pacific Palisades, Calif.: Goodyear Publishing Co., 1969.

Patterson, C. H. "The Preparation of Humanistic Teachers." *Intellect* 101(1973):195–202.

Rosenberg, Max. "Test Your H.R.Q. (Human Relations Quotient)." *Teacher* 90(1973):29.

Rubin, Louis J. "Matching Teacher, Student, and Method." *Today's Education* 62(1973):31–35.

Sale, Larry L., and Lee, Ernest W. *Environmental Education in the Elementary School*. New York: Holt, Rinehart and Winston, 1972.

Learning Module

Developing a Personal Teaching Style

Directions

This module is designed to help you in the development of a personal teaching style. To complete this module, begin with the pretest and work through the required activities. You may complete as many optional activities as you feel are applicable to your situation. Conclude with the posttest.

Pretest

Assess your present readiness for teaching by describing specific characteristics that you now possess and those characteristics that you desire to develop as a part of your teaching style.

Behavioral Objectives

Upon completion of this module you should be able to:

1. Describe specific characteristics of an effective middle school teaching style.
2. Use selected tools and procedures to measure your effectiveness in interaction with students.
3. Express specific concerns you have about becoming a teacher.
4. Contrast a minimum of three teaching approaches, indicating the relative merits of each.

Activities

(Choose those that are appropriate for you.)

1. Complete the following readings:
   a) Combs, Arthur; Avila, Donald L.; and Purkey, William. *Helping Relationships: Basic Concepts for the Helping Professions.* Boston: Allyn and Bacon, 1971.
   Chapter 3: Self-Concept.
   b) Compton, Mary F. "How Do You Prepare to Teach Transescents?" *Educational Leadership* 31(1973):214–16.

c) Flanders, Ned. *Analyzing Teaching Behavior.* Reading, Mass.: Addison-Wesley Publishing Co., 1970.
Appropriate chapters relevant to application of Flanders Interaction Analysis

d) Beegle, Charles, and Brandt, Richard M. Eds. *Observational Methods in the Classroom.* Washington, D.C.: Association for Supervision and Curriculum Development, 1973.
Chapter 7: Use of Flanders Interaction Analysis System
Chapter 8: Self-Evaluation through Video Tape Recordings

e) Hyman, Ronald T. *Ways of Teaching.* New York: J. B. Lippincott Co., 1970.
Introduction: Developing a Concept of Teaching
Chapter 10: Observing and Evaluating Teaching

f) Adams, Sam, and Garrett, John L., Jr. *To Be A Teacher: An Introduction to Education.* Englewood Cliffs, N.J.: Prentice-Hall, 1969.
Chapter 7: What is Teaching?

g) Hamachek, Don. "Characteristics of Good Teachers and Implications for Teacher Education." *Phi Delta Kappan* 50(1969):341–45.

2. Observe three middle school teachers at work in a public school classroom and write a comparative analysis of their teaching styles.
3. With the assistance of your instructor, develop competence in the use of Flanders Interaction Analysis or a related method of observational analysis.
4. Hold a conference with a college guidance counselor and complete one or more of the following:
   a) Teacher Personality Inventory
   b) Teacher Interest Inventory
   c) Teacher Personal Concerns Inventory
   d) Teacher Attitude Inventory
5. Prepare a brief lesson designed to help a selected group of learners reach an instructional objective. Audio- or videotape the lesson and discuss the results with your instructor.
6. Interview on cassette tape two middle school teachers regarding this question: What do you consider to be the essential ingredients of an effective teaching style? Discuss the tape with fellow students in teacher education.
7. Using the Education Index, review three current articles concerning characteristics of effective teaching.
8. Based on your research and related activities, prepare a brief written report concerning what you consider to be characteristics of an effective middle school teaching style.

9. Read relevant sections of *Handbook of Research on Teaching,* edited by N. C. Gage (Chicago: Rand McNally and Co., 1978).
10. Read selected chapters in *The Teacher You Choose to Be* by William A. Proefriedt (New York: Holt, Rinehart and Winston, 1975).

Posttest

Discuss what you have learned about yourself and your development of a personal teaching style.

Chapter 4

Personalizing Learning Experiences

One of the most essential steps toward personalizing experiences for middle school students is for the teachers to be their honest, sincere selves—real people! Al Cullum (1967) states the case as follows:

> When I first began teaching, there was Al Cullum the teacher and Al Cullum the person. I soon discovered that this split personality was not a healthy one for the children nor for me. I realized I had better bury Al Cullum the teacher and present Al Cullum the person, or else the school year would become monotonous months of trivia. I began to share with my students my moments of joy, my moments of love, my excitement of scholarship, and even my uncertainties. In turn, I discovered the children shared their fears, their strengths, and their hearts with me, and as a professional teacher I responded to their honesty and helped them work out their own opinions and personal values. *Sharing is a key concept* if you push back the desks successfully.

Providing humanistic, personalized experiences for students during the middle school years is top priority. Without experiencing success in middle school, students have little chance of success in secondary school. Traditionally, the public has viewed secondary schools as more important and has been willing to spend much more money on them than on elementary or middle schools. Although effective education at all levels is definitely going to cost more in the future, the greater emphasis should be placed at the elementary and middle school levels in order to assist children in developing the basic skills and concepts essential to life-long learning. Let's examine some ways in which we can make schooling a relevant, meaningful experience for emerging adolescents.

Approaches to Planning Learning Experiences

Although teachers disagree on what form planning for teaching should take, most teachers agree that effective teaching is the result of effective planning. Many variables must be considered in planning for teaching. The nature of the learner, the instructional setting, the subject matter, the available resources, and the competencies of the teacher are all very important variables to be considered.

One of the most important principles to keep in mind as a guide to effective planning is this: *The consumer should have a voice in selecting the diet.* Beginning in kindergarten, children should be given a voice in planning the instructional experiences. Under careful teacher supervision, students may be given opportunities to express their interests and needs concerning instruction. As students progress vertically in school and become more mature, they may be given increased opportunities to help the teacher plan relevant objectives, activities, and assessment processes. Certainly the expertise of the teacher should be employed to decide the degree to which students are capable of becoming involved in the planning process. It is wise to remember that an improperly planned diet generally results in indigestion!

Unit and Lesson Plans

There are generally two basic plans in middle school instruction—a unit plan and a specific lesson plan. A unit plan is a broad blueprint for a unit of study that usually contains major objectives, concepts, suggested activities, and evaluation procedures. Hanna, Potter, and Hagaman refer to a unit plan as an organization of learning experiences having the following characteristics:[1]

1. It possesses cohesion or wholeness. The goals around which the unit is organized are the unifying factor in any unit.
2. It is based on the personal-social needs of children. When children see that a unit of work is relevant to their needs, then they are usually more highly motivated to pursue it.
3. It cuts across subject lines. Greater attention needs to be directed toward an interdisciplinary studies approach to teaching that would provide opportunities for students to interrelate concepts and processes from varied disciplines.
4. It is based on modern principles of learning. It provides oppor-

1. Adapted from Lavone A. Hanna, Gladys L. Potter, and Neva Hagaman, *Unit Teaching in the Elementary School* (New York: Holt, Rinehart and Winston, 1963).

tunities for students to proceed beyond the old "study-assign-recite" method to inquiring, experimenting, collecting data, and arriving at their own conclusions.

5. It requires a larger block of time. It provides time for children to participate in a variety of activities that enable the internalization of learning. The amount of time needed for a particular unit will be dependent on the specific variables affecting each class.
6. It is life-centered. It should provide opportunities for students to relate schooling to the real-world activities of society. Schooling has often been too divorced from life outside the school.
7. It utilizes the normal drives of children. The primary needs of childhood such as the desire to satisfy curiosity, to construct, to explore, to be physically active, to share with others, to create; all these can be satisfied through an effective unit that provides for real learning.
8. It takes into account the maturational levels of children. The growth and development characteristics of the learners serve as a guide for the selection of material.
9. It emphasizes problem solving, especially of those that are relevant to the children.
10. It provides opportunities for the social development of children. Through a variety of small and large group activities, children learn to cooperate, share, accept criticism, take initiative, and develop socially acceptable behavior.
11. It is planned cooperatively by teacher and pupils. The unit plan provides an opportunity for the teacher and pupils to develop a "partnership in learning."

The lesson plan is a detailed segment of a unit plan that is designed for a specific learner or learners. It contains the same characteristics as a unit plan, but they are more specific. A suggested outline for a functional lesson plan is as follows:

Suggested Lesson Plan Guide

1. Pretest—Assesses what the learner already knows about the subject.
2. Behavioral Objectives—States what she is required to accomplish.
3. Required and optional activities—Indicates how she is to accomplish the objectives.
4. Evaluation procedures—Indicates how she is to measure her progress.
5. Resource materials—Provides listing of media and materials for use by teacher and students.

Regardless of the final format of a lesson plan, inclusion of these components will generally prove productive.

Class Meetings

Glasser (1969) has recommended classroom meetings as a vehicle for helping the teacher conduct nonjudgmental discussion with her class about what is important and relevant to them. He has identified three types of classroom meetings: the social problem-solving meeting, the open-ended meeting, and the educational-diagnostic meeting. The social problem-solving meeting involves open discussion of a problem that is relevant to the class. The teacher serves as a group leader, and the students are encouraged to examine the problem and arrive at a solution or solutions. This type of meeting has relevance for both instructional planning and improvement of class discipline.

In the open-ended meeting, children are asked to discuss any thought-provoking question that relates to their lives. The teacher does not look for any specific answers but instead attempts to encourage children to think about what they already know and to relate it to the subject being studied. Such discussion can prove extremely valuable in helping the teacher to make the curriculum more relevant.

The educational-diagnostic meeting is designed to find out what the students know or do not know following a segment of instruction. It can also be used to ascertain if teaching procedures being used in the class are effective. It should not be used, however, to grade the students. The objectivity of the process can sometimes be enhanced by asking a teacher colleague to conduct the class meeting.

The use of effective class meetings not only provides the teacher with data essential to effective lesson planning but more importantly, it establishes a cooperative relationship between the teacher and students that fosters a partnership in relevant learning experiences.

Using a Variety of Learning Guides

A learning guide consists of objective(s) and a list of materials and activities designed to help the student reach the objective. One example is the *Learning Activity Package* (LAP) or *learning module*. (For a detailed treatment of LAP, refer to Chapter 1.) A second type is the *packet* or *mini-pak* concept. This consists of a packet (could be a folder or an envelope) that has the objective(s) stated on the outside and instructions for activities on the inside. Posttests are generally kept in a central file, and children contact the teacher when they are ready to check their work. A third type is the *contract,* which will be discussed in detail later in this chapter. A fourth type is a *daily assignment sheet,* containing a list of objectives and activities from which students can choose with teacher supervision. A fifth type is a *student-developed learning guide.* A mature student who has had considerable experience in working with learning guides may be able to develop and complete her own guide with limited teacher assistance. Regardless of the type, each guide should contain such basic ingredients as a pretest, behavioral objectives, activities and materials, and a posttest.

Curriculum Contracts

A curriculum contract consists of a single unit or topic outlined by the teacher in which the student "contracts" to complete a set of learning experiences. Dunn and Dunn (1972) emphasize that using a contract facilitates learning because it provides students with the following ingredients:

1. A list of items they must learn
2. A procedure for demonstrating competency to the teacher
3. A performance criterion that indicates what they must do before they will be able to move forward to another contract
4. A choice of varied materials on their academic level
5. A choice of a variety of activities to help them reach their objectives
6. Opportunities to share what they have learned through self-selected reporting alternatives

Programmed Instruction

There are basically two types of programmed instruction—linear and branching. Teachers need to distinguish between linear and branching programs because the processes involving student learning activities are vastly different for each. *Linear programming* is a rather simplistic form of programming that involves the presentation of a stimulus, or a frame of material, to which the student makes a response. The student then compares her response to the correct response. If her response is correct, she is reinforced and permitted to advance to the next frame or stimulus. *Branching* or *adaptive programming* provides options at the reinforcement stage. Regardless of the student's response she is directed to additional material appropriate to her degree of understanding. For example, if her response is correct to item 15 of a program, she may be advanced to item 35 of a program. If her response to item 15 is incorrect, she may be directed to review material within or outside the actual program prior to advancing. Using a branching program allows students to follow different paths and different rates of progress toward their goals. (See Figure 4.1.)

As shown in Figure 4.1, linear programs present material in small amounts to students who respond by selecting either a yes/no or a multiple choice response. Branching provides alternative choices and varied subsequent actions. It is more adapted to the needs of different learners because it allows content to be skipped and remedial or more challenging sequences to be used.

Programming is very consistent with modern instructional practice with its emphasis on mastery of clearly specified content, at a specified level of

Figure 4.1

Programming Patterns

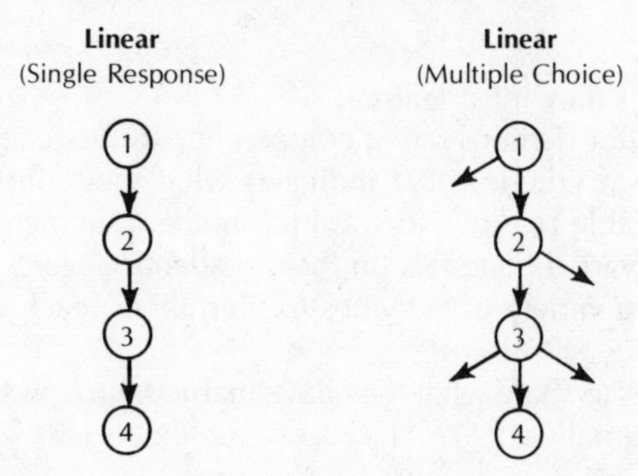

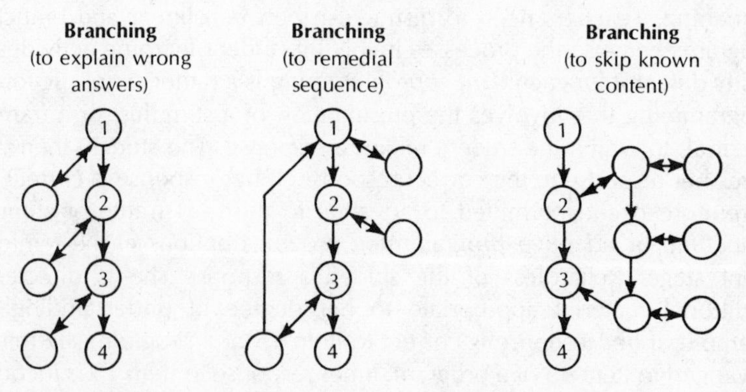

SOURCE: From James W. Brown, Richard B. Lewis, and Fred F. Harcleroad, *AV Instruction: Technology, Media, and Methods* (New York: McGraw Hill Book Co., 1977), p. 339. Used with permission.

competence, and at a pace appropriate for each learner. Programs may be produced in varied forms ranging from programmed textbooks to sophisticated programs used in computer-assisted instruction.

The process of programming may be helpful when it is applied to general instruction planning. One of the more challenging planning activities for any teacher is to write a program for a particular unit of study. This experience enables the teacher to assess her personal knowledge of the unit's content in addition to giving attention to appropriate instructional objectives and activities.

Programming is based on the stimulus-response theory of learning advocated by B. F. Skinner, Harvard psychologist. Simplified, it consists of a stimulus, a response, and a reinforcement (S-R-R). The branching form of programming offers greater opportunities for individualization than the linear form as a result of options available at the reinforcement stage.

Linear programming is especially helpful to the student who is experiencing difficulty with a given subject and needs to proceed at a rate that allows for complete development in every phase of the material. Branching is particularly helpful to the more advanced student who can master the material more rapidly and who works at a high level of self-dependence.

Developing Classroom Learning Centers

Someone once remarked, "You can homogenize milk, but you can't homogenize kids." Children with the same achievement scores on any given day are not all alike. You may find that they are similar on one variable, but you will also find that they are vastly different on many others. Rather than continuing to wrestle with the rigidity of traditional grouping patterns, many teachers are moving toward a more flexible format built around classroom learning centers. Learning centers, or stations, are small areas or tables that house carefully selected materials relating to a specific subject area. You can view the classroom as a learning laboratory characterized by two major streams of organization: (1) teaching activities, in which the teacher assumes responsibility for identifying and extending concepts and assisting children in the inquiry process, and (2) classroom learning centers, or stations, where children can go by choice or assignment to engage in a variety of personalized learning experiences. Learning centers may be established as continuing centers for the school year or as temporary centers for specific units of study.

It is very important to remember that the effective use of classroom learning centers requires the teacher to plan carefully, to continue to help children develop skills of self-dependent learning, and to engage in directed teaching when needed. Teacher-directed activities and learning centers should complement each other. For example, the teaching of certain fundamental concepts or skills relating to a particular subject may be developed in a teacher-directed group setting, and then each child may extend and internalize these concepts or skills by working in a classroom learning center.

Teaching children how to learn is a very important objective of middle school instruction. The classroom learning center facilitates this process. Moving too rapidly toward using learning centers without the students' having the prerequisite skills, however, could result in chaos. A classroom effectively organized around learning centers, however, provides each student with the following positive instructional characteristics:

1. A voice in choosing objectives, activities, and materials
2. An opportunity to progress at her own rate
3. A chance to succeed at learning tasks
4. Exposure to a great variety of instructional materials
5. Opportunities for better diagnosis and guidance by the classroom teacher
6. Optional learning experiences
7. Growth in self-assessment processes in addition to teacher's evaulation
8. Opportunities for creativity and self-expression
9. Encouragement of freedom *with* responsibility

Each classroom learning center should have an organizational structure that facilitates learning. In contrast to the traditional concept of an interest center in which a hodge-podge of materials is accumulated for browsing purposes, a learning center should contain selected materials designed to help students reach their objectives. Ingredients of the learning center should change as the needs of the students change. A stagnant, outmoded learning center will defeat the instructional intent of a center. Instead, a learning center should be attractive, organized, and stimulating in character. (A numbering or color coding of materials should help in reducing internal maintenance problems.) There is no definite "right" or "wrong" format for classroom learning centers. Experiment to determine what approaches work best in your setting. We probably know more and do less about individual student differences than any other area of schooling.

Using Games and Simulation

An instructional tool that is receiving increased attention and use in the middle school is simulation. Essentially, simulation involves structuring a real-life situation in the classroom setting for instructional purposes. You could say that a simulation is the next best thing to being "the real thing." It has been used effectively by the military in war games, by NASA astronauts to reproduce conditions in space for training purposes, and by driver's license examiners to reproduce driving conditions and situations for testing. Educational games are a type of simulation. Gordon (1970) in her excellent book, *Games for Growth: Educational Games in the Classroom,* defines a game as any simulated contest among players who follow rules with an objective of winning. The only difference, if any, between a game and a simulation is that a game usually has a winner and a simulation does not.

Although the word *game* connotes fun, educational games should emphasize the involvement of students in problem-solving and decision-making processes. If games served only to motivate students to learn, their use would be justified in the middle school. In addition to stimulating motivation and providing fun, however, they offer excellent opportunities for students in problem solving, decision making, socialization, value analysis, and development of different learning skills. A variety of excellent commercially prepared educational games that correlate with various areas of the middle school curriculum are now available. Some of these are:

Get Set: Reading-Readiness Games, Houghton Mifflin Company. This set consists of eight games designed to help children learn basic reading methods.

Economy, Industrial Relations Center, University of Chicago. This game helps children develop an understanding of the flow of goods and services in the economy.

Bushman Exploring and Gathering, Educational Development Center, Cambridge, Massachusetts. This game emphasizes cultural adaptation and the various ways in which people deal with the physical environment.

Colony, Science Research Associates. This game helps children develop an understanding of the relations between the American Colonies and Great Britain in the eighteenth century.

Environmental Values Auction, The Center for Curriculum Design, Evanston, Illinois.

Promotion, Science Research Associates, Inc. This game engages students in the complex developments of industrialization and urbanization in late nineteenth century America.

Mathematics Games, D. C. Heath and Company. This set consists of a great variety of games for helping students learn basic mathematical operations.

For a detailed description of these and other games including addresses and information for obtaining them, consult Alice Gordon's *Games for Growth: Educational Games in the Classroom.*

To help you develop a better understanding of simulation as an instructional tool, two examples are included here for your use. (See Figures 4.2 and 4.3.)

Figure 4.2

Environmental Values Auction Instrument

This simulation consists of twenty items to be sold at auction to the highest bidder, following these rules:

1. You are to pretend that you presently have *none* of the items listed.
2. You have a total of $5,000 to spend.
3. You can spend no more than $2,500 on any one item.
4. Bids must open at *no less that $50 and no more than $500* and must proceed by increments of no less than $50 and no more than $100.

Directions

This auction is not a measuring device but is designed to help clarify value priorities and valuing processes. Allocate your initial $5,000 in the first column headed "Initial $5,000 Budget" according to your own personal priorities. Select a member of your group to serve as an auctioneer. As the auction proceeds, record your bids in the column headed "Highest Amount I Bid." The auctioneer will record the winning top bid in the appropriate column and initial the name of the player who made the top bid. Only the top bidders spend money, which is subtracted from their personal bank account.

Evaluation

Ask each participant to label his or her sheet in multiples of five. Identify what all the ones, twos, threes, fours, and fives have in common. For example, each participant should identify the following categories or types of values:

Ones—personal values (self)
Twos—cultural values
Threes—other-oriented values (concern for others)
Fours—material values
Fives—environmental values

Figure 4.2 (continued)

	Initial $5,000 Budget	*Highest Amt. I Bid*	*Top Bid*
A long life free of illness	______	______	______
Travel and tickets to any cultural or athletic events, as often as you wish	______	______	______
The love and admiration of friends	______	______	______
Television	______	______	______
An unspoiled natural setting for your home	______	______	______
Complete self-confidence with a positive outlook on life	______	______	______
A complete library for your personal use	______	______	______
A happy family relationship	______	______	______
An automobile	______	______	______
A large fruit and vegetable garden	______	______	______
A very satisfying love relationship	______	______	______
The ability to speak many languages	______	______	______
A chance to eliminate sickness and poverty	______	______	______
Electricity	______	______	______
A chance to preserve endangered species	______	______	______
An understanding of the meaning of life	______	______	______
Unlimited funds for the enjoyment of music	______	______	______
A world without prejudice	______	______	______
Commercially canned and frozen foods	______	______	______
A world without air and water pollution	______	______	______

SOURCE: Adapted from The Center for Curriculum Design, Evanston, Illinois.

This simulation emphasizes a very important aspect of intermediate education that is often treated only on a limited basis—the affective dimension of values clarification. A careful analysis of it should reveal students' value priorities.

Figure 4.3

NASA—Decision by Consensus

Instructions

You are a member of a space crew originally scheduled to rendezvous with a mother ship on the lighted surface of the moon. Due to mechanical difficulties, however, your ship was forced to land at a spot some 200 miles from the rendezvous point. During reentry and landing, much of the ship and the equipment aboard was damaged. Since survival depends on reaching the mother ship, you must select the items that are most critical to take on the 200-mile trip. Below are listed the fifteen items left intact and undamaged after landing. Your task is to rank order them in terms of their importance in helping your crew reach the rendezvous point. Place the number *1* by the most important item, the number 2 by the second most important, and so on through number *15,* the least important.

____	____	*6	fifty feet of nylon rope
____	____	15	box of matches
____	____	4	food concentrate
____	____	8	parachute silk
____	____	13	portable heating unit
____	____	11	two .45 calibre pistols
____	____	12	one case of dehydrated Pet Milk
____	____	1	two 100-lb. tanks of oxygen
____	____	3	stellar map (of the moon's constellation)
____	____	9	life raft
____	____	14	magnetic compass
____	____	2	five gallons of water
____	____	10	signal flares
____	____	7	first aid kit containing injection needles
____	____	5	solar-powered FM receiver-transmitter

This is an exercise in group decision making. Your group is to employ the method of group consensus to reach its decision. This means that the assessment of the importance of each of the fifteen survival items must be agreed on by each group member before it becomes part of the group decision. Consensus is difficult to reach. Therefore, not every ranking will meet with everyone's complete approval. Try as a group to make each ranking one with which *all* group members can at least partially agree. Here are some guidelines to use in reaching consensus:

1. Avoid arguing for your own individual judgments. Approach the task on the basis of logic.

Figure 4.3 (continued)

2. Avoid changing your mind only to reach agreement and avoid conflict. Support only solutions with which you are able to agree somewhat, at least.
3. Avoid conflict-reducing techniques such as majority vote, averaging, or trading in reaching decisions.
4. View differences of opinion as helpful rather than as a hinderance in decision making.

You have thirty minutes—Go!

*Answer key.

NASA—Decision by Consensus is an example of a cognitive-oriented simulation emphasizing decision-making processes and scientific knowledge. (See Figure 4.3.)

As a teacher, you should be encouraged to develop your own simulations in addition to using commercially prepared materials effectively. Anything that occurs in life from buying groceries at the supermarket to flying in a jet plane can be simulated. Simulation is a "slice of life" that is restructured in the classroom to facilitate learning.

Concept Learning Strategies

In today's rapidly changing society, the amount of known knowledge in a given discipline is increasing at a phenomenal rate. Experts describe this growth process in terms of the "knowledge generation," the period of time in which the amount of known knowledge in a given discipline doubles. The length of the knowledge generation has now decreased to less than ten years. Obviously, many of the facts we are presently teaching middle school children will become dated or obsolete before these children complete their formal schooling. Therefore, it is far more important to teach learners how to develop concepts and extract meaning from facts and how to discover new facts than to teach them to memorize large quantities of facts.

A concept has been defined in different ways. Note the following examples. Quillen and Hanna (1961) define a concept as a general idea that is usually expressed by a word and that represents a class or group of things or actions having certain characteristics in common. A concept is a thinking unit, a vehicle for combining isolated data into a whole for communication purposes. Helping children learn concepts requires the use of carefully planned teaching/learning strategies. *A Study of Thinking*

(Bruner, Goodnow, and Austin 1956) is one of the hallmark studies of concept learning. The study consisted of twenty laboratory experiments that generated extensive data on concept formation and attainment, the different types of concepts, and the learning set of the individual for a concept-learning task. More recently, the research of David Ausubel (1968) has identified the following components in the concept formation process: (1) discriminating different stimulus patterns, (2) formulating hypotheses relating to abstracted common elements, (3) subsequently testing such hypotheses in specific situations; (4) designating some of these for a general category having a set of common attributes that cover all possible variations; (5) relating these attributes to similar ideas; (6) making a distinction between the new concept and similar concepts learned earlier; (7) generalizing the critical attributes of the new concept to all members of the class; and (8) representing the new categorical content with a symbol commonly used in our culture.

The work of Piaget (1964) and associates indicates that a child's ability to work with the broad concepts of space, time, matter, and causation depends on a type of learning that evolves from her direct sensory experiences. The voluminous research of Piaget indicates that each individual progresses at her own rate through four intellectual development periods: sensorimotor (birth to eighteen months); preoperational (eighteen months to seven years); concrete operational (seven years to eleven years); and formal operational (eleven years and over). Teachers must know these characteristics if they are to utilize appropriate concept learning strategies.

Piaget's theories are based on a lifetime of careful research, are comprehensive, and are directly related to learning. According to Piaget, as children pass through each of the four periods of intellectual development stages they develop particular thinking skills in a certain sequence. Children in any given age group will operate at different levels of thinking according to where each one is in this sequence. If in teaching the teacher does not make allowances for these intellectual differences, students may be unable to respond through no fault of their own. (See Figure 4.4.)

Gagné (1968) has suggested a model for concrete concept learning. (See Figure 4.5.)

One of the better sources of assistance in developing a concept teaching strategy is *Three Teaching Strategies for the Social Studies* by Bruce R. Joyce, Marsha Weil, and Rhoada Wald (1972). The materials consist of an instructor's manual, filmstrip, and cassette audiotape treatment of concept learning, group investigation, and role playing. The concept learning strategy consists of the following steps:

1. *Collecting data*—This involves the teacher's guiding the students in listing a great variety of data that are already a part of their experi-

Figure 4.4

Piaget's Developmental Stages and Their Characteristics

SENSORIMOTOR
Birth to approximately 2 years

— Stage is preverbal
— An object "exists" only when in the perceptual field of the child
— Basic physical experience with objects forms the foundation for later intellectual development
— Hidden objects are located through random physical movement without thought

---

PREOPERATIONAL
Approximately 2 years to 7-8 years

— Commonly satisfied with multiple and often contradictory explanations
— Tendency to focus or "center" attention on only one variable at a time
— Apparent visual contradictions do not cause conflict in thinking
— Bound to own perceptions of happenings, to what is thought to be "seen"
— Learning through simple trial-and-error rather than through logic
— Development of mental symbols and symbolic play
— Behavior and thinking are egocentric

CONCRETE OPERATIONS
7-8 years to 11-12 years

— Logic is bound to the manipulation of objects
— The concept of reversibility develops
— The concepts of conservation develop (first conservation of number, then length, followed by substance and area, then weight and, finally, volume)
— Logic begins to develop and the child learns to make groupings of classes and relations (e.g., serial ordering)

FORMAL OPERATIONS
Beginning at 11-12 years and continuing throughout life

— The ability to think abstractly without the need to work directly with physical objects
— The ability to coordinate several variables in thought or action
— The ability to combine propositions
— The ability to make systematic combinations of objects or symbols
— The ability to hypothesize, predict consequences and consider implications in new situations

SOURCE: From Oduard Egil Dyrli, "Implementing Intellectual Development Assessments" in *Implementing Teacher Competencies: Positive Approaches to Personalized Education,* James E. Weigand, editor, © 1977, pp. 7-11. Reprinted by permission of Prentice-Hall, Inc., Englewood Cliffs, New Jersey.

Figure 4.5

Gagné's Concept Learning Model

Step 1. Insure that the student repeats the concept name to acquire a stimulus-response connection.

Step 2. Have the student identify several varied exemplars of the concept and specify its name.

Step 3. Present several exemplars of the concept and several varied nonexemplars of the concept. (Having the students identify the discriminations by name is optional.)

Step 4. Present additional exemplars of the concept all at once, and request students to specify the concept name.

Step 5. Present the student with a situation containing a new instance of the concept, and ask him to identify the concept.

SOURCE: From Robert M. Gagné, *The Conditions of Learning* (New York: Holt, Rinehart and Winston, 1968), p. v.

ence. For example, the teacher could present the topic "Environment" and record students' responses to it on the chalkboard.

2. *Classifying data*—Students are guided in the process of placing related data into categories. Different learners may classify data in different ways.
3. *Labeling categories*—This involves students' developing an "umbrella" under which related data may be placed. For example, one student may group collecting trash, using returnable bottles, and recycling under the category, "Ways of Fighting Pollution." Another student may choose to use some of the same data in forming a different category or concept. (See Figure 4.6.)

By engaging learners in this type of concept learning, the teacher is emphasizing that (1) learners need to identify their present data and conceptualization level for a particular topic, (2) they need to see that concepts are formed by interrelating different data, and (3) they should understand that an effective concept learning strategy involves searching for and verifying new data from which new concepts may be formed. Concept learning enables children to develop symbolic control over their environment. To be most effective, the problem or topics explored should be those that are relevant to the childrens' lives.

A concept learning strategy is particularly valuable as a teaching tool because of its different uses. It could serve a pretest function, enabling both the students and teacher to find out what they already know about a particular subject. It can also be used effectively as a motivational tech-

Figure 4.6

Suggested Application of Concept Learning Strategy

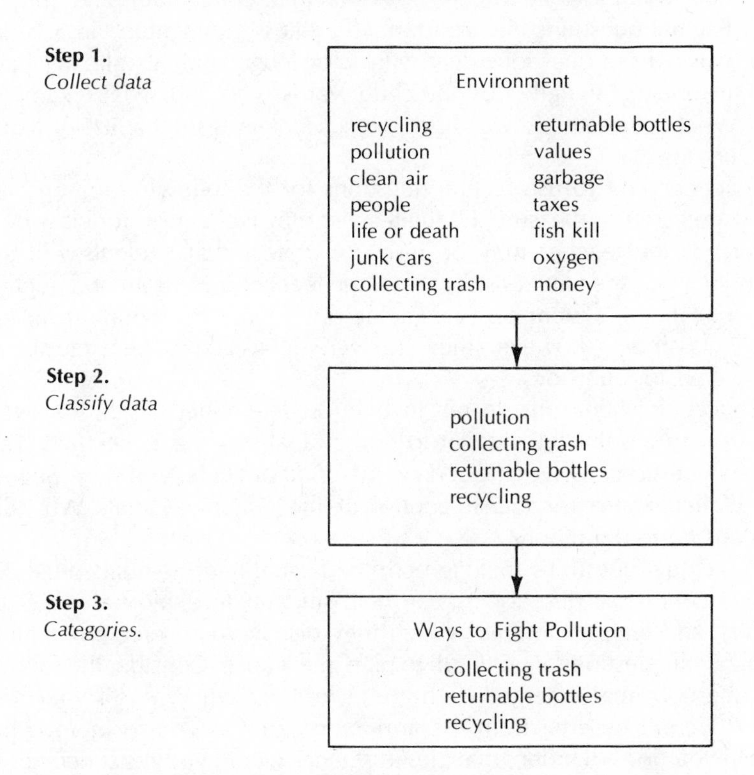

nique to involve the reluctant learner; a student who normally does not contribute in class discussion may begin to contribute more when she realizes that her ideas are acceptable and valued. The concept learning strategy is most helpful in teaching learners how to learn processes. The strategy requires the learner to inquire, to explore, to examine data, to conceptualize, and to validate facts and concepts. It may also serve as a springboard to new interests or ideas that the student had not previously encountered or considered. It helps to instill in students an appreciation and respect for each others' ideas and varying points of view. Probably the most important feature of a concept learning strategy is that it stimulates both students and the teacher to develop new ways of learning!

Questioning Strategies

Questioning is perhaps the central skill used in the teaching-learning experience. In actual classroom practice, teachers and students do make extensive use of questions. Research indicates that as much as one-third of all classroom discourse consists of questions. Teachers ask questions that tend to fall into three categories—factual, conceptual, and contextual. Factual questions elicit information that is "knowable" in a verifiable way. These questions deal with knowledge students already have and are usually signalled by the code words *who* and *what.* Examples are: What is the atomic weight of oxygen? What is the capital of North Carolina?

Teachers tend to use factual questions for the following reasons: (1) They are easier to measure, (2) the teacher may feel a need for classroom order, (3) the teacher may be insecure or fear that students will ask questions that she can't answer, or (4) the teacher may desire to maintain the educational system as it is. Factual questions are important; in too many classrooms, however, they are overemphasized to the exclusion of other types of questions.

Conceptual questions do not involve predetermined "right" answers but instead require the student to probe, analyze, and generalize. This type of question involves the code words *should, ought,* and *why*. Should the United States relinquish control of the Panama Canal? Why did humans go to the moon?

Contextual questions include both the factual and the conceptual. Effective contextual questioning can help students to explore the beliefs, values, and feelings through which they discover and create meaning. Contextual questions are difficult to plan in advance. Consider the following questions that emerged from a unit on the Civil War. "If your best friend were a deserter from the army and came to you for help, what would you do?" "Under what circumstances would you resist defending your country?" "What is the closest you have ever come to a kind of 'Civil War' in your own family?" Contextual questions are designed to stimulate students to talk about their real concerns and to examine the meaning of subject matter in the context of their daily lives.

Research in classroom discourse indicates that questions constitute about one-third of classroom discourse and teachers ask about 86 percent of the questions (Bellack et al. 1966). In contrast, students raise less than 15 percent of the classroom questions. One evidence of effective teaching is students' generating frequent, high-quality questions. The kind of questions students ask and the frequency with which they ask them may well be more important in the classroom than the kinds of questions teachers ask.

Galloway (1973) conducted a study that examined the question, Will student teachers, as a result of training, increase the proportion of questions asked that require cognitive functioning beyond recall? The subjects were prospective elementary teachers enrolled in a programmed course in introductory educational psychology at the University of Victoria in

Victoria, British Columbia, Canada. The study was conducted over a one-year period. When the questions asked in September were compared with questions asked in March, a greater percentage of the questions asked in March required cognitive functioning above simple recall. Results of the study suggest that specific training results in an increased proportion of "higher" category questions.

Enokson (1971) has developed a simplified teacher question classification model. The model allows a question to be classified simultaneously into one of two categories and on two separate scales. The first scale, cognition, is based on Bloom's *Taxonomy,* and the second, nature, is based on Guilford's *Model of Intellect.* The cognition scale contains the categories of *low* and *high. Low* requires only memory, while *high* requires the performance of higher order mental processes such as comprehension, application, analysis, synthesis, and evaluation. The nature scale includes categories of *convergent* and *divergent* questions. A *convergent* or closed question requires only a single possible answer. A *divergent* or open question requires a number of possible answers. (See Figure 4.7.)

Figure 4.7

The Simplified Teacher Question Classification Model

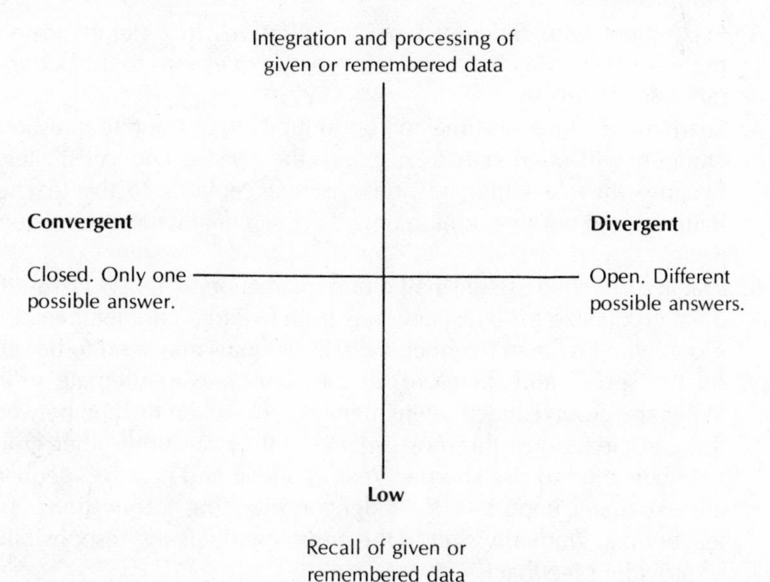

SOURCE: From Russell Enokson, "A Basic Experimental Model for Effecting Behavioral Change in the Questioning Practices of Prospective Elementary Teachers," doctoral dissertation, University of Northern Colorado, 1971.

The model permits a classification of questions that is practical and that allows for the development of questioning strategies that facilitate the inquiry process. It should be very useful in training teachers to question their students more effectively.

The effects of questions on students are varied. Students seem to learn more when questions are a part of instruction. Also, there is a positive relationship between frequent questioning and student achievement. Asking students questions about their problem-solving behavior results in their being better able to collect available information and apply it to solving specific problems. Certain kinds of questions facilitate student talk. Asking open-ended, divergent questions generally results in students' responding with longer, more elaborate statements than asking memory questions. For additional help on questioning models, see Claudia Crump's "Teacher's Questions and Cognition," *Educational Leadership* 27(1970):659.

Some practical suggestions for improving your questioning skills are:

1. Be sure the objectives of instruction are clear. Use the type of question that relates directly to the objective. If the objective emphasizes remembering information, then emphasize memory questions.
2. Monitor the questioning behavior of both yourself and your students. Use a cassette recorder to record different segments of interaction and then analyze the kinds of questions and responses employed.
3. Experiment with different types of questions in different instructional settings. Match appropriate types of questions to the needs of individual students.
4. Learn to give students time and opportunity to respond to questions. Students will often start to respond, then pause and get flustered because they fear their response is unacceptable to the teacher. Patience and positive reinforcement are essential when asking questions.
5. Practice effective use of small group interaction. In most classes, the ideal group size for a discussion is from five to eight members. In a group with less than five members, individuals may tend to be "put on the spot," and therefore all members may participate more. When the group exceeds eight members, however, the gap between the participation of the most frequent talkers and the other group members tend to rise sharply. Peer approval and positive feedback are extremely important to students responding to questions. The teacher can gradually shift to the group members the responsibility of providing feedback.

6. Using nonverbal cues such as nodding, pointing, smiling, or looking puzzled or thoughtful are ways to encourage multiple responses.
7. Teachers and students need to learn how to prompt, probe, and assist each other in focusing on the main elements of a discussion.
8. Practice the "sequence" pattern methodology: ask the question; pause; designate a student to answer the question; listen; and think.
9. Be a good verbal model for the students.

Role Playing—Humanistic Involvement

Role playing is a small group technique for dramatizing, humanizing, and actively involving learners in "real-world" problem solving. Role playing varies in difficulty from a very simplistic, charades-type activity ("You be Bugs Bunny for sixty seconds") to a very sophisticated problem-solving, instructional process. The latter format, role playing as a problem-solving tool, is generally more productive in the middle school. The process involves the following basic steps: (1) identification of a realistic problem that needs a solution; for example, what can we do to eliminate some of the problems we are having with our parents concerning homework? (2) selection of participants, hopefully volunteers, to portray certain identified roles, (3) setting up the role playing situation, (4) the role playing itself, directed toward finding a solution(s) to the selected problem, and (5) discussion and clarification of the role playing. The teacher should serve as a guide to the process with limited direct involvement. A particular role-playing situation may be reenacted by a new group of participants who may develop different solutions to the same problem. An excellent guide to using role playing in the classroom setting is *Role Playing and Teacher Education: A Manual for Developing Innovative Teachers* by Lehman (1971).

Beyond Classroom Walls

If we are to make schooling more personal and relevant for children, we must avoid the traditional concept that we should teach concepts and processes for their own sake without regard for how they relate to the world outside the school. It is indeed tragic to see teachers and students "locked" into a sterile classroom treatment of concepts that is devoid of any relationship to life outside the school. In an interview, the noted futurist Alvin Toffler emphasized this:

> We need to abandon the Neanderthal notion that education takes place only in schools. We all know that education is not just something that happens in our heads. It involves our total biochemistry. Neither does it

> occur solely within the individual. Education springs from the interplay between the individual and a changing environment. (Shane 1974, p. 73)

The teacher who desires to make schooling more relevant to society will explore a variety of processes designed to remove barriers to real-world learning. Specific attention should be given to the effective use of both professional and paraprofessional resource persons, well-planned field trips, and mass media, especially television.

Resource Persons: Help for Teachers

The teacher can enhance the realism of classroom experiences through the effective selection of resource persons. These persons include students, fellow teachers, and educational personnel; related professional personnel such as lawyers, doctors, and engineers; and senior citizens, adult volunteers, and paid paraprofessionals.

Teachers who have had unusual experiences, who have traveled, or who have special interests or talents may serve as excellent resources. Also, most communities have a variety of professional personnel who are willing to volunteer their specialized services on a carefully planned basis. Each school should keep a current file of community resource personnel, indicating the special talents, skills, or interests they would be willing to share on a volunteer basis and what time their services would be available. Some of the most helpful resources may turn out to be senior citizens or interested parents.

Paraprofessionals: Effective Use

More and more schools are using paraprofessionals to help teacher's personalize instruction. They provide an excellent source of help if certain guidelines are followed in their selection and use. The principal should select his staff, both professional and paraprofessional, not only on the basis of academic and teaching qualifications but also on the basis of personalities and interpersonal relationship skills.

If a paraprofessional *has learned* to work with children and a teacher *has learned* to use a paraprofessional in the classroom, a productive relationship emerges. Just any warm body, however, is not suited for working with middle school students!

The local school board should establish policies and procedures for effective use of paraprofessionals. The principal and his staff should identify those tasks not directly involving children that paraprofessionals could perform. Progress could then be made toward identifying the skills that the paraprofessional should possess in order to perform these tasks productively. Teachers and paraprofessionals may require some in-service experiences relating to role clarification, expectations, and productive methods of working as a team to facilitate learning. The teacher is responsible for coordinating the work of the paraprofessional. Precedent has already been clearly established for using paraprofessionals such as the dental technician to help the dentist and the licensed practical nurse (L.P.N.) to help the medical doctor. The effective use of paraprofessionals in the classroom could release the teacher to really teach!

Excursions for Learning

If wisely planned and conducted, a field trip can greatly enrich middle school learning. Teachers who know the community will be aware of some of the many opportunities for learning that are available outside the classroom and beyond the school premises. Because they will want to make some of these opportunities available to all their students, they should plan field trips for them.

Before considering field trip procedures, it would be wise for teachers to examine some of the technicalities involved. First of all, teachers should review school policies concerning field trips and the state law regarding personal liability in case of an accident. (They could probably obtain this information by consulting with the principal.) In some states, the teacher is liable in the case of an accident involving a child if the child has been taken from the school premises by the teacher. In other instances, there is an insurance arrangement whereby the school, not the teacher, will be held responsible in case of accident. When transportation is provided by the school, the child is covered by school vehicular insurance. These are some facts every teacher should be aware of before making definite arrangements for a field trip.

If a field trip is to be made beyond walking distance, the teacher should request parents' signed permissions to take each child. In many school systems, a signed blanket permission is secured from parents permitting the child to participate in any and all trips to be made by the class during the school year. Even though parents' signatures for blanket yearly permission are on file, however, it is a good idea for the teacher to advise parents of particular field trips.

Before any field trip is undertaken, the teacher and learners should be prepared. The teacher should have goals and objectives in mind along with being familiar with the place the class plans to go. The children, through previous experience, conversation, classroom discussion, and information supplied by the teacher, should have developed an attitude that will make them both eager to verify their present information and alert to make new observations and findings on the trip.

Whether the group plans to visit a privately owned or a publicly operated establishment (a bakery or a post office, for example) permission must be obtained from the proper authorities and arrangements for the trip made in advance. Trips to the woods or to grocery or hardware stores can usually be made without special appointments. In making group trips to such places as stores and markets, however, the teacher should plan the trip so that the group will not be underfoot during peak business hours.

When planning a field trip, the teacher should make sure that each child realizes the importance of following the safety rules she establishes. First of all, it must be understood that the group will always stay together. It may be a good idea, before starting out, to choose one or two leaders and "back captains." Students should not go ahead of the leaders or drop behind the back captains. Also, if the field trip is made on foot, it should be understood that the group will always stop at the street corners so that the whole group can cross the street together. When teachers let children know that this rule is not only for their safety but also for helping car, truck, and bus drivers, they tend to show the rule greater respect.

If you plan a field trip to a place too distant for walking, you must consider how the children will reach their destination. One of the most satisfactory ways of handling this, although it may be a questionable one from the point of view of liability, is to solicit the aid of parents who are known to be expert and cautious drivers. It is a good idea, however, to have two adults in each car in case of a flat tire or engine trouble. Car trouble and five ten-year-olds are not a good combination!

An appropriate field trip for middle school students would be a visit to a national military park, for example. This would be a unique learning experience because the learners would be exposed to historical facts, drawings, diagrams, and artifacts in the museum as well as actual historical battle sites, graves, and markers on the nature trails. A ranger could possibly be enlisted to give historical descriptions of the locations and articles that the children would see. All the steps of preparation listed earlier should be considered in the organization and implementation of this field trip. If a unit of history pertaining to the Revolutionary War has been taught, the information gained from this trip could be used to reinforce it.

To follow up this field trip, students could be allowed to engage in classroom discussion, each sharing a bit of knowledge gleaned from the experience. Also, several students may want to do further research on associated historical events and share their findings with their classmates.

Television: A Vehicle for Interrelationships

Television is a powerful medium with tremendous potential for helping students interrelate the "real world" with schooling. Consider, for example, the penetrating effect of viewing a man walking on the moon as opposed to the effect of reading about it in a newspaper. An effective teacher will seek every opportunity to utilize television as an instructional tool.

This medium may be used to meet a great variety of instructional needs in such activities as developing listening skills and vocabulary, creative writing, testing factual knowledge via a quiz show format, and studying dramatic structure through soap operas. The teacher should use *TV Guide* and related publications in planning units of study involving television and in guiding the viewing habits of students at home and at school. *Scholastic Teacher* provides program information and suggests teaching methods to be used with television. Many educational magazines have a special media section that may be helpful in program selection and follow-up.

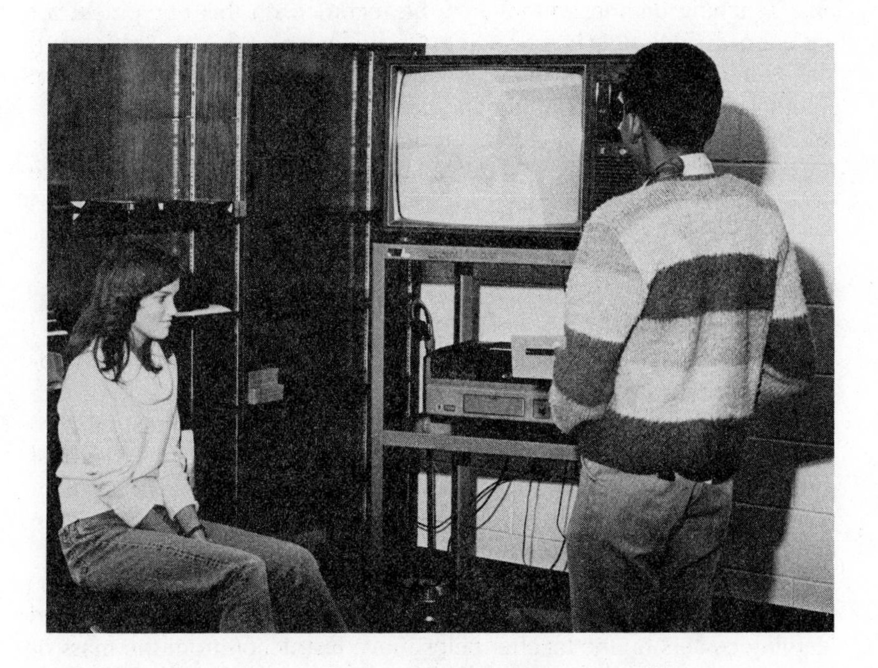

How can you use television to facilitate instruction?

Suggestions for Classroom Use of Television

Selection and use of a particular program requires careful consideration of several questions:

— Are you informed about the objectives of the program? Do they relate to your current unit of study?
— Do you need to prepare a study guide, or is there a commercially prepared guide available?
— What physical arrangements are necessary to insure effective viewing?
— Have you considered a variety of individualized follow-up activities?
— Do you plan to use earphones to enable students to view the program without disturbing others?
— Have you considered inviting television station managers to your class as resource persons?

Videotape recorders (vtr) and camera-recorder systems are becoming more widely used in classroom settings. (Of the units available, the lower cost portable units may be used most effectively by middle school learners.) Teaching demonstrations may be recorded on this equipment for various uses, including later viewing. Or, students may design, implement, and evaluate their own television program with teacher supervision. Another excellent use for the portable videotape recorder is microteaching. Microteaching involves the teacher's making a tape of her teaching performance that she can later anlayze with or without the assistance of her supervisor.

Summary

Providing humanistic, personalized experiences for children during middle school years is a top priority for teachers. Effective teaching is a product of effective planning. In planning, many variables must be considered including the characteristics of the learners, the instructional setting, the subject matter, the available resources, and your own competencies as a teacher. More relevant experiences evolve when children are also involved in this planning process.

Personalized instruction includes meeting both the academic and personal needs of the student. The use of a variety of learning guides and learning centers by the teacher helps move instruction from the mass or large group level to the individual level. These instructional vehicles enhance student's chances of reaching one of the most important goals of the middle school, learning how to learn.

The knowledge generation requires that we place greater emphasis on the use of concept learning strategies in the middle school classroom. It is far more important to help children develop concepts and meaning from facts than to teach them to memorize a large quantity of facts. If we are to make schooling more personal and relevant for students, we must teach the relationship of concepts and processes to the world outside the school.

REFERENCES

Ausubel, David P. *Educational Psychology: A Cognitive View.* New York: Holt, Rinehart and Winston, 1968.

Bellack, Arno A.; Kliebard, Herbert M.; Hyman, Ronald T.; Smith, Frank L. *The Language of the Classroom.* New York: Teachers College Press, 1966.

Brown, James W.; Lewis, Richard B.; and Harcleroad, Fred. *AV Instruction: Technology, Media and Methods.* New York: McGraw-Hill, 1977.

Bruner, Jerome S.; Goodnow, Jacqueline J.; and Austin, George. *A Study of Thinking.* New York: Science Editions, 1956.

Cullum, Albert. *Push Back the Desks.* New York: Citation Press, 1967.

Dunn, Rita, and Dunn, Kenneth. *Practical Approaches to Individualizing Instruction.* West Nyack, N.Y.: Parker Publishing Co., 1972.

Dyrli, Oduard Egil. "Implementing Intellectual Development Assessments." In *Implementing Teacher Competencies,* edited by James E. Weigard. Englewood Cliffs, N.J.: Prentice-Hall, 1977.

Enokson, Russell. "A Basic Experimental Model for Effecting Behavioral Change in the Questioning Practices of Prospective Elementary Teachers." Ph.D. dissertation, University of Northern Colorado, 1971.

Gagné, Robert M. *The Conditions of Learning.* New York: Holt, Rinehart and Winston, 1968.

Galloway, Charles G., and Mickelson, Norma I. "Improving Teachers' Questions." *The Elementary School Journal,* December 1973, pp. 145–48.

Glasser, William. *Schools Without Failure.* New York: Harper and Row, 1968.

Gordon, Alice Kaplan. *Games for Growth.* Palo Alto, Calif.: Science Research Associates, 1970.

Hanna, Lavone A.; Potter, Gladys L.; and Hagaman, Neva. *Unit Teaching in the Elementary School.* New York: Holt, Rinehart and Winston, 1963.

Joyce, Bruce R.; Weil, Marsha; and Wald, Rhoada. *Three Teaching Strategies for the Social Studies.* Chicago: Science Research Associates, 1972.

Lehman, David L. *Role Playing and Teacher Education: A Manual for Developing Innovative Teachers.* Washington, D.C.: The American Institute of Biological Sciences, 1971.

Piaget, Jean. "Development and Learning." *Journal of Research in Science Teaching* 2 (1964):176–85.

Quillen, Isaac J., and Hanna, Lavone A. *Education for Social Competence.* Rev. ed. Chicago: Scott Foresman, and Co., 1961.

Shane, June Grant, and Shane, Harold G. "The Role of the Future in Education." *Today's Education,* January-February 1974, pp. 72–76.

Learning Module

Creating Personalized Learning Experiences

Directions

This module is designed to help you increase your ability to plan and implement personalized learning experiences for learners. Begin by taking the pretest. Review your pretest results with your instructor who will assist you in selecting the appropriate objectives. Complete the required and optional activities that will assist you in reaching your objectives. Take the posttest to see what you have accomplished.

Pretest

1. Present the essential components of an effective lesson plan.
2. Discuss the characteristics of William Glasser's three types of classroom meetings.
3. Briefly list the characteristics of four types of learning guides.
4. Contrast linear and adaptive programming, giving specific examples of each.
5. Contrast Robert Gagné's concept learning model and Bruce Joyce's concept learning strategy.

Check

Review your pretest performance with your instructor.

Behavioral Objectives

Select appropriate objectives.

1. Describe three educational games appropriate for middle school use.
2. Contrast two major concept learning strategies suitable for use in the middle school.
3. Contrast a unit plan and a daily lesson plan, explaining the essential characteristics of each.
4. Discuss the basic characteristics of William Glasser's three types of class meetings.

5. Contrast linear programming with adaptive programming and give specific examples of each, using one curricular area.
6. List five important points to remember regarding the implementation of classroom learning centers.
7. Design a simulation appropriate for social studies instruction in the middle school.
8. Compare the major research findings of David Ausubel and Jean Piaget concerning concept formation by children.
9. Contrast two basic types of learning guides.

Required Activities

(Numbers in parentheses correlate with corresponding objectives.)

1. Read the first two chapters of Albert Cullum's *Push Back the Desks* (New York: Citation Press, 1967). (6)
2. Review three current periodical references regarding the use of games and simulation in the middle school. (1)
3. Interview a media specialist concerning the availability and use of programmed materials in the middle school. (1)
4. Observe three different middle school teachers in the development and use of daily lesson plans. Read relevant parts of Lavone Hanna's *Unit Teaching in the Elementary School* (New York: Holt, Rinehart and Winston, 1963). (3)
5. Review the ingredients of a curriculum contract as identified by Rita and Kenneth Dunn in *Practical Approaches to Individualizing Instruction* (West Nyack, N.Y.: Parker Publishing Co. 1972). (9)
6. Read "Class Meetings" in *Schools Without Failure* by William Glasser (New York: Harper and Row, 1968). (4)
7. Review Alice Kaplan Gordon's *Games for Growth* (Palo Alto, Calif.: Science Research Associates, 1970). (1) (7)
8. Visit a media center and preview the filmstrip/cassette package on concept learning and role playing by Bruce Joyce, Marsha Weil, and Rhoada Wald, *Three Teaching Strategies for the Social Studies* (Chicago: Science Research Associates, 1972). (2)
9. Review concept learning in Robert M. Gagné's *The Conditions of Learning* (New York: Holt, Rinehart and Winston, 1968) and Jean Piaget's "Development and Learning," *Journal of Research in Science Teaching* 2(1964):176–85. (2) (8)
10. Interview three middle school teachers who effectively use classroom learning centers. (6)
11. Practice writing Learning Activity Packages in several different curicular areas. For assistance, see "Learning Guides" in *Individualizing Instruction* by Helen Davis Dell (Chicago: Science Research Associates, 1972). (9)

12. Review three current periodical references dealing with learning centers. (6)

Optional Activities

Select additional activities to complete from the preceding list.

Posttest

Conduct an oral evaluation conference with your instructor.

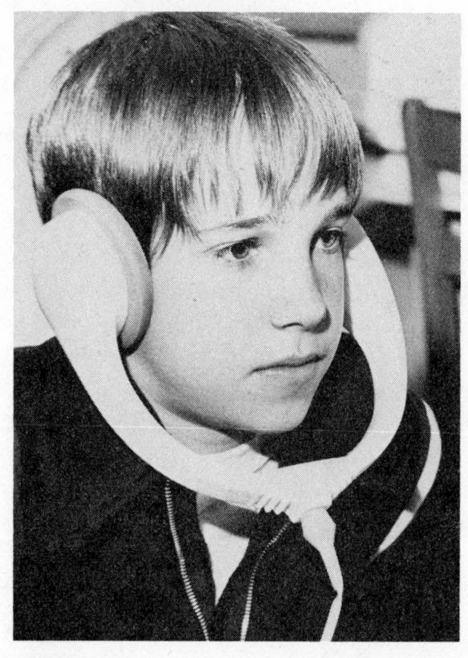

Chapter 5

Facilitating Self-Discipline

Maintaining discipline is a crucial part of good teaching. Even if a teacher really knows his subject matter, he will not be able to transmit his knowledge to his students until he has achieved effective class discipline. Remember the old maxim of generations ago, "If you can't control 'em, you can't larn 'em!"

The word *discipline* is derived from the Latin *discere,* meaning "to learn." In the early colonial, or Puritan period, of American education, the child was subjected to a rigid set of rules that emphasized the teacher's absolute authority. Strong emphasis was placed on corporal punishment, and the birch rod was regarded as a most valuable teaching tool. Therefore, discipline was viewed primarily as external in nature—imposed on the child by an outside agency.

In contrast, a concept of discipline that is receiving emphasis today is that "the best discipline comes from within." This concept emphasizes helping the learner to develop self-control. In order to do this, the learner must be taught self-management skills and provided opportunities for practicing these skills. The teacher has a responsibility to teach learners important discipline concepts such as acceptance of responsibility for your own actions, concern for others, property rights, a sense of fair play, acceptance of criticism, obedience to authority, fidelity in keeping promises, and acceptance of defeat.

Developing an Effective Rationale for School Discipline

An effective school discipline policy should be based on students' rights of American citizenship under the Constitution. Justice Abe Fortas wrote,

"The story of man is the history, first of the acceptance and imposition of restraints necessary to permit communal life, and second, of the emancipation of the individual within that system of necessary restraints" (1968, p. 59). The major focus of a school discipline policy should be to *help each individual develop responsible self-discipline*. Disciplinary policies must be in harmony with the principles of a democratic society, such as equal justice for all, respect for the rights and dignity of the individual, and humanitarian treatment for all.

Disciplinary policies should be primarily preventive and secondarily corrective in nature with emphasis being given to the *responsibilities* as well as the rights of the individual. Larsen (1972) has identified three very promising movements in American education that utilize these concepts and that may prove to have a positive effect on school discipline. They are (1) the reorganization of curriculum content to make it relevant for today's students; (2) significant movements toward individualization of instruction and a change in the role of the teacher from that of a communicator to that of an organizer and prescriber of learning experiences on the basis of individual needs; and (3) elimination of the lock-step system of grades with movement toward a self-paced, nongraded program. A teacher who is having a large number of discipline problems is generally a teacher who is implementing an instructional program that is not relevant to student needs. A modification of curriculum and instruction is often an essential step toward preventing discipline problems. Larsen states the case emphatically. "Good discipline does not create good schools. Good schools create good discipline" (1972, p. 192).

Modifying Classroom Behavior

If you were to survey the concerns of a typical group of preservice teachers, you would discover that discipline would be rather high on the list. George Gallup's "Sixth Annual Gallup Poll of Public Attitudes Toward Education" taken in 1974 revealed that lack of discipline was identified by those surveyed as the major public school problem in the United States. More significantly, discipline has been identified as the number one problem in five out of six surveys taken in recent years.

Discipline problems are as much a part of schools as reading, writing, and arithmetic. In a nationwide survey, National Education Association Research (1976) gathered data concerning the extent of school violence and discipline problems from a scientifically selected sample of public school teachers. The four problems identified most often were, in order of frequency, (1) impertinence and discourtesy to teachers, (2) theft of small items of limited value, (3) destruction of school property, and (4) theft of a serious nature. When teachers were asked to list the factors that cause misbehavior in the public schools, they most often name irresponsible parents and unsatisfactory home conditions.

Assessment Procedures

A teacher may elect to deal with a behavior problem himself, or he may collaborate with a behavioral consultant. Regardless of which approach he chooses, it is imperative that he thoroughly diagnose the learner's behavior before applying any treatment. There are several diagnostic procedures that the teacher may use. Four of the more effective tools are anecdotal records, checklists, rating scales, and assessment of target behaviors.

An anecdotal record consists of the teacher's recording specifically observed behaviors exhibited by the student. It is designed to focus the teacher's attention on the specific behaviors that are contributing to the student's problem. (See Figure 5.1.) Although the teacher emphasizes objectivity in recording data on these behaviors, the usefulness of the anecdotal record is limited because the teacher's subjective judgment is almost impossible to completely eliminate.

A checklist consists of a list of behaviors used by the teacher to indicate the behaviors that apply to a particular student. The checklist can be more objective than the anecdotal record if the items listed are clearly defined and representative of a wide range of behaviors. A disadvantage of the checklist is that it does not allow for the listing of factors that may be causing the behaviors. It can be very helpful, however, in identifying specific problem behaviors as opposed to those that are global, or general, in nature. (See Figure 5.2.)

A behavior rating scale is an adaptation of a checklist. It has the advantage, however, of providing the teacher with the means to indicate the frequency and degree of importance of a child's behaviors. (See Figure 5.3.)

A fourth diagnostic tool is the assessment of target behaviors. O'Leary

Figure 5.1

Anecdotal Record

Robert has been extremely restless in class and is constantly trying to get my attention. He is very hostile toward other children, particularly when another child receives my attention or approval. He often uses profanity on the playground and makes very unkind remarks about his parents.

SOURCE: From K. Daniel O'Leary and Susan G. O'Leary, *Classroom Management: The Successful Use of Behavior Modification* (New York: Pergamon Press, 1972).

Figure 5.2

Checklist

Child: Robert Date: 10/1/75 Teacher: Mrs. Jones

_____ 1. talks out of turn
_____ 2. feels inferior
_____ 3. bites children
__X__ 4. is restless
_____ 5. bites nails
_____ 6. throws spitwads
__X__ 7. uses profane language
_____ 8. fights older children
__X__ 9. speaks negatively about parents
__X__ 10. is jealous of attention given to other children

SOURCE: Adapted from K. Daniel O'Leary and Susan G. O'Leary, *Classroom Management: The Successful Use of Behavior Modification* (New York, Pergamon Press, 1972). Used with permission.

(1972) has outlined seven important steps in the target assessment process. The teacher should:

1. Select 1-4 behaviors on which she will focus her attention.
2. Write a detailed behavior description which is as complete and unambiguous as possible.
3. Decide which type of recording system to use. If the teacher can have someone else do the observing, continuous recording is preferred. If she is making the observations herself, she can choose either event, recording or time sampling.
4. Record the behaviors in as many situations as possible as frequently as possible (½ hour/day minimum for time sampling.)
5. Arrange for regular reliability checks (at least once a week).
6. Obtain similar observations of her own behaviors and possibly of some other children in the class.
7. Make daily summaries of her observations and record them graphically. (p. 633)

Event recording involves simply making a tally on a sheet of paper every time a behavior occurs. A time sampling procedure, on the other hand, involves selecting specific fifteen- to thirty-minute intervals during the day for recording the target behaviors. Behaviors should be recorded in a variety of situations over a period of one or two weeks in order to ascertain under what conditions they occur most frequently.

All of these techniques have limitations, particularly since the element of teacher subjectivity enters in to their use. Each technique, however,

Figure 5.3

Rating Scale

Child: *Robert* Date: *10/1/75* Teacher: *Mrs. Jones*

0 1 2	1. talks out of turn
0 1 2	2. feels inferior
0 1 2	3. bites children
0 1 2	4. is restless
0 1 2	5. bites nails
0 1 2	6. throws spitwads
0 1 2	7. uses profane language
0 1 2	8. fights older children
0 1 2	9. speaks negatively about parents
0 1 2	10. is jealous of attention given to other children

0 = no problem, 1 = mild problem, 2 = severe problem

SOURCE: From K. Daniel O'Leary and Susan G. O'Leary, *Classroom Management: The Successful Use of Behavior Modification* (New York: Pergamon Press, 1972). Used with permission.

enables the teacher to precisely identify undesirable student behaviors and provides data that may serve as a basis for a behavior modification process.

Hill (1969) has made eight helpful suggestions regarding a productive school program for helping the student achieve self-understanding:

1. The child study program of the school must be seen as primarily an effort to enhance the self-understanding of the pupils.
2. Systematic attention must be provided to help teachers improve their skills in interpreting test scores and other data to children and to their parents.
3. Pupils must be involved in discussion of education goals if they are to have experiences in school that have personal meaning and significance.
4. Children must receive a proper orientation prior to the administering of any test or inventory.
5. Individual teacher/pupil conferences must be carefully planned and must not become incidental experiences.
6. A parent/child/teacher conference may serve as a more productive reporting vehicle than the traditional report card.
7. Judgments expressed by children regarding child study procedures used in the school should be discussed in staff meetings for the purpose of improving the program.
8. The school staff should engage in carefully planned in-service experiences that emphasize ways in which human behavior is studied

and the relative merits of different ways of seeking to understand one's own behavior and the behavior of others.

Behavior modification techniques could be employed in the middle school to help students change their behavior with an ultimate goal of self-discipline. Harris (1972) has grouped these techniques into two broad categories: (1) those used to increase the frequency with which certain behaviors occur and (2) those used to decrease the frequency with which certain behaviors occur.

Techniques to Increase the Frequency of Certain Behaviors

All techniques designed to increase the child's use of a certain behavior are based on the psychological principle of positive reinforcement. For many children, the teacher's verbal feedback is sufficient to reinforce behavior. For example, the teacher may use such responses as "correct," "right," or "very good work." Material reinforcers, such as trinkets, money, and gold stars may be used to reinforce a particular behavior. In selected cases, a hug or a positive tap on the shoulder may be employed. The Premack Principle, developed by David Premack, emphasizes that each individual has high probability behaviors, which he does often or enjoys doing, and low probability behaviors, which he seldom does or doesn't like to do. A teacher could reinforce the performance of a low probability behavior such as solving math problems through the application of a high probability behavior such as participation in free play during recess. This approach involves reinforcing a learning experience with another learning experience rather than with trinkets or money.

Token Reinforcements. A token is any object that is not intrinsically valuable but is made valuable by the fact that the teacher agrees to let it be exchanged for any number of rewards called "back-up" reinforcers. For example, a child may earn a number of paper tickets that may be exchanged for very desirable objects such as candy or trinkets. A token reinforcement system enables the teacher to reward immediately and continuously, gradually increasing the amount of work required to earn a token or increasing the number of tokens required to be exchanged for a reward. Tokens generally have only short-range value, however. For example, assume that the teacher uses a candy bar as a reward. What happens when the student ceases to like the candy bar or the teacher runs out of candy bars?

Contract Plan. The contract plan involves a joint effort by teacher and student in deciding what type of rewards the student will receive for specific behaviors. The contract may be written and signed by teacher and student. One of the most important characteristics of the contract plan is that the student is involved in the decision-making process. Individual decision making is an important step toward effective self-discipline.

Techniques to Decrease the Frequency of Certain Behaviors

Unfortunately, too many teachers discover that they have to spend much time in eliminating disruptive or undesirable behaviors in addition to developing new ones. Many behaviors often interfere with learning. These include fighting, teasing, throwing objects, cheating, and many others.

Eliminating Reinforcers. One can generally assume that if a specific behavior persists it is being reinforced in some way. Therefore, the key to eliminating the undesirable behavior may be in the elimination of the reinforcement. The teacher may be unconsciously reinforcing a particular behavior. For example, dismissing the class when it is noisy may be just what the class wants. Or, peer attention could be serving as a reinforcer for a particular child, and this could be eliminated by isolating the child from the group. A teacher should be careful, however, to use positive reinforcement for appropriate behavior at the same time he is using extinction techniques.

Punishment. Although punishment only suppresses behavior rather than eliminating it, it may be effective in reducing the frequency with which some undesirable behavior takes place. Punishment need not be only physical in nature but may also include forfeiture of privileges. In fact, excessive use of physical punishment may cause a student to hate school and the teacher, or to become fearful of performing any behaviors at all.

Modeling

The technique of modeling involves the teacher's performing a behavior so that the person he is trying to teach can imitate it. This technique can be used to either increase or decrease the frequencies of student behavior. The teacher should realize that he constantly serves as a model for his students and that each student may serve as a model for another student. The type of language the teacher uses, his disciplinary techniques, his prejudices and bias, and almost all aspects of his behavior will be observed and imitated by the students.

There is general agreement among psychologists that modeling is a real and important phenomenon, but there is less certainty regarding the nature, development, and effects of modeling behavior. For example, numerous research studies have produced conflicting results on the influence of television violence and aggression on the behavior of viewers. O'Leary and O'Leary have provided an excellent treatment of modeling techniques in Chapter 5 of *Classroom Management* (1972).

Controlling the Ripple Effect

Parents and teachers have long taken the "ripple effect" for granted. They have discovered that by dealing with the deviancy of one student they are really influencing the entire class. In dealing with a deviancy, it is extremely important for the teacher to understand the difference between an *approval-focused technique* and a *task-focused technique*. An approval-focused technique places emphasis on teacher self-reference, what the teacher likes or dislikes. For example, a teacher might say, "Stop that talking because Mrs. Jones doesn't like noisy children in her room." In contrast, a task-focused technique places emphasis on accomplishing the learning task. Using this technique, the teacher might say, "If the noise continues, we will not be able to learn how to solve the problem." Task-focused techniques generally elicit more desirable student reactions than do approval-focused techniques.

Handling Classroom Aggression

In a typical classroom, there may be considerable minor aggression to which no one objects. Aggression that interferes with good teaching and learning, however, must be curbed. Redl has outlined several techniques that a teacher could use in working with aggressive behavior in the classroom (1969).

First, the teacher needs to identify the source or cause of the aggression. It may come from the home or community, it may come from within the child himself (spontaneous burst), or it may be triggered by something within the classroom environment. Aggression includes a wide range of behaviors—from reactions to boredom to personal battles with other kids. Aggression usually involves a discharge of surplus energy or temporary loss of control by the child.

A second technique involves cutting a contagion chain, or getting kids off the hook. This involves the teacher's taking action at a certain point in a child's behavior to curb it before the child and the group become involved in serious trouble.

A third technique for handling aggression is signal interference. This involves the teacher's developing a "radar" system to detect signals around the room that aggression is about to explode. All teachers need to know more about the physiological and gestural signals that indicate aggressive behavior is building up.

Another important element of working with aggressive behavior is to avoid the "dare" situation. This involves avoiding the placement of a student in a no-options situation in which he has to pretend he is really tough in order to impress others in the class.

As a teacher, you will need to control your own aggression, identifying it and analyzing the effects it is having on your students. It will be helpful to ask yourself these questions: How does my anger affect my relationship with my students? What aspects of my daily behavior tend to reduce or control aggression in my students?

As a professional, you will be charged with modifying aggression when it impedes the learning process in your classroom. You will need to apply a variety of techniques and continuous good judgment in working with classroom aggression. If you are unsuccessful or if the problem is severe, you should seek professional assistance from a fellow teacher or school psychologist.

Numerous research studies have isolated dozens of variables that are associated with disruptive students, including socioeconomic status, academic achievements, IQ, race, sex, age, number of siblings, and whether or not parents are divorced. It is beyond the scope of the school's ability to change most of these variables. One variable that could be related to student disruption and may have implications for teaching, however, is the student's self-concept as a learner. Branch and others conducted a research study in four middle schools in North Florida. The study involved a randomly selected population of 208 disruptive students and a comparison group of 208 nondisruptive students. Two instruments were used to obtain data on the students' self-concepts as learners: the Florida Key (1973) and the school-academic subscore of the Self Esteem Inventory (1967). The Florida Key is designed to assist the teacher in identifying his students' self-concepts as learners. To do this, it uses the teacher's ratings of a student in regard to eighteen overt classroom behaviors. The Self Esteem Inventory (SEI) is a self-report instrument consisting of fifty-eight items and yielding a total score and five subscores.

The inferred and professed academic self-concepts of disruptive and nondisruptive students were compared, and multivariate analyses of variance were conducted. Analysis of the data revealed significant differences between the scores of disruptive and nondisruptive students on the Florida Key, with disruptive students scoring significantly lower. Analysis of variance of the school-academic subscale of the SEI revealed a significant difference between disruptive and nondisruptive students, with the scores of disruptive students being significantly lower. The basic conclusion of this study was that a persistent relationship exists between a student's self-concept and the student's disruptive or nondisruptive behavior.

The "turtle technique" described by Robin (1976) has been used successfully to help students decrease aggressive classroom behavior.

Though originally intended for use with emotionally disturbed children, the technique has implications for success in helping normal children control their impulses towards aggressive behavior. The technique involves four components: the "turtle response," relaxation, problem solving, and peer support. Children are taught to react to their impulses to be aggressive by: (1) imagining that they are withdrawing into a shell, putting their heads down, and closing their eyes, (2) relaxing their muscles to cope with tensions, and (3) using social problem solving to generate acceptable alternative responses. Peer group members are instructed to support appropriate use of the technique. For a detailed treatment of the turtle technique, see Schneider and Robin (1974).

Establishing Order in an Inner-City Middle School

Teachers, students, and parents are becoming increasingly concerned about the quality of discipline in the schools. This concern is particularly acute in inner-city schools, where school administrators have found limited solutions to discipline problems. Sanders and Yarbrough (1976) reported on a project in an urban school setting in Texas that was successful in bringing order to an inner-city middle school.[1] The project was called Project ORDER (Organization for Responsibility, Dependability, Education, and Reality), and the program design was based on four assumptions:

1. That much student behavior results from a feeling of impersonalness and anonymity due to large enrollments and limited teacher contact
2. That lack of instruction in attitudes, values, and behavior within the school contributes to the disciplinary problems
3. That a majority of any school's serious behavior problems are caused by a small minority of the students
4. That much alienation and misbehavior is caused by a faulty curriculum

Over a two-year period, Project Order applied these assumptions in the following ways:

1. Teachers and students were organized into small clusters for most of the day to foster students' feelings of identity and personal responsibility.

1. From Stanley G. Sanders and Janis S. Yarbrough, "Bringing Order to an Inner-City Middle School" in *Phi Delta Kappan* 58 (1976): 333–34. Used with permission.

2. A blend of ideas from transactional analysis, reality therapy, values clarification, and other therapies were used to satisfy student needs.
3. A CIC (Crisis Intervention Center) was provided for students with behavior problems too severe to be treated in the regular classroom. The CIC was staffed by a special teacher and an aide who employed special psychological methods to help the student. Once acceptable behavior was developed, the student was able to return to regular classes.
4. A strong effort was made to adjust the curriculum to the needs of learners, especially their affective needs.

Results of the project were:

1. The number of discipline problems handled by teachers decreased by 63%.
2. The number of cases referred to the principal's office dropped by 77%.
3. The use of corporal punishment was reduced by 93%.
4. The number of suspensions was reduced by 20%, a significant decrease.

Two significant complementary themes emerge from careful examination of this project. Modern approaches to educational psychology with special emphasis on classroom implementation and modification of curriculum and teaching methods can have a significant impact on discipline within the school when they are used together.

Facilitating Self-Management

As teachers, or behavior modifers, one of our major tasks is to decrease the amount of dependence a child has on adults. In addition to moving toward an ultimate goal of self-discipline, a student with self-management skills will be able to learn effectively even when the teacher or parent is absent.

Developing Self-Management Skills

The Individual Guided Motivation (IGM) program developed by Klausmeier and associates emphasizes a motivational-instructional procedure in which small-group conferences are used to develop self-directed prosocial behavior (1972). IGM is a component of the complete system of elementary education called individually guided education (IGE). (The individually guided motivation (IGM) system is described in detail in a bound volume and in five sound-and-color films designed to assist teachers in learning how to carry out the various motivational processes.)

A major thrust of the program is to eliminate potential discipline problems through the application of motivational principles in two major areas: care of property and relations with people. The small-group conference is a primary vehicle employed by the teacher to help students discuss and reason out problems and develop alternative courses of action to deal with them. The emphasis of the program is on helping students rely more on themselves and less on adult authorities for guiding their behavior. Each student involved in the program is assisted in setting reasonable goals and receives praise for achieving them. IGM may serve as a helpful model for stimulating an individual teacher to develop new approaches to teaching self-discipline.

Carefully consider the following suggestions for helping students develop self-management skills:

1. Teach children to go to recess or a special activity only after they feel that they have completed assignments qualifying them for the special activity.
2. Utilize a variety of individualized instructional materials including contracts and Learning Activity Packets.
3. Involve students in establishing and enforcing rules for school behavior.
4. Teach individual students to self-instruct regarding problem behaviors. For example, a child may be taught to "count to ten" when he is angry.
5. Give students directions only once, avoiding the "repetition syndrome.
6. Encourage students to get instructional materials themselves and return them to their proper places, use and maintain audiovisual equipment independently, organize discussion groups independently, tutor each other whenever possible, and take the initiative to ask for help from adults when necessary.

Students must be taught the fundamental skills of self-management that this list of instructional responsibilities encompasses. This process is not automatic; every teacher, however, must regard it as an integral element of the instructional program.

Contingency Management: A Systematic Approach to Self-Discipline

Contingency management is a contracting system in which students' successful completion of tasks is consistently rewarded by free time activities they select for themselves. When this system is used, students and teacher enter into an agreement that consists of two major elements: (1) the teacher promises to provide free time for students to participate in self-chosen activities they enjoy; and (2) the students agree to complete a specific amount of academic work in order to "earn" their free time. The major features of contingency management are based on the work of Lloyd Homme et al. (1970). Since receiving a reward is made contingent on task completion, contingency management is particularly effective with the slow learner, the child who is "turned off" to learning, and the student whose behavior patterns inhibit his own learning as well as that of his classmates. The goal of a contingency management system is for the classroom situation to be arranged in a way that facilitates students' efforts to manage their own contingencies effectively.

Langstaff and Volkmor (1975) have developed a comprehensive contingency management program consisting of four sound filmstrips and a programmed text that contains structured tasks and activities. The program emphasizes the use of positive reinforcement in teaching academic skills and building students' self-respect. Some of the basic ingredients of the program are presented here in descriptive form:[2]

> **Contract:** an agreement (written or verbal) between teacher and student stating a specific task or amount of work to be done and the reward available upon completion of the work or task.
> **Cycle:** a specific amount of classroom time (usually 20–30 minutes) during which students complete tasks and then participate in reward activities.
> **High Probability Behaviors (HPBs):** behaviors which are enjoyed by the individual and which he frequently chooses to engage in when given the opportunity.
> **Low Probability Behaviors (LPBs):** behaviors which occur infrequently and which the teacher would like to increase.
> **RE Menu:** a written list of activities from which students may choose during free time. The menu is generated cooperatively by the students and the teacher.
> **Reinforcing Event (RE):** activities (HPBs) and materials chosen by the students for reward.
> **Schedule:** a carefully planned, written outline of the daily program in the classroom.
> **Task Area/RE Area:** two divisions of the classroom, task area for completion of student-selected reward activities.

This approach emphasizes students' contracting for a series of short

---

2. From Anne L. Langstaff and Cara B. Volkmor, *Contingency Management* (Columbus, Ohio: Charles E. Merrill Publishing Co., 1975) pp. 103–4. Used with permission.

individual assignments or tasks for which they receive frequent and immediate reinforcement via the REs.

Planning and implementing a contingency management program involves the following steps:

1. *Set up the reinforcement menu.* The menu is a list of reward acitivities (REs) from which students may choose after completing a required task. A menu could contain some of the following:
   watching TV
   tutoring another student
   looking at a magazine
   going to the library
   doing homework assigned in other classes
   feeding fish
   building a model airplane
   listening to records

   Students must complete their assigned tasks before selecting activities from the reinforcement menu regardless of what items have been listed on it.
2. *Arrange the classroom.* It may be helpful to divide the classroom into two areas: a task area where students can work on required academic assignments and an RE area where students can spend time on reinforcement activities. Before a classroom is arranged, careful consideration should be given to such factors as physical features of room, size of group, and availability of materials and equipment.
3. *Schedule time.* The school day should be organized to provide students with appropriate task time and RE time. The teacher should use a nonverbal signal system (notes on the chalkboard, lights, or a bell) to indicate to students that it is time to move from one activity to another. Students should be allowed to go to the RE area only when they have completed their assigned tasks or have made an acceptable attempt to do so.
4. *Plan tasks for students.* In the initial stages of the program, difficulty of assigned tasks should fall slightly below students' competency levels so that they might experience success. As the students become more versed in use of the system, tasks should become more difficult; the teacher should observe students at work and modify tasks as necessary. A general practice is for the teacher to design tasks that may be completed in approximately fifteen minutes.
5. *Explain the system to the students.* Explanation of the system may be presented through a group discussion. Careful attention should be given to involving the students in discussing the procedures, com-

ponents, rules, and signals used within the system. The teacher should emphasize that problems will be cooperatively worked out by both teacher and students.

Application of basic principles of contingency management may be extremely helpful in developing a classroom environment that is conducive to learning. Hankins (1973) has stated the case as follows:

> How to manage children in the classroom is a major concern of today's teachers; lack of ability in classroom management is a major reason for teacher failure. The success or failure of an instructional program depends on the teacher's ability to establish and maintain a classroom environment that is conducive to learning. (p. 84)

Barriers to the Development of Self-Discipline

Here are some of the more common barriers or problem areas relating to self-discipline:

1. Improper match between teacher and student personalities
2. Poor or rigid teaching methods
3. Authoritarian teacher who dominates the classroom
4. Lack of student input concerning development and implementation of classroom discipline procedures
5. Lack of opportunities for students to find success through self-dependent learning activities
6. Obsolete or irrelevant subject matter
7. Poor home conditions that do not facilitate self-dependency
8. Punishment of a total class for the misbehavior of an individual student
9. Classroom conditions that cause the student to become too dependent on the teacher or another student
10. Rigid instructional organization patterns that do not allow the student to function creatively and independently

The teacher should continuously work toward the removal of any barrier that impedes students in becoming more responsible for their own behavior.

Self-Administered Behavior Therapy

Most discipline policies in schools today are based on some or all of the following traditional notions about discipline: (1) Teachers operate under a legal and moral sanction known as *in loco parentis* (in lieu of parents),

(2) discipline serves as a primary function of helping a child "fit in" to a group of society, (3) discipline is viewed as "being good for the child," essentially a process of replacing evil with good, and (4) discipline is required to keep an institution alive.

Instead of emphasizing rigidity and conformity, a more modern concept of discipline recognizes that teachers must provide for diversity and uniqueness in individuals within a framework of freedom with responsibility. A developing tool designed to facilitate this goal is self-administered therapy. Clement (1973) emphasizes that a child should be taught how to analyze his own behaviors and to administer his own behavior therapy. This process involves the child's rewarding himself for productive behavior. It would appear that self-administered behavior therapy is far less offensive to many psychologists than behavior modification strategies, which are administered by someone other than the child himself.

A self-administered behavior therapy approach could involve the following steps:

1. The teacher could ask the child to identify the things he does at school that others like and dislike including those things the teacher wishes he would do.
2. The teacher could ask the child to select one problem behavior and record the number of times it occurs.
3. The teacher and child could sign a contract stating that the child will receive ten cents per day for merely turning in the behavior record or that he will reward himself with points for correcting or modifying his behavior productively.
4. If the point system is used, the child would receive a reward (for example, an airplane ride or a trip to the fair) when he has accumulated a certain number of points. The teacher and pupil could negotiate this reward in exchange for a selected number of points.
5. A later contract could involve the child's giving himself points for studying, thereby emphasizing a positive instructional element in exchanging points for a reward.
6. The desired result is that the child will become increasingly more responsible for his own behavior and continuously seek to improve it.

Each teacher should be encouraged to experiment with various approaches to helping students develop a self-administered behavior therapy program. The elements of individual programs will vary depending on the characteristics of the individual students involved and the professional judgments of the teacher.

Practical Guides to Effective Discipline

There are many practical suggestions that can be helpful when attempting to achieve good student discipline. Teachers should consider the following:

1. Avoid "either-or" situations. Whenever a teacher establishes a "do this or else" situation with a child, the teacher usually loses the respect of the child, who may become withdrawn or hostile. This loss may be delayed, but it will come.
2. Always give a child an outlet. Allow him to be able to withdraw graciously from a situation that he has created and that has turned out to be unpleasant. For example, a child should be allowed to withdraw from an unpleasant group situation maintaining a positive self-image.
3. Discuss feelings and difficulties with children rather than threatening them. Give youngsters a chance to unload their feelings.
4. Avoid using the group as a threatening device designed to coerce a student to adopt a certain behavior. Try to remember that an individual who is on trial before his group is a very lonely figure.
5. Avoid using techniques that take pleasure away from the slow learner because he has not been able to finish his work.
6. Try to remember that all behavior is caused. Do your best to understand all student behavior and its causes.
7. Don't try to always be right. It is impossible.
8. Plan activities for children that are challenging to them and that they will be willing to undertake. Many problems arise due to students' boredom.
9. Help your class establish its own standards of conduct.
10. Be the first to admit your own mistakes.
11. Cultivate the art of giving directions.
12. After your students have started working on a project, avoid interrupting them. Unnecessary interruptions create distractions that can lead to trouble.
13. Focus on a child's strong points. Frequently the child with behavior problems in your room is a child seeking attention.
14. Listen. Children will respect you for recognizing their right to be heard.
15. Ask yourself this question: Who does the most talking in your class? If you do, you're talking too much!
16. Know how children learn. Think through your daily curricular experiences. Are they geared to the interests and the abilities of the children in your class?

17. Try not to take unacceptable behavior as a personal affront. Reject the behavior, but not the child.
18. Show a sense of humor. Let the pupils know that you are a good-natured, cheerful, and happy individual who is capable of laughing *with* them and *at* yourself.

The following test is designed to help you analyze your emotions.[3] Understanding your own feelings should make you better able to understand the feelings of your students and to achieve more effective classroom discipline.

> Take a sheet of paper and try to finish each of these statements. Some of these statements may make you blush, but no one else need see them. This is simply a test for facing oneself. Be truthful!
>
> 1. I hate . . .
> 2. I wish . . .
> 3. I fear . . .
> 4. I love . . .
> 5. I hope . . .
> 6. I'm embarrassed when . . .
> 7. The thing that bothers me most is . . .
> 8. The thing I am most afraid of is . . .
> 9. I want most to be . . .
> 10. Regarding myself, I feel . . .
> 11. The person who worries me most is . . .
> 12. I am most cheerful when . . .
> 13. I am deeply happy when . . .
> 14. My greatest interest in life is . . .
> 15. The person who means the most to me is . . .
> 16. The ones who love me most are . . .
> 17. In leisure time, I like most to . . .
> 18. I have great respect for . . .
> 19. My health is . . .
> 20. My ability is . . .

Classroom Social Climate

The social climate—the feelings that exist among pupils and between them and the teacher—is a crucial factor in helping each student develop self-discipline. Nerbovig and Klausmeier (1969) have categorized social climates as cooperative, competitive, repressed, and anarchic. In order to establish a cooperative climate in the classroom, the teacher should use

---

3. From Paul H. Landis, *Your Marriage and Family Living* (New York: McGraw-Hill, 1969), p. 15. Used with permission.

skill in organizing and directing small-group activities. Effective group activities help each child to develop socialization skills and contribute toward high morale in the classroom. The teacher must be cautious in releasing control, however, because sudden freedom for students may result in anarchy in the classroom.

A competitive climate should also be a friendly climate. Because our society is competitive, students need to learn how to use competition in a positive and effective way. The emphasis should not only be on winning, however, but also on learning to follow the rules and practice integrity. For positive competition to occur, the following conditions must be present:

1. Competition should involve students of approximately the same achievement level.
2. Rules should be established and enforced.
3. The objective for which students are competing should not be so difficult to achieve that students are forced cheat.
4. Students' losing should not result in their experiencing feelings of inferiority but in gaining a more realistic understanding of personal strengths and weaknesses.

The teacher must be careful to prevent the development of a punitive, competitive climate that is characterized by uncivilized behavior, the strong's taking advantage of the weak, or the poor performer's withdrawing from activities.

A repressed climate is characterized by limited or no pupil participation in planning and goal-setting activities. An apathetic, repressed class is one in which the students are so heavily dominated by the teacher that they have given up on individual initiative and simply do as they are commanded. A covertly repressed class is one in which the students are united in a common bond of resentment and resistance toward the dominance of the teacher. The students functioning in this type of climate use varied tactics to irritate the teacher including breaking pencils, clearing their throats loudly, blowing their noses, throwing objects, and other similar tactics. Repressed climates force children to direct their energies toward defeating the leader rather than successfully completing their learning tasks.

Of the different types of social climates, an anarchic climate has the most negative effect on students. It is chaos! It is characterized by no standards of conduct and no planned activities. The type of student behavior usually found in this climate is undisciplined and disruptive.

An effective classroom social climate does not just happen automatically. The teacher has to practice humane mental and social guidance techniques in order to facilitate a partnership with the students and develop an effective social climate. Especially important for the teacher to develop are face-to-face communication and group behavior skills. The following instrument, "Self-Appraisal Exercise," can be used to help the teacher assess his own skills in these areas.[4]

> This form is designed to help you think about your behavior in groups. First, read over the scales, and on each one place a check indicating the place on the scale that describes you as you *usually* act in this group.
>
> After marking all the scales, pick out the three or four along which you would most like to change. On these scales, draw an arrow above the line to indicate the desirable direction for *changing* your behavior and the *extent* of *change you seek.*

1. Ability to listen to others in an understanding way.

1	2	3	4	5	6	7
INATTENTIVE UNRECEPTIVE						OBSERVANT SENSITIVE LISTENING

2. Ability to influence others in the group.

1	2	3	4	5	6	7
NO INFLUENCE						ALL MY PROPOSALS ACCEPTED

3. Tendency to build on the previous ideas of other group members.

1	2	3	4	5	6	7
GO MY OWN WAY						USE THEIR IDEAS

4. Likely to trust others.

1	2	3	4	5	6	7
DISTRUST						TRUST

5. Willingness to discuss feelings (emotions) in a group.

1	2	3	4	5	6	7
RETICENT						VERY FREE

4. From David W. Johnson, *Reaching Out: Interpersonal Effectiveness and Self-Actualization,* © 1972, pp. 27–28. Reprinted by permission of Prentice-Hall, Inc., Englewood Cliffs, New Jersey.

6. Willingness to be influenced by others.

1	2	3	4	5	6	7
	CLOSED					GO ALONG WITH SUGGESTIONS

7. Tendency to run the group.

1	2	3	4	5	6	7
	NO DESIRE OR EFFORT					TRY TO GET MY WAY IN GROUP

8. Tendency to seek close personal relationships with others in a group.

1	2	3	4	5	6	7
	NO INTEREST IN OTHERS					VALUE INTIMACY

9. Reaction to critical comments about own behavior in a group.

1	2	3	4	5	6	7
	RESENT, DEFENSIVE					GENUINELY WANT CRITICISM

10. Awareness of the feelings of others.

1	2	3	4	5	6	7
	UNAWARE, UNINTERESTED IN THEIR FEELINGS					SENSITIVE, EMPATHIC, RESPONSIVE

11. Degree of insight into the *why* of behavior—own and others.

1	2	3	4	5	6	7
	NO INSIGHT INTO BEHAVIOR					EXCEPTIONAL SELF-INSIGHT

12. Reaction to conflict and antagonism in the group.

1	2	3	4	5	6	7
	AVOID IT, QUICKLY HARMONIZE, SHRINK FROM IT					USE IT CONSTRUCTIVELY, CREATIVELY

13. Reaction to expressions of affection and warmth in the group.

1	2	3	4	5	6	7
EMBARRASSED AVOIDS OR REJECTS						DELIGHTED

14. Reaction to opinions opposed to mine.

1	2	3	4	5	6	7
ARGUE, REJECT OPPONENTS						EXPLORE DIFFERENCES READILY

Breckenridge (1976) described several techniques that significantly changed a deteriorating school climate in just one year. The school climate was characterized by divisions among staff, rumors about teachers, student fights on the playground, unpleasant incidents in the classroom, and tension between teachers and principal. As a result of a staff development seminar on "climate control," the faculty implemented a program to improve the social climate of the school. First, a modified brainstorming technique called "1–3–6" was used to identify the major problems. Each teacher participating in the group privately listed all the concerns they had about the school. Later, teachers met in groups of three to combine their lists into one. Finally, each group of three met with another group to combine lists again. In this way, the following thirty-two items of staff concern were identified and ranked according to priorities:

1. There is tension between teachers and principal.
2. Competition and backbiting exist among the teachers. Also, they are not engaging in needed self-evaluation.
3. Communication among parents, staff, and students is needed.
4. Teachers are swamped by innovative programs and the resulting pressures.
5. Guidelines for discipline are needed.
6. Student input in decisions is lacking.
7. Staff needs to make use of more resources to remedy problems.
8. Earlier recognition of behavioral and academic problems is needed.
9. Racial, social, and academic differences are not accepted by all.
10. There is too much academic pressure on teachers.

Some of the selected procedures that the faculty used to improve the situation were:

1. Faculty committees were formed to work on different items on the problem list.
2. Students were involved in drawing up rules for the school.
3. The student council was revitalized and became a productive organization working with the principal and teachers.
4. Parents were involved with school committees designed to enhance the school climate.
5. A school-community newspaper was published.
6. Teachers began to praise each other, and it became contagious.
7. A new format for faculty meetings was designed to involve teachers in planning agendas, time schedules were provided, and efforts were directed toward keeping meeting brief but meaningful.
8. The principal modified his schedule to provide time for informal discussions with teachers and students.

The main conclusion to be drawn from this study is that the social climate of an individual school can be improved when the individuals within the school identify the problems and work cooperatively toward improving the situation. It can be done!

Summary

There are many varied concepts of discipline. The two major concepts are: (1) external discipline, which is imposed on the learner from the outside, and (2) internal discipline, which helps the learner develop self-control. Application of the latter concept offers the greater potential for positive mental development. The learner should be taught self-management skills and provided opportunities for applying these skills in varied settings. The major focus of a school discipline policy should be to help each individual develop responsible self-discipline.

The teacher should employ a variety of diagnostic processes in identifying student behaviors that should be increased or decreased in frequency. The appropriate application of contingency management principles is essential to the development of self-discipline in students.

REFERENCES

Branch, Charles V.; Purkey, William V.; and Damico, Sandra B. "Academic Self-Concepts of Disruptive and Nondisruptive Middle School Students." *Middle School Journal,* December 1976, pp. 15–17.

Breckenridge, Eileen. "Improving School Climate." *Phi Delta Kappan* 58(1976):314–18.

Clement, Paul W. "Training Children to be Their Own Behavior Therapists." *Journal of School Health* 43(1973):615–20.

Coppersmith, S. A. *The Antecedents of Self-Esteem.* San Francisco: W. H. Freeman, 1967.

Dell, Helen Davis. *Individualizing Instruction.* Chicago: Science Research Associates, 1972.

Fortas, Abe. *Concerning Dissent and Civil Disobedience.* New York: New American Library, 1968.

Gallup, George H. "Sixth Annual Gallup Poll of Public Attitudes Toward Education." *Phi Delta Kappan* 56(1974):20–33.

Harris, Mary B. *Classroom Uses of Behavior Modification.* Columbus, Ohio: Charles E. Merrill Publishing Co., 1972.

Hill, George E., and Luckey, Eleanore Braun. *Guidance for Children in Elementary Schools.* New York: Appleton-Century Crofts, 1969.

Homme, Lloyd; Csanyi, A. P.; Gonzales, M. A.; and Rechs, J. R. *How to Use Contingency Contracting in the Classroom.* Champaign, Ill.: Research Press, 1970.

Johnson, David W. *Reaching Out: Interpersonal Effectiveness and Self-Actualization.* Englewood Cliffs, N.J.: Prentice-Hall, 1972.

Klausmeier, Herbert J.; Frayer, Dorothy; and Quilling, Mary B. *Individually Guided Motivation, Guidelines for Implementation.* Experimental copy. Madison, Wis.: Wisconsin Research and Development Center for Cognitive Learning, 1972.

Landis, Paul H. *Your Marriage and Family Living.* New York: McGraw-Hill, 1969.

Langstaff, Anne L., and Volkmor, Cara B. *Contingency Management.* Columbus, Ohio: Charles E. Merrill Publishing Co., 1975.

Larsen, Knute. *School Discipline in an Age of Rebellion.* West Nyack, N.Y.: Parker Publishing Co., 1972.

Nerbovig, Marcella, and Klausmeier, Herbert J. *Teaching in the Elementary School.* New York: Harper and Row, 1969.

O'Leary, K. Daniel, and O'Leary, Susan G. *Classroom Management: The Successful Use of Behavior Modification.* New York: Pergamon Press, 1972.

Purkey, William; Gage, B. N.; and Graves, W. "The Florida Key: A Scale to Infer Learner Self-Concept." *Educational and Psychological Measurement* 33(1973):979–84.

Redl, Fritz. "Aggression in the Classroom. *Today's Education,* September 1969, pp. 30–32.

Robin, Arthur. "The Turtle Technique: An Extended Case Study of Self-Control in the Classroom." *Psychology in the Schools* 13 (1976):449–53.

Sanders, Stanley G., and Yarbrough, Janis S. "Bringing Order to an Inner-City Middle School." *Phi Delta Kappan* 58(1976):333–34.

Schneider, Marlene, and Robin, Arthur L. "The Turtle Technique: A Method for the Self-Control of Impulsive Behavior." Unpublished manuscript. Point of Woods Laboratory School, State University of New York, Stony Brook, 1974.

Learning Module

Facilitating the Development of Self-Discipline

Directions

This module is designed to help you enhance your ability to facilitate the development of self-discipline in middle school students. Begin by taking the pretest, then select appropriate objectives and complete appropriate activities. Prepare your own posttest in order to evaluate what you have accomplished.

Pretest

1. Write a brief statement indicating your personal views on the concept that "the best discipline comes from within."
2. Briefly identify three primary causes of misbehavior in the middle school classroom.
3. Contrast task-focused control techniques with approval-focused control techniques.
4. Contrast a self-administered behavior therapy program with an extrinsically oriented behavior modification approach to discipline.

Check

Discuss pretest results with your instructor.

Behavioral Objectives

Select those that are appropriate for you.

1. Discuss the effective use of four assessment tools in the diagnosis of a child's behavior problem.
2. Discuss the application of two approaches designed to increase the frequency of certain behaviors in a classroom setting.
3. Experiment with selected approaches to modifying aggressive behavior among a group of middle school students.
4. Outline a process for helping a middle school teacher develop a classroom program that facilitates student self-management.
5. Contrast Nerbovig and Klausmeier's four categorized social climates.

Activities

Select those that correlate with your objectives.

1. Read sections in *Classroom Management: The Successful Use of Behavior Modification* by K. Daniel O'Leary and Susan G. O'Leary (New York: Pergamon Press, 1972) regarding behavior assessment processes and use of behavior modification techniques. (1) (2) (3)
2. Review three readings on aggression in the classroom including Fritz Redl's "Agression in the Classroom," pp. 302–8 in *Learning to Teach in the Elementary School,* edited by Hal D. Funk and Robert T. Olberg (New York: Dodd, Mead and Co., 1971). (3)
3. Review the section on development of self-discipline, pp. 145–80 in *Teacher and Child* by Haim Ginott (New York: Macmillan Co., 1972). (4)
4. Describe some of your own ideas concerning disruptive behavior. Interview two teachers on the same topic and compare your ideas. (1) (2) (3) (4) (5)
5. Conduct a survey of discipline practices employed by parents of children in a specific class. Contrast the practices used by the parents with those used by the teacher. Summarize the results. (1) (3) (4)
6. Review *Classroom Uses of Behavior Modification* by Mary B. Harris (Columbus, Ohio: Charles E. Merrill Publishing Co., 1972) for assistance in increasing or decreasing certain behaviors in a classroom setting. (2)
7. Read the section on social climates, pp. 555–60 in *Teaching in the Elementary School* by Marcella Nerbovig and Herbert J. Klausmeier (New York: Harper and Row, 1969). If possible, visit several middle school classrooms and identify or categorize social climates according to Nerbovig and Klausmeier. (5)
8. Review the concepts involved in Individually Guided Motivation (IGM) and try to use them with some middle school pupils. For information, see p. 92 in *Individually Guided Motivation, Guidelines for Implementation,* Experimental copy, by Herbert J. Klausmeier, Dorothy A. Frayer, and Mary B. Quilling (Madison, Wis.: Wisconsin Research and Development Center for Cognitive Learning, 1972). (4)
9. Write down three actions a teacher could take and three he should avoid when a pupil misbehaves. Collect additional ideas from classmates and develop a list based on general agreement. (1) (2) (3) (4) (5)
10. Interview two school psychologists on the topic, "Helping the Student Develop Self-Discipline." Compare their ideas with your own. (1) (2) (3) (4) (5)
11. Interview a random sample of middle school pupils concerning their

views on discipline. Focus particularly on their ideas regarding development of self-discipline. (1) (2) (3) (4) (5)

Posttest

Write a brief essay summarizing what you have learned from your experiences.

Chapter 6

Evaluating and Reporting Pupil Progress

One of the most complex and challenging functions that a teacher performs is that of evaluating and reporting pupil progress. As a prospective teacher, you should spend considerable energy in developing competence in this area. This chapter is designed to help you develop competence and confidence in evaluating and reporting pupil progress.

Measurement and Evaluation

Two basic concepts, measurement and evaluation, are often misunderstood by teachers. Measurement is a process of obtaining quantitative data on a learner's progress. Evaluation, a more comprehensive concept, is a process of comparing data with a standard or making a judgment about the data. In essence, measurement involves collecting data, and evaluation involves analyzing data and using it to improve learning. Measurement and evaluation are continuous processes integral to effective teaching. It is very important to avoid the "pitstop evaluation" syndrome or "test every Friday" practice. These segmented approaches to evaluation are basically unproductive because they are not consistent or comprehensive. The evaluation process, however, must be comprehensive to be effective. Don't overemphasize any one variable, such as an IQ test score or achievement test score, to the extent that you overlook data regarding a student's interest or health, for example. Although group competition is a fact of life, your classroom evaluation system should encourage the learner to compete primarily with himself.

Evaluation can be defined as a process of collecting data relating to an individual student's progress and making a valid judgment on the basis of that data. The characteristics of evaluation are as follows:

1. It is related to the objectives of instruction; it is comprehensive in nature.
2. It is focused on the individual child, not on his performance compared with others.
3. It utilizes a variety of instruments and processes designed to collect both qualitative and quantitative data.
4. It is a continuous process.
5. It involves comparing data to a standard and making valid judgments on that basis.
6. It provides information for reporting to parents and keeping records concerning a student's progress and for improving curriculum.

Evaluation in a personalized instructional program is significantly different from evaluation in a traditional group-centered program. Evaluation in a group-centered program is usually based on the comparison of each student's progress with the group norm or the performance of other students in the class. In contrast, a personalized approach to evaluation emphasizes assessing an individual student's behavior to determine if he can meet stated learning objectives. When this approach is used, it is imperative that the student receive continuous oral and written feedback—understandable information that enables the student to analyze his own progress toward reaching the objectives.

Bloom and associates (1971) have emphasized that measurement may assume two different roles: formative and summative. Measurement is formative when it is used as a diagnostic measure of performance. Formative measurement is criterion-referenced, indicating the level of a student's progress with regard to predetermined standards.

Summative measurement is terminal or end-of-instruction measurement. It could be criterion-referenced and utilized in comparing an individual to a proficiency continuum, or it could be norm-referenced if a decision needs to be made regarding the student's rank among a group of individuals.

Criterion- versus Normative-Based Tests

A competency approach to instruction involves effective measurement. Wentling (1973) states that the measurement of competencies can be considered from two points of reference: norm reference and criterion reference. The more common one with which most teachers would be familiar is norm reference. Using a norm-referenced approach to measuring competencies involves the use of the normal curve and the comparison of students with other students, either in the immediate or an external norm group. This traditional type of measurement is designed to discriminate among individuals and select the better students. Mental ability tests, aptitude tests, and most grades and teacher ratings are of the norm-reference type. Norm referencing focuses on ordering and comparing students to other students rather than on what the individual student knows or can accomplish.

Criterion-referenced measurement focuses on competencies. It gives us information regarding a student's present behavior as compared to a standard. The driver's licensing test required by most states is an example of criterion referencing. The individual taking the test must meet a predetermined standard—in this case, a specific number of correct answers—before he is granted a license. How his score compares to the scores of others taking the test does not affect his obtaining a license.

What is the difference between a criterion-referenced test and a normative-based test? Criterion-referenced tests measure student progress toward specific objectives. They measure the degree of a student's mastery of material that is taught and learned in a specific time frame. Criterion-referenced tests serve as a tremendous asset for the teacher who is individualizing instruction.

In contrast, normative-based tests measure children in relation to each other rather than in an individualized manner. When individualizing instruction, the teacher's objectives and methods are likely to be different from the ones the test publisher assumes that he uses. To be more specific, a normative-based test contains test items that do not tap the information the students have actually learned.

Norms are a way of describing, by statistical methods, the test performance of specific groups of students of various ages and/or grades. Norms are used to describe average, below average, and above average performances. Grade, age, and percentiles are commonly used types of norms.

Norm-referenced tests can be used effectively for the following purposes:

1. General assessment of student ability
2. General assessment of student achievement
3. Diagnostic assessment in the classroom
4. Assessment of school programs and instructional procedures
5. A means of comparing the general achievement level of various schools, districts, and regions throughout the nation

Some pitfalls of using norm-referenced tests are:

1. The norms are prepared on the basis of the median scores of many pupils in many school systems. These may be suitable standards of

attainment for the average pupil but too high for slow pupils and too low for pupils who are above average in mental ability.
2. It's difficult to find a standardized test that parallels the objectives and grade placement of the local school.
3. If the teacher believes that he is to be rated on the basis of his pupils' test scores, he may have a tendency to teach for the tests only.
4. Unjustified comparisons of one child to another may be made using test scores.

Brazziel (1972) has presented six major advantages of using criterion-referenced tests. These tests do the following:

1. Permit direct interpretation of learner's progress toward reaching specific behavioral objectives.
2. Assist the teacher with individualized instruction.
3. Eliminate the situation in which half of the students "lose" or fall below the median.
4. Consist of summative tests that enable the teacher to measure student progress regularly and consistently.
5. Reduce the pressure on teachers to "teach to the test."
6. Provide the teacher with a vehicle for compiling a comprehensive record of the child's development.

Characteristics of a Good Test

The characteristics of a good test are validity, reliability, objectivity, and practicality. In order for a test to be valid, it must measure what it sets out to measure. For example, a history teacher might attempt to maintain validity in constructing a test by including questions representative of the important concepts and facts he has taught the learner. There are four types of validity:

1. *Content validity*—This involves a systematic comparison of test content with the behavior the test is designed to measure.
2. *Predictive validity*—This refers to the effectiveness of a test in predicting future performance. The predictive validity of a readiness test, for example, may be determined by a follow-up study to determine if pupils with high scores tended to advance more satisfactorily than those with low scores.
3. *Concurrent validity*—This refers to the relation between scores on a test and some other performance criterion, such as student grades or a psychological report obtained at the same time the test is given.
4. *Construct validity*—This refers to the validity of the inferences made from a test score about the characteristics of the person taking the

test. For example, an "anxiety" test has construct validity if differences in the test performances of individuals can be based on individual differences in the set of behavioral characteristics we identify as anxiety-produced. In order to establish construct validity, you must also carefully consider content, predictive, and concurrent validity.

A test is reliable when and if it measures accurately and consistently. Stated in other terms, a test is reliable if it obtains similar results when it is administered under similar circumstances on different occasions. A test has objectivity if two competent judges, independently scoring test papers, arrive at comparable scores for each paper graded. Determining the practicality of a test involves considering its cost per copy, the administration time, ease of scoring, possible reuse of test books, and related economic factors. Validity and reliability, however, are the two most important characteristics of a good test.

Constructing Teacher-Made Tests

The first step in the construction of a teacher-made test is to determine what should and will be tested. The test should be prepared in terms of the specific objectives of the specific unit of study being tested; it should measure what it purports to measure. If the teacher has clearly stated instructional objectives in behavioral terms, they can be readily translated into test items. Therefore, behavioral objectives may serve as a "blueprint" for a valid examination.

The second step is to give careful consideration to the type of test or format that will be used. Most teacher-made tests are either multiple-choice, essay, completion-item, or true-false. Let's briefly consider some suggestions for effective construction of each type.

The multiple-choice test enables the teacher to measure a large body of knowledge in an efficient and economical manner. The following criteria should be applied to a multiple-choice test:

1. The key proposition or *stem* of each test item should be stated in the form of a proposition or a problem. For example: The first thing to do on learning of a case of typhoid fever in the community is to:
2. The suggested answers or *alternatives* should be very carefully constructed so that all items have plausibility. Unless they have some plausibility, the choice of answer will be so easy for the student that it will pose no problem.
3. The wording of the questions should be appropriate for the reading level of the learners.

4. Whenever possible, the test item should emphasize knowledge of concepts or principles as opposed to knowledge of isolated facts.
5. It is usually better to state a problem in a positive form rather than in a negative one.
6. Items should not contain grammatical, contextual, or other irrelevant clues.

The essay test would appear to be more valid than the objective test for certain purposes. For example, the essay test would be a more logical choice for appraising writing abilities such as organizing materials or treating a topic logically, clearly, and comprehensively. A limitation of the essay-type examination involves the difficulties encountered in grading it. Studies have indicated that the same grader may assign significantly different grades to the same essay test if he grades them on two separate occasions. Hulten (1925) involved twenty-eight experienced high school English teachers in grading a theme and then grading it again two months later. The study revealed that fifteen teachers who gave passing marks on the first marking failed the paper in the second marking, and eleven teachers who failed the paper the first time assigned a passing grade on the second marking.

More recently, Marshall (1967) conducted a study in which 700 teachers marked the same essay examination. All teachers were instructed to grade on content alone in accordance with an outline of desired content. Thirteen forms of the essay were used with varying numbers of spelling, grammar, and punctuation errors introduced in each. The study revealed that teachers are influenced by the quality of the composition even when instructed to grade only on content. The lowest grades were assigned to the essay examinations that contained spelling errors only and those that contained grammatical errors only.

A few suggestions for improving the use of essay tests are:

1. In phrasing a question, present a clear delineation of the nature and scope of the answer desired.
2. A more adequate sampling of students' knowledge of content is possible by using a large number of questions requiring brief answers rather than a small number of questions requiring lengthy answers.
3. Develop a scoring key based on appropriate points per response.
4. Practice grading one question for all papers to reduce the "halo" effect. (The "halo" effect refers to an evaluator's tendency to allow the response given to one question to influence the evaluation of other questions in the same test.)

5. Practice writing answers to your own test questions. This should assist you in refining the questions.

The completion-item test is best used for measuring recall of specific information. One problem associated with the completion or fill-in-the-blank exam is that it may encourage rote learning on the part of students.

To improve the quality of completion-item tests, you should:

1. Leave blanks for important words or phrases, not trivial details.
2. Avoid lifting statements directly from the text as it encourages rote learning.
3. Avoid using irrelevant cues like *a* or *an* before a blank and making blanks correspond to the length of the fill-in word.

The true-false test has the advantages of sampling a large body of content in a short testing time, and it can be scored objectively. A major weakness is that so few things are so clearly right or wrong, answers are often debatable.

Here are a few pointers to help you construct true-false tests:

1. Provide students with reasonably short items that contain precise language. Avoid words subject to double meanings.
2. Avoid ambiguous statements.
3. Avoid using such words as *always, absolutely, never,* and *usually.*
4. Avoid making negative statements, especially those using the word *not.*
5. Avoid using confusing symbols such as O for true and + for false.

It would appear that for most testing purposes the multiple choice and essay formats are the most desirable choices for middle school use.

As a prospective middle school teacher, you need to carefully examine your concept of the role of examinations in assessing pupil progress. Many educators have expressed concern that teachers spend so much time "getting the learners ready" for examinations that they ignore intellectual development levels. Postman and Weingartner (1969) express this concern as follows:

> A "course" generally consists of a series of briefings for the great Trivia contest. It is a kind of rigged quiz show. And it seems to work only if the participants value the "prize." The "prize," of course, is a "grade." An appropriate grade permits the participants to continue playing the trivia game. All the while, let's not forget very little, if any, substantial intellectual activity is going on. (p. 152)

If this is true, it indicates that too many teachers and students believe that the possession of information for recall represents learning. Therefore, the emphasis is not on evaluation of the student's understanding and application of concepts and processes but on his ability to memorize and regurgitate facts. Renner, Shepherd, and Bibens (1973, p. 276) stress that "the current overemphasis on testing is the principal ailment of education in the United States, and possibly in the world. Most testing procedures have little to do with intellectual growth, which must be the primary concern of the schools for the reason that there is no other institution in our culture as equipped to foster that growth."

Tittle (1973) conducted a study of sexist bias in educational tests. The work, supported by the Ford Foundation, analyzed educational achievement tests for the extent to which their content reflected bias and sex-role stereotypes of women. The study involved recording all nouns and pronouns and content stereotypes. The major findings were:

1. With one exception, each test battery showed a higher frequency of usage of male nouns and pronouns than female nouns and pronouns.
2. The content bias in favor of males did not appear to be primarily a function of language usage, but rather of content selection.
3. Some test items implied that the majority of professions are closed to women.
4. The study revealed that most of the tests, like other instructional materials in education, contained numerous sex-role stereotypes.

Each teacher should become more cognizant of the influence of sex-role stereotyping in educational tests and the degree to which it influences the evaluation of the student.

Appraising Affective Behavior

Although professional test developers have been quite successful in the development of a variety of reliable and valid instruments to measure cognitive learning, very few instruments have been developed to measure affective learning. The lack of attitude assessment instruments for young children is very apparent. Beere's (1973) research illustrates the type of affective instrument development that is needed. The research involved the development of an attitude assessment instrument appropriate for use with groups of early elementary school children. This instrument used a measurement technique involving oral and pictorial presentation of items with pictorial response choices.

The response choices are represented by five faces that vary in expression from very happy to very sad. Of the forty items included in the instrument, thirty-two are in the oral presentation style, and eight are pictorial. For twenty-two of the oral items, a favorable attitude is indicated by marking one of the happy faces (Figure 6.1); for ten of the oral items a favorable attitude is expressed by marking one of the sad faces. Also for the eight pictorial items, a favorable attitude is expressed by marking one of the happy faces. Specifically, each item has five possible response choices that range from very happy to very sad. The Beere instrument is very similar to a Likert scale (an attitude instrument developed by R. Likert in 1932). The advantages include ease of construction, administration, scoring, and interpretation. A manual for administration and analysis of data accompanies the instrument.

Brown and MacDougall (1973) conducted a study designed to examine the impact of teacher consultation on the affective perceptions of elementary school children. The study involved an in-service program for fourteen female elementary school teachers in an urban elementary school setting in Virginia. Two-hour training sessions were held after school for six consecutive weeks. The training sessions engaged the teachers in observing, discussing, and analyzing videotapes made by themselves and by their colleagues in their individual classrooms. Each teacher received a private critiquing session during which only her positive teaching behaviors were noted. Each teacher then shared her videotapes with her colleagues. The group presentations enabled the teachers to observe a wide range of possible positive behaviors in addition to those they currently used themselves.

To examine the effect of teachers' training experiences on the pupil

Figure 6.1

One Pictorial Item and Response Choices

SOURCE: From C. A. Beere, "Development of a Group Instrument to Measure Young Children's Attitudes Toward School," *Psychology in the Schools* 10(1973):309. Used with permission.

population, a Personal Competence Inventory developed by Brown and MacDougall was administered to the pupils in grades three through six. An analysis of the data obtained upheld the proposition that if teachers are given opportunities to examine, discuss, and model behaviors that have been judged to be effective in the classroom, then the children they teach will regard themselves more positively.

The study suggests the following: "(1) teachers are influenced by the socioeconomic status of the child; (2) a teacher's style of interaction teaches children how to perceive their classmates; (3) teachers are not generally influenced by a child's race or sex; and (4) teachers and pupils tend to agree on perceptions of school work tasks, but no such congruence was observed for social skill tasks" (Brown and MacDougall1973, pp. 344–45.).

The Sentence Completion Form developed by Feldhusen, Thurston, and Benning (1966) is an easily administered, yet reasonably reliable and valid, measure of the general adjustment of school children.[1] It should be used in conjunction with other measures such as teacher observation of a child's behavior. It could be used to identify socially approved or disapproved tendencies in children, although, at this point, it is designed more for describing current behavior than predicting future behavior. Test items are as follows:

1. I like . . .
2. I want to know . . .
3. I am sorry that . . .
4. Boys . . .
5. A mother . . .
6. My greatest fear . . .
7. I can't . . .
8. Other kids . . .
9. The future . . .
10. I need . . .
11. I am best when . . .
12. What bothers me most . . .
13. At school . . .
14. My father . . .
15. I secretly . . .
16. Most girls . . .
17. My greatest worry is . . .
18. I don't like . . .

---

1. From J. F. Feldhusen, J. R. Thurston, and J. J. Benning, "Sentence Completion Response and Classroom Social Behavior," *Personnel and Guidance Journal* 45(1966):165–70. Copyright 1966 American Personnel and Guidance Association. Reprinted with permission.

19. My daydreams . . .
20. My life's job will be . . .

In developing the instrument, the authors compared sentence completion responses of ninety-six children whose classroom behavior was socially approved with responses of ninety-six children whose behavior was socially disapproved because it was aggressive and disruptive. Socially approved behaviors included industry, productivity, good-naturedness, ambition, cooperation, and responsibility. Socially disapproved behaviors were disrupting the class, bullying others, throwing a temper tantrum, and talking back to the teacher. The Sentence Completion Form may be used to obtain extremely important data that the teacher may use in assisting individual students with affective behavior development and in improving the quality of classroom social behavior.

How can middle school learners be assisted by the schools to monitor their own behavior? Most methods used by teachers in the past to control children placed little or no responsibility on the student to evaluate his own behavior. Some examples of these methods are the teacher's being present, scolding, smiling, pleading, giving praise or privileges, or threatening intervention by parents or principal.

Mazza and Garris (1972) conducted a research project designed to allow students to assess their own behavior and to establish behavioral goals that they might deem desirable. Students selected to participate in the project were in the upper three grades of elementary school. A summary of the major steps in the project is as follows:

1. The student's classroom behavior was videotaped by the teacher without his knowledge.
2. A verbal assessment by the student of his own behavior was tape-recorded prior to the student's viewing of the videotape. In other words, the student was asked to talk about his behavior before viewing it.
3. The student viewed the videotape.
4. The student was asked to compare his initial assessment on tape (Step 2) with the videotape.
5. The teacher asked the student specific questions about his behavior to assist him in seeing areas where he might make improvements. The teacher avoided making judgments.
6. In some instances, the videotape was reviewed for clarity.
7. The teacher assisted the student in setting realistic behavioral goals. Goals were the student's own choices, however. The entire process was repeated at a later date to allow the student to reassess his progress.

This procedure should have unlimited applications in an elementary school setting in self-assessment and self-concept development processes. The affective dimensions of student development require careful analysis; as we previously noted, they are often neglected.

Record Keeping

It is very important for the teacher to develop a personalized record-keeping system that is simple, functional, and productive. Dell (1972) has developed a classroom record-keeping model that will quickly provide information in four areas of major concern: (1) curricula data, (2) individual student progress reports, (3) individual student work schedules, and (4) behavior modification schedules. It is advisable to keep individual student files containing records appropriate to each student's needs.

A curricula data list would include goals, objectives, and learning guides for a particular subject area. This information should be recorded in a format that can be used for the teacher's curriculum counseling with the student. It is advisable to work out a series of letter and number designations for subject areas and specific objectives. For example, consider the following system:

Primary objectives	1-200	Language Arts	(La)
Intermediate objectives	200-400	Social Studies	(Ss)
Junior high	400-800	Mathematics	(Ma)
High school	800-1500	Music	(Mu)

An example of the application of this system is seen in the diagnosis that an intermediate level student could work on La 220. Any system similar to this one that assists teachers in identifying appropriate learning objectives and approximate levels could be used.

Individual student progress reports help the teacher and student plan the student's work and provide a system for reporting his progress to parents. A great variety of progress reports are being developed and used by creative teachers throughout the nation. One example is a card that contains the student's name and his learning objectives, which are listed around the periphery of the card. A paper punch is used to mark each objective as the student completes it. (See Figure 6.2.)

Individual student work schedules are an important part of record keeping. A variety of forms may be used. For example, a student who has developed sufficient self-management skills could use a work schedule card that would include the following data: name, number of objectives, date of expected completion, date of completion. It could be designed for the student to use over a period of several days. On the other hand, the

Figure 6.2

Individual Student Progress Report

1/2/3/4/5/6/7/8/9/10/11/12/13

23		14
24		15
25		16
26		17
27		18
28		19
29		20
30		21
31		22

32/33/34/35/36/37/38/39/40/41

SOURCE: From *Individualizing Instruction* by Helen Davis Dell. © 1972, Science Research Associates, Inc. Reprinted by permission of the publisher.

work schedule for the student needing short-range goals might include objectives and activities for only one day. Regardless of the format used, a work schedule's emphasis should be on helping the student grow in self-management skills and wise utilization of his time.

Behavior modification schedules are helpful in developing effective learning habits and social behaviors. Behavior modification involves specific techniques used by a teacher to modify, change, or maintain student behaviors. The teacher may reinforce behaviors through use of verbal praise and nonverbal expressions, tokens, or desirable activities. The teacher should use discretion, however, particularly in the use of tokens. Activity reinforcers are especially appropriate for young children and emphasize intrinsic rather than extrinsic reinforcement. To reinforce desired behavior, the teacher may give students a variety of recreation or work privileges, such as helping in the classroom in leadership of activities, playing a game with a friend, reading a chosen book, taking messages for the teacher to other parts of the school, or working in a preferred subject area. Regardless of the reinforcement procedures he uses, the teacher should keep a record of procedures and results.

Dean (1972) has identified certain dangers in record keeping that we need to guard against. One problem is that it is possible to be so busy recording data that we never get around to the important tasks of planning and teaching. We need to be certain that the data we record is accurate. A teacher should always guard against leaving negative statements on a permanent record that may not prove to be true later after a child has experienced a change in behavior or has simply matured. We must develop a true professional attitude so that we will not be worried about writing statements about a child for fear it might color the expectations of the colleague who meets him next.

Criteria for Evaluating an Individualized Classroom

In order to judge the degree of individualization in any classroom the teacher should follow these selected criteria:

1. Instructional objectives should be stated in specific behavioral terms and assigned individually to students.
2. Students should be able to achieve the objectives with a minimum of teacher assistance.
3. Students should be allowed to choose some instructional objectives on their own.
4. A great variety of learning modes should be employed by the teacher and students.
5. A great variety of evaluation modes should be employed by the teacher and students with increasing emphasis on self-evaluation.
6. Student records and progress reports should emphasize individual progress rather than group norms.
7. Students should display increasing ability to work independently.
8. A variety of multimedia materials should be used by learners to reach variable objectives.
9. The teacher and learners should develop a variety of cooperative relationships, resulting in an environment conducive to personalized learning.
10. The teacher should fill a variety of roles, including the role of learner.

Reporting Pupil Progress

The process of reporting a pupil's progress requires careful consideration and selected skills. It also serves several important functions:

1. It enables the child and parent to view the child's progress in reaching specific objectives.
2. It aids in helping the child develop a meaningful and valid self-concept.
3. It functions as a tool for enlisting parents' support and cooperation in the educational process.
4. It requires the teacher to periodically rethink his teaching.
5. It communicates school values to the community.

There are four major ways of reporting pupil progress:

1. *Informal reporting by the student.* This involves the child's discussing with his parents what he learns and does at school, sharing samples of work completed or expressing interests that are a result of school experiences. The teacher does not direct this method but may assist by holding verbal evaluation periods during the school day.
2. *Parent participation at school.* This process of reporting includes inviting parents to observe or participate in school activities such as American Education Week activities, classroom projects, field trips, or work with school-community groups. Parents may also observe their children in actual classroom situations if invited.
3. *Written report to parents.* This takes many forms including the traditional A-B-C report card, rating instruments, and written statements.
4. *Parent-teacher conference.* This approach involves the parent and teacher in discussing the child's progress and in cooperatively developing a plan for continuously improving it.

Conducting a Parent-Teacher Conference

Herman (1968) has indicated that the following steps and procedures are important to follow in conducting a successful parent-teacher conference:[2]

1. The purpose of the conference should be clearly defined in order that both teacher and parent may understand why a conference is needed.
2. Careful preparation by the teacher is imperative. The parent should be contacted well in advance and a convenient time arranged. Make a thorough review of the student's record and have appropriate data and samples of the student's work available. Select an appropriate setting for the conference.
3. Practice positive, professional procedures during the conference. Greet parents warmly. Help the parent to feel at ease and to understand that your job is to help the child through a cooperative relationship. Present the problem or purpose of the conference in an honest, open manner. Listen and allow time for the parents to talk and share their feelings about the child. Do not take written notes

---

2. Adapted from Barry E. Herman, "The Parent-Teacher Conference," *Catholic School Journal,* November 1968, pp. 7–8. Used with permission.

but make mental reminders. Avoid use of educational jargon and adapt language to the parent. Use positive expressions. For example, "can do more when he tries" instead of "lazy," "could do neater work" instead of "sloppy," and "extremely self-confident" instead of "stubborn." Seek cooperative, realistic solutions.

4. A plan for follow-up is essential. A brief review should be conducted so that both parent and teacher understand what has been accomplished during the conference. Specific follow-up procedures for both parties should be clarified. Conclude the conference on a positive note.
5. Avoid conducting conferences only when there is a problem. Also conduct conferences to report positive data on students. This will help eliminate the "oh, what has he done now" fear that parents sometimes have regarding conferences.

If properly implemented, the parent-teacher conference can be one of the best methods of reporting pupil progress. In addition, it can be extremely valuable in building a bridge of cooperation between home and school.

Using Written Reports

A personalized instructional program that places emphasis upon a student's competing primarily with himself requires a written report significantly different from the traditional A-B-C report card. The letter-grade system focuses on comparison with a group norm; although it does give parents an index of their children's progress, it is basically a very limited reporting device. If a child is doing very poorly, it does not analytically indicate *where* and *how* he is doing poorly. It can also encourage the parental practice of making unjust sibling comparisons.

An effective written report provides specific information concerning the student's strengths and weaknesses and his developmental learning pattern. It should give attention to personal-social progess in addition to academic progress.

Summary

Evaluating and reporting pupil progress is one of the most important functions that you will perform in teaching. A concise conception of measurement and evaluation is essential to effective teaching. It is extremely important to emphasize the assessment of individual student progress in relation to personalized objectives rather than in comparison with a group norm.

Criterion-referenced tests are generally more desirable than normative-based tests. Criterion-referenced tests measure student progress toward specific objectives. More attention needs to be given to the appraisal of affective learning, however, as well as to the use of a greater variety of cognitive test items. Every teacher should employ a variety of processes designed to enable the student to more effectively assess his own progress.

Parent-teacher conferences and written reports that provide specific information on the student's progress in relation to his capabilities are the most effective reporting processes. You should greatly enhance your measurement and evaluation competencies through application of the concepts and processes presented in this chapter.

REFERENCES

Beere, C. A. "Development of a Group Instrument to Measure Young Children's Attitudes Toward School." *Psychology in the Schools* 10(1973):308–15.

Bloom, Benjamin S.; Hastings, J. T.; and Madaus, G. F. *Handbook of Formative and Summative Evaluation of Student Learning.* New York: McGraw-Hill, 1971.

Brazziel, William F. "Criterion-Referenced Tests." *Today's Education,* November 1972, pp. 52–53.

Brown, Jeannette A., and MacDougall, Mary Ann. "The Impact of Teacher Consultation on the Self-Perception of Elementary School Children." *Education* 93(1973):339–45.

Dean, Joan. *Recording Children's Progress.* New York: Citation Press, 1972.

Dell, Helen Davis. *Individualizing Instruction.* Chicago: Science Research Associates, 1972.

Feldhusen, John F.; Thurston, John R.; and Benning, James J. "Sentence Completion Response and Classroom Social Behavior." *Personnel and Guidance Journal* 45(1966):165–70.

Herman, Barry E. "The Parent-Teacher Conference." *Catholic School Journal,* November 1968, pp. 7–8.

Hulten, C. E. "The Personal Element in Teacher's Marks." *Journal of Educational Research* 12(1925):49–55.

Marshall, J. C. "Composition Errors and Essay Examination Grades Reexamined." *American Educational Research Journal* 4(1967):375–85.

Mazza, Paul, and Garris, Donald. "Shared Student Self-Evaluation." *Personnel and Guidance Journal* 50(1972):745–48.

Postman, Neil, and Weingartner, Charles. *Teaching as a Subversive Activity.* New York: Delacarte Press, 1969.

Renner, John W.; Shepherd, Gene D.; and Bibens, Robert F. *Guiding Learning in the Elementary School.* New York: Harper and Row, 1973.

Tittle, Carol Kehr. "Women and Educational Testing." *Phi Delta Kappan* 55(1973):118–19.

Wentling, Tim L. "Measuring the Achievement of Competencies." *Educational Technology* 13(1973):48–50.

Learning Module

Evaluating Pupil Progress

Directions

This learning module is designed to help you develop competency in the application of appropriate evaluation and reporting procedures. What is evaluation? What are some effective procedures to use in the evaluation of a learner's progress? Can you effectively utilize a variety of pupil assessment tools in a middle school setting? To complete this learning module, start with the pretest, work through the appropriate activities, and conclude with the posttest.

Pretest

Read each question carefully and then answer to the best of your ability.

1. Define in your own words your concept of the term *evaluation*.
2. Contrast evaluation and measurement.
3. List and explain three informal evaluation processes and three formal evaluation processes.
4. What are the characteristics of an effective teacher-made test?
5. List three specific self-assessment tools and explain their application in a middle school setting.
6. What are some important guidelines for pupil-teacher and teacher-parent conferences?

Check

Review your pretest performance with your instructor. Based on your results, select the appropriate objectives.

Behavioral Objectives

1. Select the objectives that are appropriate for you. Describe and discuss intelligently several concepts relating to the evaluation of pupil progress.
2. Explain the application of five informal evaluative procedures and five formal evaluative procedures.
3. Discuss some specific self-assessment tools and procedures for middle school use.

4. Write appropriate true-false, short-answer, multiple-choice, and essay test items.
5. Use a variety of record-keeping procedures designed to assess pupil progress.

Required Activities

1. Read Chapter 4, "Evaluating Student Progress," and Chapter 7, "Record Keeping," in Helen Dell's *Individualizing Instruction* (Chicago: Science Research Associates, 1972). Write a brief summary of the major concepts presented.
2. Read pp. 1–15 in Clarence H. Nelson's *Measurement and Evaluation in the Classroom* (London: Macmillan & Co., 1970). Explain the function of measurement and evaluation in the classroom.
3. Refer to pp. 50–75 in C. M. Lindall's *Measuring Pupil Achievement and Aptitude* (New York: Harcourt, Brace and World, 1967) and pp. 204–71 in Julian C. Stanley's *Measurement in Today's Schools* (Englewood Cliffs, N.J.: Prentice-Hall, 1964). Answer these questions:
   a) Explain the construction of completion, multiple-choice, true-false, matching, and essay tests.
   b) What are some guidelines for effective test construction?
   c) What criteria are used for analyzing and interpreting test scores?
   d) Plan a well-constructed test and use it in a classroom setting.
4. Discuss the application of five informal and five formal evaluation procedures. Refer to Chapters 2 and 7 of Robert Thorndike's *Measurement and Evaluation in Psychology and Education* (New York: John Wiley and Sons, 1967).

If you now feel competent in your knowledge and understanding of evaluating pupil progress, its purposes, and some of the techniques involved in it, then proceed to *Optional Activities*. If you need more assistance, refer to *Enrichment Activities*.

Enrichment Activities

These are optional; you may do any or all of the following:

1. Prepare a simulation dealing with two situations:
   a) a teacher-parent conference that is conducted in an effective, professional manner
   b) a teacher-parent conference that is conducted very poorly.
2. Interview a guidance counselor on the topic, "Assessing Pupil Progress."
3. Visit several local middle school classrooms and collect samples of the pupil assessment tools and procedures that are in use. Hold a conference with your college instructor.

Optional Activities

Do any *four* of the following activities.

1. Tape-record an interview with five selected middle school teachers, obtaining their ideas and suggestions on evaluating pupil progress. Prepare a written, comparative summary of the interview.
2. Analyze a traditional report card. Then, based on your own research and experience, design a more personalized, effective instrument.
3. Prepare a self-appraisal questionnaire and use it with a group of learners. Refer to Chapter 12 in Thorndike's *Measurement and Evaluation in Psychology and Education* if you need help.
4. Using *Education Index,* review three current periodical references concerning the evaluation of pupil progress.
5. Prepare a booklet of concrete examples of ways to keep daily records, plot pupil progress, and so forth.
6. Read three current articles regarding parent-teacher conferences. Contact a local middle school teacher and arrange to observe a parent-teacher conference.

Posttest

Respond to the following:

1. Compare the major considerations involved in using multiple-choice test items with those involved in using essay items.
2. Describe four specific purposes of evaluation instruments.
3. Design a student report card for parents that will reflect the philosophy of personalized instruction.
4. Plan a well-constructed test and administer it to an individual pupil.
5. Conduct a teacher-pupil conference and a teacher-parent conference. Evaluate your planning, implementation, and follow-up procedures.
6. Discuss the concept of self-assessment. Outline three specific tools or procedures that could be used for self-assessment by a middle school pupil.
7. Design three appropriate record-keeping instruments for recording pupil progress in a middle school setting.

Chapter 7

Assessing Teacher Competencies

To effectively assess teaching competence, we must collect as much related objective data as possible by utilizing a variety of procedures. A technique for assessing a teacher's competence that has been used since the beginnings of formal education is evaluation by someone other than the teacher herself. The external evaluator could be an administrator, a fellow teacher, supervisor, or even a student. Pairs of teachers have found success in observing and evaluating each other. Too little attention has been given to helping the teacher develop and utilize effective self-evaluation processes. Self-assessment resulting in improved teacher performance should become an integral part of teacher evaluation. Let's examine some specific processes involved in assessing teacher competencies.

Purposes of Teacher Evaluation

The evaluation of teachers is an extremely complex, important process. If you were to interview a random sample of teachers, administrators, and supervisors concerning the focus or purpose of this process you would no doubt discover many varied opinions. Some individuals would see evaluation as a process that provides analytical data to the teacher that she can use to become familiar with her own strengths and weaknesses and to engage in a process of self-improvement. Others would emphasize evaluation's function in categorizing teachers with little thought being given to helping them improve their teaching skills.

Evaluation is a value judgment process; unless qualitative description, analysis, and interpretation precede it, poor results will occur. Bolton (1973) has identified six major functions of the teacher evaluation process:

1. *Improvement of instruction*. There is general agreement among educators that this is the most important purpose.
2. *Rewarding superior performance*. Too often in the past this purpose has been accomplished with excessive emphasis being placed on subjective rather than objective data.
3. *Modification of assignment*. Effective application of promotion or change in assignment results in better staff morale and a better instructional program.
4. *Protection of the individual and the organization*. From a legal standpoint, responsibility for the operation of school programs is delegated by the state to the local district and from there to the teacher. Society holds the schools accountable for reaching certain goals. Effective evaluation is legally essential to both the school and the teacher.
5. *Validation of the selection process*. More effective evaluation of existing staff provides data essential to the proper selection of new staff members. This practice needs greater emphasis in the future.
6. *Promotion of individual growth and self-evaluation*. An effective self-evaluation process involves continuous diagnosis of teaching, which is essential to good teaching.

After an extensive review of research and practice connected with evaluation of teachers on a nationwide basis, Jones (1972) developed the following conclusions:[1]

1. There is considerable disagreement in the reports of education research as to what the effective teacher is.
2. Teachers generally focus their professional development on the points of evaluation used to measure their performance.
3. Secondary students tend to rate their teachers' general performance more accurately than do supervisors, other teachers, or principals.
4. Most teacher evaluation forms are so vague that teachers regard them as having very little value.
5. Teachers want to participate in self-evaluation processes.
6. Almost all public school evaluation procedures identify individual teacher deficiencies but fail to provide effective guidance toward self-improvement.

---

1. From Anthony S. Jones, "Realistic Approach to Teacher Evaluation," *Clearing House* 46(1972):474–81. Used with permission.

7. Most in-service education for teachers does not include a follow-up designed to assess any change in teacher performance.

Based on these conclusions, Jones (1972) proposed the following objectives for a realistic program of teacher evaluation:

1. Evaluation items should focus on the kind of teacher characteristics found in a particular school system at a particular time.
2. Students should participate in the evaluation of teachers.
3. Vague and irrelevant items should be eliminated from teacher evaluation procedures. Items beyond the evaluator's scope of understanding or awareness should also be eliminated.
4. Teachers should have an opportunity to evaluate their own teaching.
5. Every evaluation item should be accompanied by a professional development or in-service counterpart. For example, if a teacher is found deficient in classroom management skills, he should be provided with an opportunity to participate in an in-service workshop or college course designed to remove the deficiency.
6. There should be an evaluative follow-up immediately following all in-service educational experiences.

Evaluation Strategies

There are presently three major strategies employed in the evaluation of a teacher. The traditional and most widely used strategy has been to evaluate the teacher education program under which the teacher was trained. A second strategy involves measuring the progress of pupils taught by the teacher. Finally, a more recent emphasis has been placed on measuring the competencies or actual teaching behavior of the teacher. After careful consideration of various strategies, Soar (1973) concludes that systematic observation appears to be one of the more promising assessment procedures for measuring teaching skill. Some of the advantages of this strategy are as follows:

1. It measures the teacher's performance that is most directly under her control.
2. It permits the faculty and administration of a school or school system to agree on what teaching behaviors are most important.
3. The teacher is able to obtain feedback on her teaching that is essential to her self-improvement.
4. The teacher is able to engage in action research that should result in improved instruction.

Helping the Teacher with Self-Appraisal

The results of extensive research on the teaching-learning process in the classroom indicate that no specific style of teaching can be designated as the best model for everyone to follow. Instead, teachers need to employ self-appraisal to find and develop the style that is most effective for them. Roberson (1971) has developed the Teacher Self-Appraisal Observation System for the use of teachers in improving their instruction. The TSA system consists of three aspects of teacher classroom behavior: methods, objectives, and expressions. (See Figure 7.1.) The system includes nine possible methods, nine levels of objectives, and seven levels of verbal and nonverbal expressions.

To use the TSA system, the teacher follows specific steps:

1. She develops a lesson plan describing the objectives she intends to accomplish and the methods to be employed.
2. She videotapes the lesson, views the tape, and codes a set of TSA cards according to methods, objectives, and expressions used during the lesson. A code is recorded at every ten-second interval for each category.
3. After the videotape has been coded, the deck of TSA cards are computer processed to provide feedback that can be used to compare the planned performance with the actual performance.
4. The data can be carefully analyzed in order to provide suggestions for improvements.

The TSA program is based upon the following assumptions (Roberson 1971):

> 1. Teaching is basically people behaving together, with learning as their objective.
> 2. There is one mode of successful or "good" teaching.
> 3. The participant must be aware of a need to change, in order for lasting change to occur.
> 4. Teaching behavior changes most readily when the teacher is provided an audio or video record of his teaching. (p. 471)

Flanders Interaction Analysis

Flanders (1970) has developed a system to observe and record pupil-teacher verbal interaction. There are ten categories in the system with seven focusing on teacher talk, two on student talk, and one on silence or confusion. (See Figure 7.2.)

The Flanders system can be used by an outside observer or by the teacher herself listening to a tape recording of classroom interaction. The

Figure 7.1

TSA Observation Terms and Definitions

Category	Subcategory	Term and Definition
METHODS	Closed	Lecture—teacher talk or information giving.
		Demonstrate—teacher supplements talk with visual clues or external props.
		Direction—teacher commands or insists students comply.
		Question—teacher interrogative request for specific information.
		Mastery—teacher drills or practices specifics with students.
		Problem Solving—teacher sets or poses a situation which requires the student to arrive at a predetermined solution.
	Open	Clarification—teacher permits the student to express or elaborate feelings, opinions, or thoughts without interruption.
		Inquiry—teacher pursues and challenges student statements, or permits students to question.
		Dialogue—teacher allows students to interact, react, and discuss a topic or idea with interjections but not inhibiting behavior.
OBJECTIVES	Affective	Receive—teacher intends the student to listen or be conscious of current classroom activity.
		Respond—teacher intends for the student to comply.
		Value—teacher intends for the student to realize the worth of information, idea, belief, or concept by utilizing words such as "good," "beautiful," "excellent," etc.
	Cognitive	Know—teacher intends the student to recall specific information for which there is only one correct answer.
		Comprehend—teacher intends the student to translate, interpret in his own words, predict, or summarize given material.
		Apply—teacher intends the student to use the information in a situation that is different from the situation in which it was learned.
		Analyze—teacher intends the student to separate, compare, and establish relationships between concepts, information, and ideas.
		Synthesize—teacher intends the student to combine previous learned information and concepts into an original entity that satisfies the student.
		Evaluate—teacher intends the student to make a choice or selection from a predetermined number of alternatives.
EXPRESSIONS	Verbal	Support—teacher praises, repeats student response, or uses student idea.
		Helping—teacher repeats statements or gives cues and assistance that aid student.
		Receptive—teacher indicates to a student that the lines of communication are open.
		Routine—teacher expressions that cannot be categorized, as encouraging or inhibiting.
		Inattentive—teacher disinterest or impatience displayed by statements such as "hurry up," "not now," etc.
		Unresponsive—teacher openly ignores student question, request, or response.
		Disapproval—teacher admonishes, reprimands, or threatens student.
	Nonverbal	Support—teacher gestures, facial expressions, and voice tone that convey approval.
		Helping—teacher gestures and pointing that assist students.
		Receptive—teacher maintains eye contact with students.
		Routine—teacher movements that cannot be coded as encouraging or inhibiting.
		Inattentive—teacher does not maintain eye contact or body gestures that demonstrate an unwillingness to listen.
		Unresponsive—teacher gestures that openly ignore a student request.
		Disapproval—teacher frowns, gestures, and voice tones that convey dissatisfaction with student behavior.

SOURCE: From Wayne E. Roberson, "Teacher Self-Appraisal: A Way to Improve Instruction," *Journal of Teacher Education* 22(1971):469–73. Used with permission.

Figure 7.2

Categories for Interaction Analysis

TEACHER TALK	*Indirect Influence*	1.* ACCEPTS FEELINGS: accepts and clarifies the feeling tone of the students in a nonthreatening manner. Feelings may be positive or negative. Predicting or recalling feelings are included.
		2.* PRAISES OR ENCOURAGES: praises or encourages student action or behavior. Jokes that release tension, not at the expense of another individual, nodding head or saying, "un hm?" or "go on" are included.
		3.* ACCEPTS OR USES IDEAS OF STUDENT: clarifying, building, or developing ideas suggested by a student. As a teacher brings more of his own ideas into play, shift to category five.
		4.* ASKS QUESTIONS: asking a question about content or procedure with the intent that a student answer.
	Direct Influence	5.* LECTURING: giving facts or opinions about content or procedure; expressing his own ideas, asking rhetorical questions.
		6.* GIVING DIRECTIONS: directions, commands, or orders to which a student is expected to comply.
		7.* CRITICIZING OR JUSTIFYING AUTHORITY: statements intended to change student behavior from nonacceptable to acceptable pattern; bawling someone out; stating why the teacher is doing what he is doing; extreme self-reference.
		8.* STUDENT TALK—RESPONSE: a student makes a predictable response to teacher. Teacher initiates the contact or solicits student statement and sets limits to what the student says.
		9.* STUDENT TALK—INITIATION: talk by students which they initiate. Unpredictable statements in response to teacher. Shift from 8 to 9 as student introduces own ideas.
		10.* SILENCE OR CONFUSION: pauses, short periods of silence and periods of confusion in which communication cannot be understood by the observer.

*There is NO scale implied by these numbers. Each number is classificatory; it designates a particular kind of communication event. To write these numbers down during observation is to enumerate, not to judge a position on a scale.

SOURCE: From Ned A. Flanders, *Analyzing Teaching Behavior,* © 1970, Addison-Wesley, Reading, Massachusetts. Used with permission.

procedure involves the recording of a numeral that corresponds with a category appropriate to the verbal interaction taking place. Verbal interactions should be recorded on the recording matrix moving down the column at a rate of every three seconds. (See Figure 7.3.) When recording, you always begin with silence (10) and end with silence (10). You may record up to twenty minutes of verbal interaction on one recording matrix.

Please observe carefully the following excerpt from a fourth grade geography lesson. (See Figure 7.4.) The data concerning verbal interactions taking place during the lesson can be analyzed by using an analysis

Figure 7.3

Recording Matrix

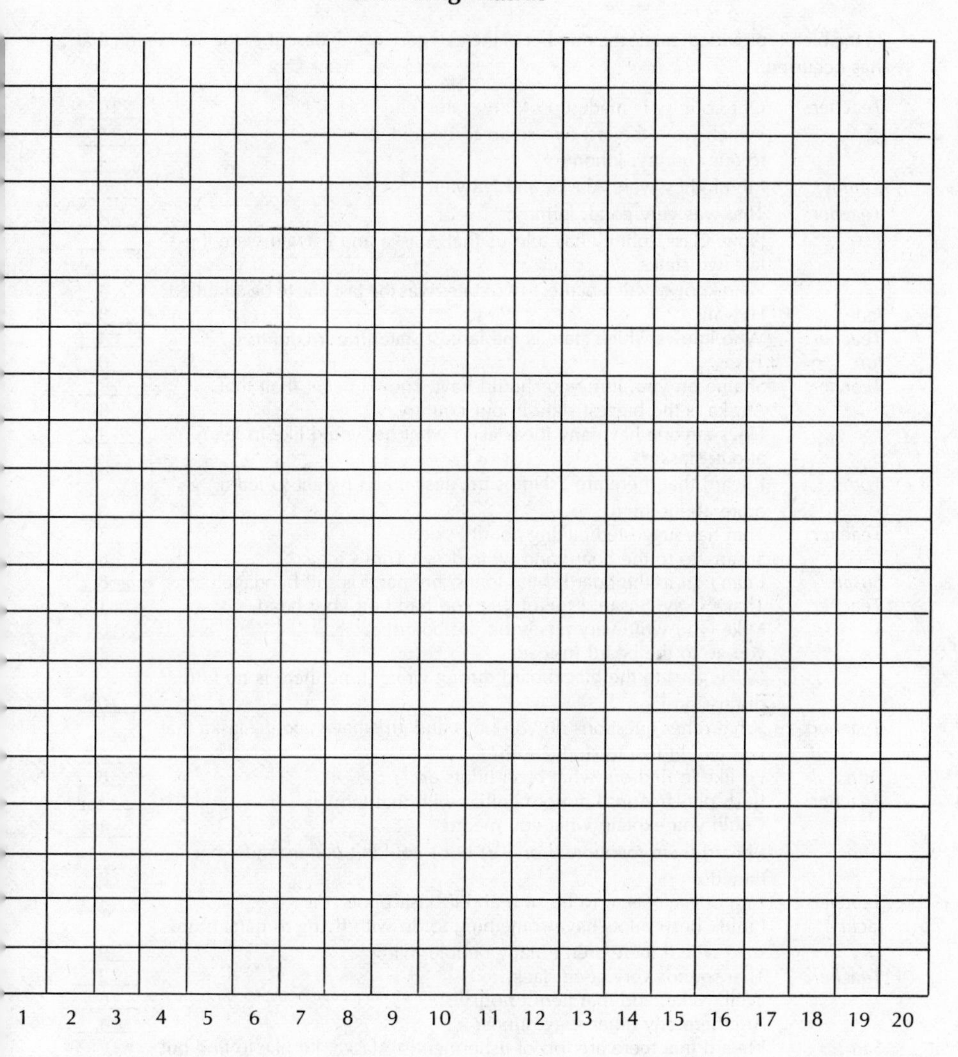

matrix. (See Figure 7.5.) In order to effectively use the analysis matrix, follow these guidelines:

1. Numbers are tallied in the matrix one pair at a time. For example, assume that your first two numbers in the first column of your

Figure 7.4

Excerpt from a Fourth Grade Geography Lesson

In the blanks provided, place the number of the category which describes the interaction that has occurred.

Teacher:	Our country is made up of fifty states	10
	Which were the last two states to be added	5
	to our country, Johnny?	4
Johnny:	I think they were Alaska and Hawaii.	8
Teacher:	That was very good, Johnny;	2
	Now, class, Johnny has told us that Alaska and Hawaii were the last two states.	3
	Who knows which of these two states was the last one to be admitted?	4
Jane:	Hawaii.	8
Teacher:	Who knows which state is the largest state in our country?	4
Jim:	Texas.	8
Teacher:	Shame on you, Jim; you should have known better than that.	7
	Alaska is the biggest state in our country.	5
	Does anyone have any ideas as to what he would like to learn about Alaska?	4
Tom:	I heard that there are Eskimos in Alaska, and I want to learn more about them.	9
Teacher:	Tom has suggested talking about Eskimos.	3
	Susan, go to the board and write down Tom's idea.	6
Susan:	I can't go to the board, Miss Jones, my hand is still bandaged.	8
Teacher:	That's okay, Susan, I forgot that you had hurt your hand.	1
	Mike, you write very nicely on the board,	6
	you go to the board instead.	2
	(Mike goes to the blackboard during which time there is no further discussion.)	10
Teacher:	What other questions do you boys and girls have about Alaska that you would like to study? Ann?	4
Ann:	I'd like to find out what bush pilots do.	8
Teacher:	Bush pilots? Ann, I'm not familiar with that term.	3
	Could you explain what you mean?	4
Ann:	I heard them mentioned on TV, but I couldn't understand what they do.	8
Teacher:	Ann doesn't seem to be sure about bush pilots . . .	3
Jack:	I think bush pilots have something to do with flying to parts of the state where there aren't many people living.	9
Teacher:	That sounds very good, Jack.	2
	Well, Mike, add that item to our list.	6
	Are there any other suggestions?	4
Sam:	I heard that there are lots of fishermen in Alaska. I'd like to find out what kind of fish they catch.	9
Teacher:	Sam would like to find out what kinds of fish are caught in Alaska.	3
	You will learn something about Alaska's economy.	5
	Would that be agreeable with everyone? Rick?	4
Rick:	Do you mean that if we study the economy of Alaska that that's all we'll study?	9
		10

SOURCE: From Ned A. Flanders, *Analyzing Teaching Behavior* (Reading, Mass.: Addison-Wesley, 1970). Used with permission.

Figure 7.5

Analysis Matrix

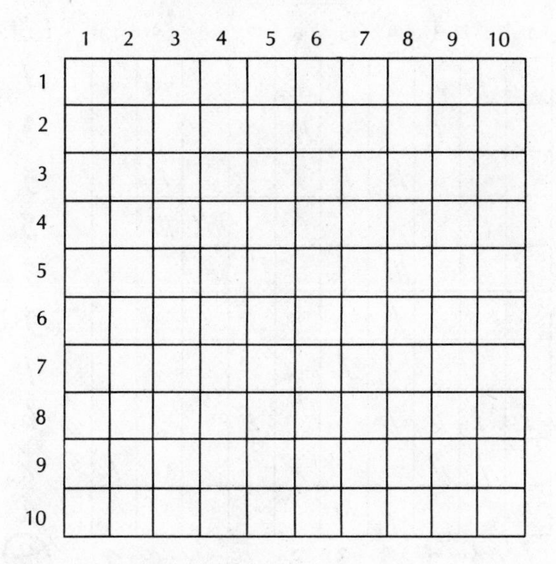

recording matrix were 10 and 5. The first pair of numbers on your matrix would then be 10/5.

2. The first number in the pair designates the row, and the second number designates the column. Recordings are made by use of a tally mark.
3. Each successive pair of numbers overlaps with the preceding pair. (Last number of first pair becomes first number of second pair. For example, in a sequence of 10, 5, 4 the second pair would be 5/4.) All the data are recorded in the row/column (R/C) pattern. (See Figure 7.6.)
4. Tallies are totalled by both row and column.
5. An analysis of the data may be completed by using two basic processes:
   a) cell analysis—total the number of times a specific numeral appears. For example, how many times did the teacher praise or encourage the students? Answer = 3. How many times did the teacher accept or use ideas of students? Criticize?
   b) I/D ratio. Total the number of tallies for the first four columns (1-4) and divide by the total for columns 5-7. For example, INDIRECT/DIRECT = 17/2 = 2.4. This would indicate a relatively high indirect influence. An I/D ratio of 1 would indicate that the teachers indirect and direct influence are equivalent. A

Figure 7.6

Tallied Analysis Matrix

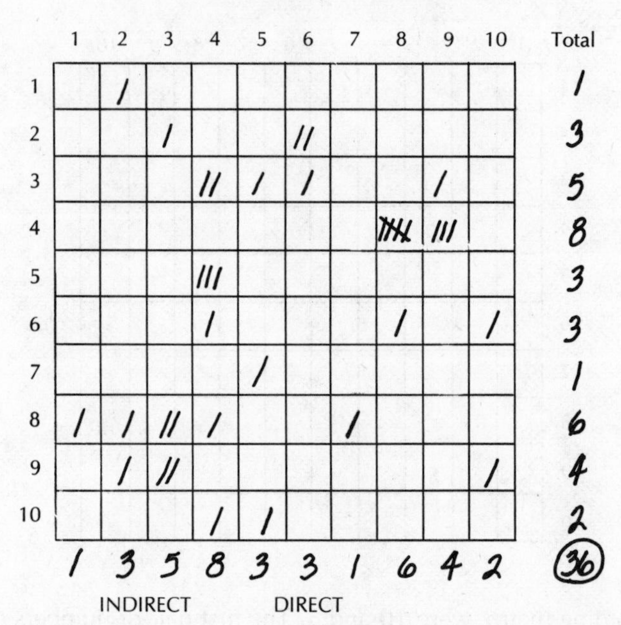

	1	2	3	4	5	6	7	8	9	10	Total
1		/									1
2			/			//					3
3				//	/	/			/		5
4								/////	///		8
5				///							3
6				/				/		/	3
7					/						1
8	/	/	//	/			/				6
9		/	//							/	4
10				/	/						2
	1	3	5	8	3	3	1	6	4	2	(36)

INDIRECT DIRECT

generally applicable statement would be as follows: The higher the I/D ratio, the greater the teacher's emphasis on indirect influence.

It is very important to remember that no "ideal" is indicated by the Flanders system. It simply gives the teacher a reliable, accurate account of the type of verbal interaction that is occurring in her classroom. The desirable I/D ratio, for example, is dependent on the type of verbal interaction that a teacher believes is desirable.

The strength of the Flanders system lies in its emphasis on self-analysis and self-improvement. The individual teacher may identify her own strengths and weaknesses and modify her behavior accordingly. She should, however, collect different samples of data during different classes and on different occasions before developing analytic conclusions. Careful use and follow-up of the Flanders system can result in positive changes in the quality of verbal interaction in the classroom.

Teaching Analysis Sheet

Any teacher evaluation procedure employed by a supervisor should emphasize use *with* teachers rather than *on* teachers. If teachers feel that

Figure 7.7

Teaching Analysis Sheet

A—Excellent	B—Good	C—Average
D—Below Average	F—Poor	0—Does not pertain to this course

INSTRUCTOR EVALUATION

A B C D F 0 Knowledge of subject matter.
A B C D F 0 Is willing to admit error or lack of knowledge about a certain area.
A B C D F 0 Interest and enthusiasm for subject.
A B C D F 0 Interest and attention of class.
A B C D F 0 Ability to stimulate your interest in subject.
A B C D F 0 Definite, clear-cut presentation of subject matter.
A B C D F 0 Criticizes students' efforts on a constructive basis.
A B C D F 0 Voice qualities (pleasant, easily heard, etc.)
A B C D F 0 Awareness of students' failure to understand.
A B C D F 0 Understanding attitude toward students' efforts and problems.
A B C D F 0 Approachability of instructor.
A B C D F 0 Freedom of student to express his own ideas.
A B C D F 0 Preparation for class meetings.

COURSE EVALUATION

A B C D F 0 Clarity of course objectives.
A B C D F 0 Use of recent research and material in this field.
A B C D F 0 Logical arrangement of topics and material.
A B C D F 0 Clear examples and illustrations.
A B C D F 0 Use of examples that make course interesting.
A B C D F 0 Effective use of class time.
A B C D F 0 Clarity and readability of text.
A B C D F 0 Value of text for course.

MARKING EVALUATION

A B C D F 0 Value of exams for measuring your knowledge.
A B C D F 0 Clarity of assignments and exams.
A B C D F 0 Fairness of grading system.
A B C D F 0 Is the amount of work required appropriate for credit received?
A B C D F 0 Uses tests for actual learning situations, after they have been returned.
A B C D F 0 Prompt return of assignments and exams.

SOURCE: From James R. Marks, Emery Stoops, and Joyce King Stoops, *Handbook of Educational Supervision* (Boston: Allyn and Bacon, 1971), pp. 525–26. Used with permission.

results of evaluation will be used to penalize them, they will be very reluctant to reveal their own weaknesses and problems. On the other hand, if they view evaluation as a process that is going to help them improve their professional status, they will be much more eager to participate. Teachers should be encouraged to use self-appraisal techniques

Figure 7.8

Checklist
How Do I Rate as a Teacher?

KEY: Indicate A for excellent
B for very good
C for passable
D for poor, needs improvement

1. Do I create a happy, relaxed, but business-like atmosphere? ______
2. Is order and control inherent in my approach to classroom management? ______
3. Am I conscious of each student's potentials and needs? ______
4. Do I avoid judging students by adult standards? ______
5. When a student does not reach my standards do I search for causes? ______
6. How do I encourage initiative and orginality? ______
7. Has every student confidence that I will try to see his problem from his point of view? ______
8. Do I have conferences with each student as often as possible? ______
9. Do students come to me for advice voluntarily? ______
10. Do I recognize symptoms of withdrawal, timidity, unsociableness, and discouragement as being especially serious? ______
11. Am I impersonal in dealing with behavior problems? ______
12. Do I analyze behavior problems through a systems analysis approach? ______
13. Are specific instructional objectives, stated in terms of observable changes in behavior and performance, definitely formulated? ______
14. Do I stimulate my students by scheduling field trips, audio-video-presentations, motion pictures, special reports, open-forums, guest speakers, and other attention-getting and interest-stimulating techniques? ______
15. Do I consider both students and subject matter as I plan for instruction? ______
16. Do I use the materials of instructional technology, including the simplest audio-visual aids, regularly and with purpose? ______
17. Do I capitalize on each student's personal environment? endowments? ______
18. Am I aware of each student's interests? ______
19. Am I mindful of individual differences, abilities, and needs? ______
20. Do I give all students equal opportunities and equal attention? ______
21. Do I help students to form good work habits? ______
22. Do I teach students how to study effectively? ______
23. Are students assuming more and more responsibility for their own improvement? ______
24. Is each student's attention span increasing? ______
25. Is there evidence that students are increasing in self-control, initiative, and originality? ______
26. Do students attack difficult problems eagerly? ______
27. Does a large percentage of students participate in class discussion? ______
28. Do I summarize ideas and generalization regularly? ______
29. Do I supply each student with knowledge of results? ______
30. Do I make the subject so clear and vital that students are highly stimulated? ______
31. Do I begin each class session promptly and keep things moving without appearing to hurry? ______

Figure 7.8 (continued)

32. Do I encourage students to assist each other? _____
33. Do I expect to be more than a good teacher? _____

Consider yourself as a superior teacher if you scored 25 or more items as excellent or very good. If you marked less than 15 items as excellent or very good, you may do well to enroll in a graduate course in professional education and/or psychology, to seek the aid of your colleagues in education, to consult professional texts and journals, and/or to enroll in in-service educational programs.

SOURCE: From James R. Marks, Emery Stoops, and Joyce King Stoops, *Handbook of Educational Supervision* (Boston: Allyn and Bacon, 1971), pp. 526–28. Used with permission.

and be given effective supervisory assistance in their use. Marks (1971) has developed a teaching analysis sheet and checklist that could serve as a very helpful guide to teacher self-evaluation. (See Figures 7.7 and 7.8.)

The student teacher should have ample opportunity to engage in a variety of self-evaluation procedures. Carefully examine Figure 7.9 and assess your progress to date.

Teacher Education Exit Criteria

One of the major contributions of the competency-based teacher education movement has been an increased emphasis on the teacher trainee's mastery of specific competencies before graduating from the teacher preparatory program. Teacher educators are now required to obtain more concrete, specific data about the preprofessional's progress. Consequently, considerable attention is presently being given to the development of effective exit criteria for the student teacher. (See Figure 7.10.)

Follow-Up Studies

Teacher education institutions are currently experimenting with procedures for the assessment of graduates at the end of one or more years of teaching experience in the field. Sandefur and Adams (1973) have reported the results of a model for the evaluation of teacher education graduates at Western Kentucky University. The rationale for the model was based on two major premises: (1) A sufficient body of research data existed from which generalizations could be drawn of the characteristics of good teaching and good teachers, and (2) classroom observational systems and other evaluative tools had been developed that enabled educators to evaluate the products of teacher education programs.

Figure 7.9

Appraisal of Experience in Student Teaching

Indicate in the appropriate space at the right the extent of your participation in the various experiences listed below. Also indicate by a check mark in the appropriate space the value of the experience to you.

ACTIVITY OR EXPERIENCE	Extent of Participation				Evaluation of the Experience		
	None	Too Little	About Right	Too Much	Of Great Value	Of Some Value	Of Little or No Value
1. Observed the supervising teacher at work							
2. Observed teachers other than the supervisor							
3. Held conferences with individual pupils							
4. Taught a small group of pupils							
5. Gave a demonstration before a class							
6. Organized, arranged, and used a bulletin board							
7. Graded papers							
8. Planned, developed, and taught one or more major units of work							
9. Planned and carried out field trips or excursions							
10. Prepared, proctored, and scored an examination over work covered in the major unit							
11. Conferred with principal or teachers other than supervisor on problems							
12. Started a file of materials useful in teaching							
13. Supervised a study hall, lunch room, or noon hour activity							
14. Held or observed conferences with parents							
15. Attended, planned, or presented an assembly program							
16. Participated in or observed a school club program							

Figure 7.9 (continued)

ACTIVITY OR EXPERIENCE	Extent of Participation				Evaluation of the Experience		
	None	Too Little	About Right	Too Much	Of Great Value	Of Some Value	Of Little or No Value
17. Attended a P.T.A. meeting							
18. Attended a faculty meeting							
19. Participated in homeroom activities							
20. Helped plan, attended, or sponsored a student social activity							
21. Participated in some community project							
22. Helped a student to accept his responsibility for good behavior							
23. Observed a student council meeting							
24. Read professional magazines							
25. Made a special effort to get acquainted with the special abilities, interests, and problems of individual students							
26. Assisted with school publications ...							
27. Assisted with or observed athletic events							
28. Utilized audio-visual aids							
29. Studying all available records of pupils							
30. Directing study							
31. Making daily health observations ...							
32. Taking care of physical conditions of room							
33. Keeping attendance records							
34. Making use of community resources for teaching							
35. Experience in teaching unusual students: retarded or exceptional underline which one(s)							
36. Aiding in filling out state registers							

Figure 7.9 (continued)

ACTIVITY OR EXPERIENCE	Extent of Participation				Evaluation of the Experience		
	None	Too Little	About Right	Too Much	Of Great Value	Of Some Value	Of Little or No Value
37. Experience in preparing report cards							
38. Loading buses							
39. Supervising reference work in the library							
40. Public talks and appearances							
41. Others of importance (please list)							

SOURCE: From Gardner-Webb College, Boiling Springs, North Carolina. Used with permission.

The format of this model involves obtaining data from four sources:

1. Career line data regarding promotions, advanced degrees, writing, research, professional activity, and teacher mobility
2. Direct classroom observation data on teaching behavior
3. Student, peer, and supervisor ratings
4. Standardized measures

All evaluative instruments are administered during the student teaching experience and at the conclusion of the first, third, and fifth years of teaching. To make the model financially feasible, a random sample of twenty elementary and twenty secondary teachers are evaluated annually.

The data are processed and stored in computers for use in statistical studies and related feedback. Copies of an annual report on the data are given to all faculty of the college of education. The type of evaluative data that can be collected with this type of follow-up study should be very valuable to the individual teacher education graduate in addition to facilitating improvements in the teacher preparatory program.

Checklist of Personalized Instructional Practices

Ensworth (1973) has developed the following self-evaluative guide for helping the teacher to evaluate her instructional practices (see pp. 177–78):

Figure 7.10

Exit Criteria for Teacher Education Graduates

Name of Student ____________________

Home Address ____________________ Home Phone ________

Teaching Field(s) ____________ Time in Student Teaching ________

Cooperating School ____________ Address ____________

Supervising Teacher ____________ College Supervisor ____________

Major: _____Early Childhood _____Intermediate _____(9–12) Major: _____

Area of Concentration ____________ _____

Second Concentration ____________ Total Semester Hrs. _____ QPR _____

PART I—ACADEMIC AND PROFESSIONAL ACHIEVEMENT

A. INSTRUCTIONAL PROGRAM PERCENTAGES

1. General Education Component _____%
2. Specialization Component _____%
3. Professional Education Component _____%

B. INSTITUTIONAL ACHIEVEMENT SCORE REQUIREMENTS:

1. Entrance into the Education Curriculum

   a. STEP English, 15 %ile
   b. STEP Math. Concepts, 15 %ile
   c. STEP Soc. Studies, 15 %ile
   d. STEP Science, 15 %ile
   e. Tenn. Self-Concept: (Determined by the Education Dept. on an individual student basis.)

2. NTE Composite, 950

C. ACHIEVEMENT SCORES OF APPLICANT:

1. SAT Verbal _____
2. SAT Quant. _____
3. Purdue Eng. _____%ile
4. Academic Progress (Math.) _____%ile

Figure 7.10 (continued)

5. Otis Mental Ability _____%ile
6. N.D. Reading (Vocab.)_____%ile
7. N.D. Reading (Comp.)_____%ile
8. STEP English _____%ile
9. STEP Math. Concepts _____%ile
10. STEP Science _____%ile
11. STEP Soc. Studies _____%ile
12. Tenn. Self-Concept Scale: _____Normal, _____Deviant
13. Undergraduate Record Exam. Aptitude ____, Quant. ____, Field ____
14. NTE Composite _____
15. Other _____

PART II—PERFORMANCE IN STUDENT TEACHING

Code: 1 = Inferior, 2 = Below Average, 3 = Average, 4 = Above Average, 5 = Superior

A. GUIDELINE 1—APPLICATION OF ACADEMIC AND PROFESSIONAL KNOWLEDGE (Check Appropriate Rating)	1	2	3	4	5
1. Demonstrates comprehensive knowledge of academic subject.					
2. Possesses in-depth knowledge of the area of specialization.					
3. Understands growth and developmental characteristics of the learners being taught.					
4. Utilizes appropriate materials and media.					
5. Employs a variety of teaching strategies.					
6. Demonstrates knowledge of curricular design and implementation					
7. Applies effective measurement and evaluation procedures.					
8. Demonstrates knowledge of historical and sociological foundations of education.					

Figure 7.10 (continued)

	1	2	3	4	5
9. Demonstrates skill in helping pupils become more self-dependent learners.					
Comments ______					
*TOTAL POINTS					

B. GUIDELINE 2—CLASSROOM CONTROL (Check Appropriate Rating)	1	2	3	4	5
1. Demonstrates ability to guide and control the classroom in a businesslike, impartial and disciplined manner.					
2. Demonstrates competency in establishing relevant objectives based on diagnosis and thereafter formulating plans to attain them and implement when necessary.					
3. Exhibits skill in using varied instruction strategies to aid and interest slow learners, disadvantaged, average, and gifted students.					
4. Demonstrates resourcefulness in using varied instructional materials to achieve a maximum learning environment.					
5. Exhibits competency in diagnosing group and individual needs and is able to group children for effective learning activities.					
6. Exhibits skill in identifying various problems dealing with discipline and differentiating between possible solutions.					
7. Develop and maintain proper mental and social guidance, through good student-teacher relationships.					

Figure 7.10 (continued)

	1	2	3	4	5
8. Demonstrates skill in working cooperatively with students to create best learning environment possible.					
9. Demonstrates skill in human relationships through showing respect and understanding for all students.					
Comments ________					
*TOTAL POINTS					

C. GUIDELINE 3—EXPERTISE IN THE AREA OF HUMAN RELATIONS (Check Appropriate Rating)	1	2	3	4	5
1. Is able to communicate well with students.					
2. Shows ability to communicate with parent, racial, and ethnic groups in the community.					
3. Has good rapport and interaction with other teachers, supervisors, and administrators.					
4. Relates well and inspires others by his ability to motivate morale of those he teaches and works with.					
5. Has a positive approach rather than a negative attitude.					
6. Works well with home and school.					
7. Is able to guide effectively students with individual differences.					
8. Will accept constructive criticism with a positive attitude and work to better himself.					

Figure 7.10 (continued)

	1	2	3	4	5
Comments					
*TOTAL POINTS					

D. GUIDELINE 4—PROFESSIONAL ATTRIBUTES (Check Appropriate Rating)	1	2	3	4	5
1. Will go beyond the call of duty, is not satisfied with doing only what is required.					
2. Is sincere in his actions and professional attitude.					
3. Exhibits excellent qualities of leadership.					
4. Has a good sense of humor.					
5. Is willing to learn and grow professionally.					
6. Is interested in and actively participates in community affairs.					
7. Participates in curriculum development.					
8. Is able to plan, organize, and motivate.					
9. Attends extra-class and social activities related to education.					
10. Is ethical in his relationship with all people.					
11. Keeps records accurately and efficiently.					
12. Is able to adjust to differing situations and demands.					
Comments					
*TOTAL POINTS					

Figure 7.10 (continued)

E. GUIDELINE 5—PERSONAL AND SOCIAL CHARACTERISTICS (Check Appropriate Rating)	1	2	3	4	5
1. Is free of fears and worries about trivial things.					
2. Shows no sudden shifts in mood.					
3. Is appropriately dressed for the occasion.					
4. Is physically and mentally alert.					
5. Is free from distracting and irritating mannerisms.					
6. Speaks clearly, distinctly and has an accepted, natural accent.					
7. Sets goals and exhibits the self-discipline needed to achieve them.					
8. Is adaptable and is challenged by new situations.					
9. Places the welfare of the group before self.					
Comments ______					
*TOTAL POINTS					
GRAND TOTAL OF POINTS					

*Total Points means number of checks in columns

GENERAL ESTIMATES OF ABILITY

Check Appropriate Rating				
5 Superior	4 Above Average	3 Average	2 Below Average	1 Inferior

Endorsements:

Student Teaching Supervisor ______________________

For Teacher Education Committee ______________________

SOURCE: From Gardner-Webb College, Boiling Springs, North Carolina. Used with permission.

Checklist

1. Do you retain a sense of humor with children? staff members?
2. Can you laugh at yourself?
3. When phrasing questions, do you include clues to the correct answers?
4. Do you encourage more reluctant students to participate in class?
5. Do you respect children as intelligent human beings?
6. Do you encourage boys and girls to show love? anger on occasion?
7. Do you encourage children to cope with all of their emotions and to be honest about them?
8. Do you arrange study patterns so that bright children and slow learners can work together?
9. Do you have specific ideas to develop the special interests and talents of individual children? Are they designed to boost positive self-images?
10. Do you treat children as individuals? Do you have plans to help each child establish and achieve his own goals?
11. Do you respect the ideas of young children? Do you think they may have something to teach you as well?
12. Do you encourage children to bring you their problems?
13. Do you have plans to develop your children's creativity through different media (literature, art, oral expression)?
14. Do you utilize home and community resources? Do you plan to talk with each child and his parents in their home?
15. Does your classroom provide as many areas of interest as possible to stimulate a desire to learn?
16. Are your classroom surroundings attractive as well as instructional?
17. Are there manipulatives for children to use in the classroom?
18. Are there displays throughout the room from which children can learn and which reflect their own creativity?
19. Are you willing to put in a number of extra hours each evening and weekend to prepare exciting activities for students? Or do you do so grudgingly?
20. Do you have hobby centers such as aquariums, terrariums, and gerbil pens in the classroom?
21. Do you make a wide variety of high-interest books available?
22. Do you encourage children to know where to find correct answers rather than learning them by rote?
23. Do you let children participate in the making of classroom rules?
24. Do you make each student feel successful in some way?
25. Do you give students opportunities to make decisions?
26. Do you attempt to establish an atmosphere of cooperation?
27. Do you give criticism fairly and constructively?
28. Can you empathize with children about how it feels to be a youngster?

29. Do you honestly like working with children even though some aren't very likeable?
30. Are your students aware that if they try their best, they will not be faulted?
31. Do you make assignments compatible with each child's ability?
32. Do you enter into children's games on the playground?
33. Do you invite many different resource people to speak to children? [2]

Summary

Teacher evaluation should focus on helping the teacher identify her strengths and weaknesses and provide data that enables the teacher to engage in a positive self-improvement process, which should ultimately result in the improvement of instruction for children. Emphasis should be placed on teacher self-evaluation through application of a variety of processes. Historically, insufficient attention has been given to developing and utilizing effective self-appraisal instruments and processes for teachers.

There are three major strategies most often used in the evaluation of a teacher: (1) evaluation of the teacher education program under which the teacher was trained, (2) measurement of the growth of pupils taught by the teacher, and (3) assessment of the competencies and actual teaching behavior of the teacher. Of the three, the third assessment strategy appears to be the most promising. By replacing guesswork and excessive subjective data with a variety of objective data on teaching performance, each teacher should be able to improve her performance. More importantly, children will profit from more effective teaching.

REFERENCES

Bolton, Dale L. *Selection and Evaluation of Teachers*. Berkeley, Calif.: McCutchan Publishing Co., 1973.

Ensworth, John. "Checklist." *Instructor* 83(1973):45.

Flanders, Ned A. *Analyzing Teaching Behavior*. Reading, Mass.: Addison-Wesley Publishing Co., 1970.

Jones, Anthony S. "Realistic Approach to Teacher Evaluation." *Clearing House* 46(1972):474–81.

Marks, James R.; Stoops, Emery; and Stoops, Joyce King. *Handbook of Educational Supervision*. Boston: Allyn and Bacon, 1971.

---

2. From John Ensworth, "Checklist," *Instructor* 83(1973):45. Used with permission.

Roberson, E. Wayne. "Teacher Self-Appraisal: A Way to Improve Instruction." *Journal of Teacher Education* 22(1971):469–73.

Sandefur, J. T., and Adams, Ronald D. "A Case Study of Second-Year Teacher Education Graduates." *Journal of Teacher Education* 24(1973):248–49.

Soar, Robert S. "Accountability: Assessment Problems and Possibilities." *Journal of Teacher Education* 24(1973):205–12.

Learning Module

Teacher Self-Evaluation Processes

Directions

This module is designed to help you develop competence in the process of evaluating your own teaching. To complete this module, begin with the pretest and work through the required activities. You may complete as many optional activities as you believe applicable to your needs. Conclude with the posttest.

Pretest

1. Briefly discuss six major functions of the teacher evaluation process.
2. Discuss how to effectively use the Roberson Teacher Self-Appraisal Observation System.
3. Explain how to compute an I/D ratio using the Flanders Interaction Analysis System.
4. Based on use of a videotape recording, describe what you consider to be your strongest teaching characteristics.

Check

Review your pretest with your instructor.

Behavioral Objectives

Select those that are most applicable to you.

1. Describe three major purposes of teacher evaluation.
2. Effectively implement the Roberson Teacher Self-Appraisal Observation System in an elementary classroom setting.
3. Audiotape a segment of verbal interaction involving a teacher and group of students. Analyze the taped segment using the Flanders Interaction Analysis System.
4. Objectively evaluate your own teaching competencies by using a self-evaluation instrument or exit criteria instrument.
5. Videotape your own classroom interaction segment and analyze the results.

6. Obtain feedback from the students you are teaching or from fellow teacher trainees by using the Marks Teaching Analysis Sheet.

Required Activities

(Numbers in parentheses correlate with corresponding objectives.)

1. Read pp. 99–102 in Dale L. Bolton's *Selection and Evaluation of Teachers* (Berkeley, Calif.: McCutchan Publishing Corp., 1973) and Anthony S. Jones' "Realistic Approach to Teacher Evaluation" (*Clearing House* 46(1972):474–81). (1)
2. Interview a middle school teacher regarding the various ways in which she evaluates her own teaching. Discuss your findings with your instructor. (1) (4) (5)
3. Read relevant segments of Ned A. Flanders' *Analyzing Teaching Behavior* (Reading, Mass.: Addison-Wesley Publishing Co., 1970). (1) (3) (5)
4. Review the self-evaluation instrument and exit criteria (p. 168) in Chapter 7 of this book. (4)
5. Read "Teacher Self-Appraisal: A Way to Improve Instruction," by Wayne E. Roberson (*Journal of Teacher Education* 22(1971):469–73). (2)
6. Arrange an appointment with your instructor or a media specialist for a practice session in the effective use of the videotape recorder in a classroom setting. (3) (5)
7. Review the use of the Teaching Analysis Sheet in *Handbook of Educational Supervision* by James R. Marks, Emery Stoops, and Joyce King-Stoops (Boston: Allyn and Bacon, 1971). (4) (6)
8. Conduct a conference with a public school supervisor regarding the teacher evaluation processes she employs. (1) (6)
9. Arrange to teach in a local middle school setting. Videotape a segment of your teaching and analyze your nonverbal behavior with the assistance of your instructor or the cooperating middle school teacher. (5)

Optional Activities

Select from the preceding list of activities those that you have not completed or develop your own relevant options.

Posttest

Based on the data you have obtained and the concepts and processes you have learned, prepare your own "Teacher Self-Assessment Profile" and measure your own competencies. Discuss the completed instrument with your instructor.

Part 3

The Middle School Program

Chapter 8

Establishing a Middle School Curriculum

What is a curriculum? What is a middle school curriculum? Historically, the term *curriculum* has referred to the subjects taught in school. This concept, in the minds of the public and in the minds of many people in the education field, suggests that there is a fixed body of knowledge that all students should learn. Another concept of curriculum involves a curriculum guide, a document setting forth a course of study or a list of the course offerings of an educational institution. A more modern concept suggests that a school's curriculum includes all student experiences for which the school accepts responsibility. A curriculum develops when people, ideas, and things are brought together in a dynamic relationship within a school setting. A middle school curriculum is more than mere course offerings set down on paper; in reality, it is the actual learning experiences of emerging adolescents that take place under the responsibility of the middle school. Rather than being fixed and rigid in nature, it should be flexible, varied, and responsive to the continuously changing needs of middle school students.

Basic Principles of Curriculum and Instruction

The development of an effective middle school curriculum requires the application of validated principles of curriculum and instruction. The most important principle to apply in developing middle school curriculum is that the curriculum must be designed around the characteristics and needs of the emerging adolescent. The diversity and uniqueness of the students in the middle school must be the focus of its curriculum.

Learning experiences should be based on the specific needs and capabilities of emerging adolescent learners.

Tyler (1950) has presented three major criteria for organizing learning experiences: continuity, sequence, and integration. *Continuity* emphasizes the vertical reiteration of major curriculum components. For example, if an important objective of the science curriculum is the development of skills in reading and interpreting science materials, it is essential to provide recurring and continuing opportunities for these skills to be practiced and developed. Therefore, as the learner progresses year after year through the middle school curriculum, specific skills or concepts should be reviewed. *Sequence* is a major criterion that is related to continuity in curriculum. It emphasizes, however, not mere duplication of instruction but broader and deeper treatment of a specific skill as it is revisited at a higher level. For example, the learner may be introduced to a particular skill at the fifth-grade level and later review the skill in greater depth at the sixth- or seventh-grade level. Continuity and sequence are two very important principles relating to the vertical organization of curriculum.

In contrast, *integration* emphasizes the horizontal relationship (within a course or a school year) of curriculum experiences. The application of this criterion helps to insure that what the learner masters in one area of the curriculum may be applied or related to another area of the curriculum. This results in a more unified, interdisciplinary learning experience. For example, if a learner develops skill in use of the scientific method in a science course, opportunities should be provided for the learner to apply this skill in social studies and related areas of the curriculum. Appropriate application of the integration principle may result in more unified learning, less emphasis on acquiring isolated facts, and avoidance of gaps and duplication in learner experiences.

It is essential that objectives of the middle school curriculum be stated in terms of characteristics of the emerging adolescent population as defined in the local school-community setting. Although emerging adolescents possess some universal characteristics, identification of the specific needs of the local school population is critical in any curriculum development venture. Such *needs assessment* data provide a frame of reference for local curriculum planning and evaluation. Since the middle school occupies a strategic position between the elementary and high school, attention must be given to the impact its curriculum has on the *articulation* of the local kindergarten through high school program. Changes in a community's middle school curriculum present significant implications for changes in the elementary and high school programs.

Application of the fundamental curriculum planning principles of continuity, sequence, integration, needs assessment, and articulation, is essential in establishing an effective middle school curriculum. Let's look briefly at some specific pitfalls that may be encounterd in middle school curriculum planning.

Pitfalls to Avoid in Middle School Curriculum Planning

Much publicity and criticism has arisen around the controversy involving the junior high versus the middle school. The labels, however, do not mean that much. It is what is happening inside the programs of each school—what is happening to the emerging adolescent—that is really important. Solutions to curricular problems cannot be found by dealing in labels, by jumbling and juggling grades, or by engaging in related surface changes that do not involve significant changes in school philosophy, curriculum, and teacher competencies. From its inception in the United States around 1905, the junior high has emphasized two major programs: a terminal program stressing vocational education that was designed for the majority of students who were dropouts by grade nine and an introduction to a high school type program that was designed for the small number of students that were going on to secondary and postsecondary work. Over the years, some characteristics have evolved in the junior high program that many educators believe are undesirable for emerging adolescents. Briefly, some of these undesirable characteristics are:

1. A "watered-down" version of the senior high curriculum that is not specifically designed for and relevant to the needs of the emerging adolescent. A major criticism is that the curriculum is designed to focus on what is going to happen later in the student's career rather than on the experiences of the present period of transescence.
2. Too rapid a transition from the relatively secure self-contained elementary school program to the rigidly organized, departmentalized junior high program.
3. Emphasis on vocational education as a separate curricular track designed primarily for the lower academic achievers rather than on career education for all students.
4. Emphasis on interscholastic sports for a few students rather than on appropriate health and physical fitness programs for all students.
5. Curricular offerings that stress "getting them ready for high school" rather than introducing a variety of exploratory experiences in tune with the evolving interests and needs of the emerging adolescent.
6. Teachers who are not properly trained to teach the middle school learner. Too often elementary school teachers are moved up or

high school teachers are moved down to teach the emerging adolescent.

7. Inadequate provision of guidance personnel specifically prepared to assist the emerging adolescent learner.
8. Excessive emphasis on norm-referenced evaluation processes to the neglect of criterion-referenced evaluation processes.
9. Limited cooperative curriculum planning designed to enhance curricular articulation on a kindergarten through high school continuum.
10. Emphasis placed on juggling grades (5–8, 6–7, 5–9) rather than making significant internal curricular changes based on the characteristics and needs of emerging adolescents.

Avoiding these pitfalls is essential to the development of an appropriate middle school curriculum. What then are some essential *guidelines* for the establishment of a modern middle school curriculum?

Needs Assessment: Critical Step in Curriculum Planning

Too often curriculum planners make changes in existing curricula or develop new curricula based upon limited or invalid data. More and more schools are engaging in "needs assessment" processes before initiating formal changes. A variety of procedures may be included within a needs assessment process, including surveys of the opinions of students, faculty, administration, and the public; examination of the school's goals and purposes by the faculty and administration, longitudinal studies of graduates of the school; surveys on financial resources and the public's ability to support the school program; and the use of supportive data to determine the most immediate and long-range needs of the school population.

One of the most helpful needs assessment tools is the student opinion survey. Since the students are going to be the "curricular consumers," they should have significant input into the curriculum-planning process. Coffland (1975) provided an example of how the use of a Kleinett Student Inventory revealed some very helpful data in a Florida middle school. The Kleinett instrument is a Likert-type scale that asks the student to respond to seventy-five items relating to her teacher, her class, and her schoolwork. In the Florida study, the instrument was read to all students in small groups so that even those students with reading difficulties would understand the questions. Group mean scores were tabulated and used as indicators of the students' opinions toward the school. Student responses to the seventy-five items provided data that proved to be extremely helpful when curricular changes were considered. This study illustrates only one of the ways a needs assessment process can be initiated.

Guidelines for Establishing a Middle School Curriculum

The modern middle school program should possess certain essential characteristics. These characteristics are incorporated in the following guidelines:

1. Rather than mimicking the secondary school program, the curriculum should be intellectually stimulating, rich in options and exploratory experiences, and built on learning acquired during the elementary school years. A typical middle school learner population will be characterized by great variability in capability, interest, and achievement. The curriculum should therefore be flexible, emphasize self-pacing, and provide for both acceleration and remediation. The curriculum should emphasize that the learner, not the program, is most important.
2. The instructional organization pattern should be transitional in nature, incorporating the secure features of self-containedness with the benefits of interaction with varied teachers and students. An organizational pattern that contains large-group, small-group, and independent study is very desirable. The middle schooler needs exposure to various teachers, preferably through a localized team format in which two or more teachers work with a group of students within the same classroom setting, as opposed to a rigid departmental format. Many middle school students lack the emotional maturity essential to functioning successfully in a rigidly departmentalized, high school mode.
3. The curriculum should maintain a proper balance of the cognitive, affective, and psychomotor domains of learning. In the cognitive area, emphasis should be given to mastery of the basic skills and concepts of the various academic disciplines with specific attention to life-long learning skills. In the affective area, the students' development of a personal value system and positive self-concept should be emphasized. In the psychomotor area, the significant physiological changes of transescence require a personalized health and physical education program that emphasizes physical fitness, personal hygiene, family-life education, and carry-over sports for all students. High school type team sports for a few students should be de-emphasized until the latter stages of the middle school.
4. Career-based curricular experiences should be provided for all students, not just the lower academic achievers. Career awareness/exploration experiences should be interrelated with all academic areas. For example, when a math concept is being taught, the teacher should demonstrate to the student how the math concept may be applied in the world of work. In addition to the efforts of

academic teachers, career exploration teachers within a career exploration laboratory should help students learn more about jobs and career opportunities. (See Chapter 12 for a thorough treatment of this concept.)

5. The school evaluation and pupil progress reporting system should emphasize student assessment based on the progress made in relation to each student's own ability. Secondary emphasis should be placed on assessment in terms of the norm. The emerging adolescent needs competition; productive and psychologically healthy competition evolves through students' competing with their own level of ability. The use of teacher-made, criterion-referenced tests enables students to compare their level of attainment with past accomplishments. The type of data obtained from these tests allows both teacher and student to develop meaningful, reachable goals. Students also need to know how they stand in relation to class, school, state, and national norms. This type information, however, is not as conducive to promoting individual progress as criterion-referenced data. Standardized testing should be de-emphasized during the middle school years.
6. Provisions should be made for helping the exceptional learner within the middle school setting. Varied services and competent personnel should be provided to assist the regular classroom teacher in diagnosing, teaching, and evaluating exceptional learners. There should be particular attention given to often-neglected gifted students in addition to provisions made for educable mentally retarded and handicapped students and students with related exceptionalities. Unless the regular classroom teacher has received training in working with exceptionalities, mainstreaming (the practice of placing exceptional children in regular classroom settings) should be held to a minimum.
7. Each teacher and student should be provided with effective guidance services. Guidance personnel should be specifically trained to work with the emerging adolescent, avoiding the "counselor model" as practiced in secondary education. Emphasis should be given to promoting effective student self-discipline in a wholesome learning environment.

Middle School Program Characteristics

Let's look briefly at some specific program characteristics and identify appropriate trends and practices in middle school curriculum development. Gross (1972) conducted a comprehensive study of 1,337 middle schools to identify their perceived purposes, functions, and characteristics. Results of the study revealed the following conclusions:[1]

Grade-Level Organization. Sixty-four percent of the schools involved in the Gross study included grades six through eight, whereas slightly less than one-third (32.9 percent) encompassed grades five through eight. These findings show that middle school curriculum planners are adopting the 5-3-4 pattern of grade organization more often than the 4-4-4 plan. (These findings were later confirmed by Raymer [1974]). There seems to be general agreement that the ninth grade is more closely related to the grades above than to the grades below. No one particular type of organization, however, will work in every school district, and careful attention should be given to local variables and considerations.

School Size. If the middle school is to fulfill its purpose of providing personalized experiences and curricular alternatives for each student, attention must be paid to the significant variable of enrollment size. Approximately 65 percent of the schools reporting in the Gross study indicated an enrollment of 700 students or less. In addition, 16.5 percent reported enrollments in the 700–900 range, 8.8 percent in the 900–1100 range, and slightly more than 8.0 percent in the 1000–1500 range. A desirable enrollment for a modern middle school seems to be 700 to 900 students.

Required versus Elective Experiences. The middle school has the serious responsibility of providing for the general education of its students. In doing this, it should offer exploratory activities to students in order to enhance their experiential background and to provide them with a broad base of knowledge from which to make academic and career decisions. Gross concluded that almost all middle schools require the following subjects of all students: English or language arts, mathematics, science, social studies, health, and physical education. A great variety of exploratory courses were identified including speech, foreign language, arts and crafts, shop and home economics, typing, vocal music, instrumental music, and modern math.

Cocurricular Activities. All of the schools surveyed by Gross reported cocurricular programs, band being the activity most often reported. Other activities reported in descending order of importance were chorus, intramural athletics for boys, student government, intramural athletics for girls, student publications, and clubs.

---

1. From Bernard M. Gross, "An Analysis of the Present and Perceived Purposes, Functions, and Characteristics of the Middle School," Ph.D. dissertation, Temple University, 1972. Used with permission.

Mini-Courses. The mini-course concept has become increasingly popular in the middle school. In general, noncredit courses are cooperatively planned by teachers and students and are geared to the students' changing interests. For that reason, the courses vary in length from two to six weeks. The following are examples of mini-courses:

Newspaper Production	Drug Seminar
Poetry	TV News
Myths and Legends	Folk Dancing
Writing Lab	Speed Reading
Current Events	Parlor Games
History of European Sports	Photography
Logic	Fishing
Chess	Stock Market
Map Reading	Fun with Words
Oceanography	Storytelling
Animal Behavior	The Laser

Instructional Organization Patterns. Almost 85 percent of the schools reporting in the Gross study indicated that they used team teaching in some form. Less than half of the schools reported using paraprofessionals as team members. Only about 25 percent of the schools reported having some type of block-of-time program. The model school day was six hours long and consisted of seven periods of forty to forty-five minutes, including lunch. Gross also found that the average class size among those reporting was in the range of twenty-five to twenty-nine students. Class size appears to be an extremely critical factor in the consideration of increased individualized instruction for students. Educators should therefore make a definite attempt to resist pressures being exerted on schools to increase class size.

On the basis of studies conducted by Gross (1972) and Raymer (1974), current literature and related research, and the author's own middle school visitation and related field work, the following middle school curricular trends are proposed:

1. A middle school organization pattern has emerged that most often contains grades six, seven, and eight within a 5-3-4 framework.
2. A middle school total enrollment number averages between 700 and 900 students.
3. All middle schools require English, mathematics, science, social studies, health, and physical education at all grade levels.
4. The most often-offered electives are instrumental music, vocal music, and foreign languages.

5. The majority of cocurricular activities involve music and athletics.
6. The typical school day is six hours long, consisting of seven periods of forty to forty-five minutes each including lunch.
7. Average class size is twenty-seven students.
8. Mini-courses based on current student interests appear to be increasing in number within middle schools.
9. Team teaching is the most often identified instructional organization pattern.
10. A greater emphasis on a comprehensive personalized health and physical education program has emerged, focusing attention on personal hygiene, family living, and physical fitness for all students rather than on athletics for a few students.

Back to Basics Movement: Implications for the Middle School

"Back to the basics!" This adamant cry has been heard often during the past few months. The cry puts both school administrators and scholars on the defensive. What do back-to-basics advocates really want? Although this list is not comprehensive, Brodinsky (1977) has presented a few of the points made by advocates of back-to-basics:

1. Eliminate electives and related frills, and increase the number of required courses.
2. Eliminate such "social services" as guidance, sex education, and driver education.
3. Place greater emphasis on patriotism and the free enterprise system within the schools.
4. Spend most of the elementary school day emphasizing reading, writing, and arithmetic.
5. Reinforce the concepts of dress codes, teacher dominance, and corporal punishment.
6. Teaching methods should emphasize drill, homework, and testing.
7. Eliminate social promotions and "rubber diplomas."
8. Graduation from grades and graduation from high school should be permitted only after students have demonstrated mastery of material through testing.
9. Ban innovations and social experimentation in the schools.

One of the by-products of the back-to-basics movements has been the evolution of a performance-based curriculum. When this type of curriculum is used, the student must demonstrate minimal competency prior to moving to the next grade or level. State legislatures, state boards of education, and state departments of public instruction have all moved forward in the minimal competency movement. Florida school districts have established the policy of moving pupils forward, grade by grade, on the basis of performance rather than on social promotion. By 1979, Florida districts will have to establish performance levels for high school graduation, and boards of education will be authorized to award differentiated diplomas on the basis of the varying achievement levels of the graduates. Virginia's Standards of Quality Act of 1976 required the State Board of Education to set up minimum statewide educational objectives and statewide tests in reading, language arts, and math. In Oregon, several steps have been taken to develop performance indicators and raise high school graduation requirements.

The seventh annual Gallup Poll on education (1975) revealed that citizens were dissatisfied with the quality of learning taking place in the nation's elementary and secondary schools. The poll also indicated that nearly 60 percent of all parents would, if given the option, send their children to alternative public schools that emphasize strict discipline and the three Rs. The number of alternative or "fundamental" schools has, in fact, been increasing throughout the United States.

Colleges have long complained that the typical high school graduate is unprepared for college. Officials cite the drop in national test scores to indicate the need for secondary schools to return to basic skills.

What are the implications of the back-to-basics movement for the development of middle school programs? The implications are numerous and far-reaching. Some of the implications could be classified as positive and some as negative. Some of the positive ones include:

1. Emphasis on students' mastery of fundamental skills in language arts and arithmetic during the elementary school years
2. Focus on assisting the teacher reestablish effective classroom discipline that is conducive to learning
3. Movement away from application of the social promotion concept
4. Movement toward restoring public confidence in the value of the high school diploma and in public education in general
5. Less emphasis on mass education and greater attention to individualized instruction
6. More careful delineation of goals and purposes of the school with appropriate goal-setting evaluation processes

Some possible negative implications include:

1. Excessive emphasis on testing, with teachers actually "teaching to the test."
2. An excessive swing of the pendulum back toward a rigid, sterile

curriculum that does not respond effectively to the needs and interests of the emerging adolescent learner.
3. A tendency toward dehumanizing the learning process with an overemphasis on basic facts and skills.
4. A failure to clarify what is basic. What is basic to one group of people is not necessarily basic to another.
5. An effort to remove or decrease the number of exploratory activities that are so critical toward helping emerging adolescents enhance their experiential background and that provide a base of knowledge from which they can make academic and career decisions.

What is needed in the development of a productive middle school curriculum is an effort on the part of educators to capitalize on the positive elements contained in various school philosophies. In such an effort, the conservative back-to-basics philosophy could contribute an awareness of a more precise delineation of middle school purposes and objectives, greater attention to students' mastery of specific survival learning skills, and restoration of confidence in the quality of education. Curriculum planners, however, must guard against allowing the pendulum to swing too far backwards, resulting in a lack of application of what has been learned about learners, teaching, and learning during the last fifty years.

Values Clarification in the Middle School Curriculum

People of all ages often become confused about values. Emerging adolescents of today are confronted with many more value choices than those of previous generations. In addition, the complexity of the times has made the act of choosing more difficult. Therefore, teaching values clarification, and more specifically, helping the student to develop a process of values clarification, should undergird the middle school curriculum.

Traditionally, teachers have used several approaches to values instruction that have been generally unproductive.

1. Moralizing is a direct attempt to inculcate adults' values in the young. This approach is becoming less effective for two main reasons. First, youth are exposed to moralizing in the home, school, church, peer group, media, and so many other places that they tend to become confused; and second, moralizing does not help the student to develop a valuing process for selecting the best and rejecting the worst elements contained in the various value systems

or value positions. Moralizing tends to have a surface effect, influencing students' words but little else.

2. The "let them do and think what they want" approach isn't effective. Emerging adolescents don't need adults running their lives, but they do need advice and help.
3. Modeling is an approach that has been used for years. The idea behind this approach is that the teacher acts as an attractive, living values model that students will want to emulate. The basic problem with this approach is that students are exposed to so many different models that they have difficulty deciding which one to emulate. Teachers, parents, movie stars, friends, and other adults all provide different models.

We recognize the need for helping the emerging adolescent with values. What approach should be employed within the middle school curriculum? Louis Raths (1966) developed an approach that is systematic and educationally sound. The emphasis in Raths' approach is not on the content of people's values, but on the *process of valuing*. This approach involves the following seven subprocesses:

Prizing one's beliefs and behaviors
1. prizing and cherishing
2. publicly affirming, when appropriate

Choosing one's beliefs and behaviors
3. choosing from alternatives
4. choosing after consideration of consequences
5. choosing freely

Acting on one's beliefs
6. acting
7. acting with a pattern, consistency, and repetition

The values-clarification approach does not attempt to "preach" or "teach" any particular set of values but instead attempts to help students utilize the seven processes of valuing in their own lives. With this approach, the teacher uses methods and materials that help students:

1. Become aware of the beliefs and behaviors they prize
2. Consider alternative modes of thinking and acting
3. Bring their beliefs and actions into closer harmony
4. Practice making choices and evaluating the actual consequences of their choices

Values clarification should be interwoven in the various academic areas of the middle school curriculum. For example, the strategy could be especially applicable to an ecology unit in which students are involved in environmental decision making. It could also be readily applied to instruction in math, history, health or any area of the curriculum. Simon, Howe, and Kirschenbaum (1972) have provided seventy-nine practical strategies for teachers and students to use in values clarification. They advocate that the goal of values clarification is to involve students in practical experiences that help them become aware of their own feelings, ideas, and beliefs so that they will make conscious and deliberate decisions based on *their own value systems.* For an additional reservoir of values clarification strategies, consult Howe and Howe (1975).

Values clarification strategies should be interwoven into the fabric of the middle school curriculum. They should not be set apart as a separate entity such as "values time" or a rainy-day "gimmicks and games" activity. All of schooling should enhance the student's personal decisionmaking skills and help her develop a valuing process that has meaning and purpose.

Interdisciplinary Design

The type of curriculum design used in a middle school can have great influence on the quality of its students' learning. For example, a separate subject design in which each subject is taught by a different teacher often provides a very fragmented pattern of information for the learner, giving her few clues to what is most significant. Tanner (1975) distinguishes between a multidisciplinary and an interdisciplinary curriculum. A multidisciplinary curriculum has emerged as a "laminated" curriculum consisting of separate subjects being glued together as individual layers instead of being synthesized into a whole. In contrast, an interdisciplinary design interrelates the conceptual threads and processes of the various disciplines using reinforcement and a minimum of redundancy. For example, within the framework of an interdisciplinary science course, the learner should learn that the processes of scientific inquiry, that is, the scientific method, are not unique to only one particular discipline but are critical to the study of any science. McCarthy (1972) has provided an excellent example of how an interdisciplinary unit could be developed for middle school learners.

Interdisciplinary Unit—"The Sea Around Us"

Middle school students acted as volunteers to aid in an experimental activity conducted during an intensive, month-long in-service program for middle school personnel in Fort Lauderdale, Florida. During the program, a unit was developed that demonstrates how teachers and students can use events of national interest as motivation for practicing basic skills and learning new concepts. The United States had just launched Apollo 11, and the entire world was about to watch the first moon walk, the return trip to earth, and the splashdown. Because of the school's proximity to Cape Kennedy and the natural geography of the environment, student and staff interest in the space project was very high. One interdisciplinary team and its students agreed to study certain aspects of the sea and relate them, when possible, to the Apollo project.

The mathematics teacher and the social studies teacher on the team worked with students in helping them to trace routes leading to the splashdown area. After the students had indicated that they would like to travel to the target area on the Queen Elizabeth, a former passenger ship permanently based in the Fort Lauderdale area, the math teacher gave them each a ditto sheet containing the information they would need to do this. (See Figure 8.1.)

Figure 8.1

The Sea Around Us—Mathematical Aspect

Your mission is to charter the Queen Elizabeth now located in Port Everglades, Florida. After chartering the Queen, you must plot a course that will take you to an area in the Pacific Ocean where you will assist in recovering Apollo 11. The location of the splashdown area is 175 degrees east, 10 degrees north. Your goal, after considering the factors listed below in addition to other discoveries you make, is to get to the target area as quickly as possible. Give the course you will take, the total hours of the trip, and the time and date of your arrival.

You will have to consider the following:

A. Latitude
B. Longitude
C. Time
D. Ocean currents
E. Possible courses to the splashdown area
F. Ship capabilities
G. Length of the Queen Elizabeth—1083 feet
H. Draft—56 feet
I. Length of anchor chain—165 fathoms
J. Fueling range based on a twelve-boiler operation:
    1. 30 kts. for 3500 miles
    2. 15 kts. for 6000 miles
    3. 25 kts. for 4500 miles

SOURCE: From the book *The Ungraded Middle School* by Robert J. McCarthy. © 1972 by Parker Publishing Company, Inc., West Nyack, New York. Used with permission.

The social studies teacher worked with her pupils on map and globe skills, and students plotted various courses for the trip. She also secured a film entitled *The Restless Sea,* which helped many youngsters comprehend the geographic factors that had to be considered in reaching their destination. Other films produced by Jacques Cousteau were also used to highlight points raised by the pupils in their investigations.

The English teacher on the team, with the cooperation of the librarian, had all the books in the library dealing with the sea moved into the classrooms where they were available for immediate student use. In her vocabulary development, she focused on the following terms, all of which were directly related to the topic under discussion:

1. bathysphere
2. plankton
3. oceanography
4. desalinization
5. algae
6. Mohole Project
7. current
8. undertow
9. continental shelf
10. thermocline
11. hydrosphere
12. sounding
13. fathom
14. time
15. dredge
16. scuba
17. trenches
18. buoy
19. modules
20. tide
21. edible
22. mariner
23. prime meridian
24. drift
25. knots
26. course
27. bends
28. triests

The science teacher on the team worked with the students in exploring some of their ideas about life in the sea, both plant and animal. Because the students were eager to touch and feel examples of plant and animal life found in the sea, a teacher took some of them out on a boat to gather specimens. They caught fish and brought in several varieties of seaweed that could be used in the classroom by other students. For several days the pupils went about dissecting the fish, looking at the seaweed through a stereo viewer, and viewing some filmloops about sea life. Students were also asked to find answers to the following questions:

1. What are fish?
2. How do fish take in oxygen?
3. What is their means of travel?
4. What is the purpose of fins?
5. How are fish able to rise in the water?

At this point in the unit, the English teacher began working with some pupils on their written expression. He also aided them in keeping a log of their activities throughout the three-week period that the unit was being explored.

Certain members of the related arts team also joined in the undertaking. The art teacher supervised interested students in painting sea scenes and decorating the classrooms of the interdisciplinary team with materials designed to fit in with the sea theme. The physical education staff also worked with some students on the basic principles of surfing and body navigation through water. Two young high school graduates were invited in to speak with the students about where they surf, why they surf, composition and structure of a surfboard, and techniques of surfing. The class was very receptive to their presentation and responded with many questions.

This interdisciplinary unit, developed in the course of a three-week summer session through the cooperation of students and staff was most successful. It helped students to develop certain fundamental skills while enabling them to see that many of these skills applied to several different subject matter areas. It also helped the school staff to see that a teaching approach based on student interests can work in helping youngsters achieve worthwhile objectives.

Model Middle School Programs

Let's look briefly at some model middle school programs.[2] In addition to studying these examples, you may want to visit some middle schools in your area.

Centerville Middle Schools, Washington Township, Ohio

Centerville Middle Schools are located in a rapidly growing section of Ohio near Dayton. The educational preparation of the people in the area is high; one-third are college graduates, and approximately 90 percent are high school graduates. Three middle schools serve the district, each accommodating 600 students in grades six, seven, and eight.

The expressed purposes of the Centerville Middle Schools are to help boys and girls become self-actualizing persons, to help them refine the basic skills initially acquired in elementary school, and to individualize their instruction. The teachers are organized into teams. Some teams are interdisciplinary, and some are organized around a single discipline. Each team is assisted by teacher aides. The teams are responsible for

---

2. The material on Centerville Middle Schools and Del Mar Community Intermediate School is adapted from Leslie W. Kindred, Rita J. Wolotkiewicz, John M. Mickelson, Leonard E. Coplein, and Ernest Dyson, *The Middle School Curriculum* (Boston: Allyn and Bacon, 1976). Used with permission.

instruction in the major curricular areas of language arts, social studies, mathematics, and science. Specialized teachers provide instruction in physical education, typing, music, foreign languages, and unified arts.

The curriculum is organized around a theme or "umbrella" topic. For example, themes in English might include animals, folklore, the sea, semantics, or careers. The teachers are very much involved in curriculum planning, specifically, through the preparation of Unipacs or related learning packets to be used by each child.

An interesting feature of the school program is its daily schedule. The schedule provides for blocks of time that are teacher scheduled and unstructured time that is student scheduled. The block format provides opportunities for teachers to use a variety of teaching strategies and grouping patterns. The student-scheduled time is built into the sixty-minute noon hour. After eating their lunch, students may take part in a variety of activities in the gymnasium or outside the school, work on projects, or just relax.

A unique experience is provided for sixth-grade students via a one-week school camping experience at the Grant Life Science Center, a sixty-acre park operated jointly by the township and the school district. The typical practice is for approximately thirty students and one science teacher to arrive at the center on a Tuesday and stay for the remainder of the week. A variety of projects and experiments are conducted in environmental education at the center.

At Centerville, significant efforts are directed toward individualizing instruction through use of Unipacs, open environment, grouping based on students' needs and interests, a well-equipped media center, and personal attention by the teacher. The school program includes the essential components of a school designed to meet the needs of an emerging adolescent learner.

Del Mar Community Intermediate School

The Del Mar Middle School is in the Reed Union School District, Marin County, California. The parents in the community are generally well educated and have high aspirations for their children.

The Del Mar School faculty perceives the middle school as placing a particular value on the differences of students and helping them to cope with the various change processes of the emerging adolescent period. The faculty also believes that the application and uses of subject matter should be taught and that diagnosis of pupil needs is the major basis for individualized instruction.

The Del Mar School is really two schools: an intermediate school and a middle school. The intermediate program is for grades seven and eight and is organized around three integrated subject areas: (1) humanities, (2) math-science, and (3) creative arts, Spanish, physical education, and exploratory areas. A smaller ungraded middle school program for students in grades six, seven, and eight is also provided. That program is organized around teaching teams representing the major subject areas, supported by specialists in physical education, foreign languages, and the unified arts.

One significant feature of the school organization pattern is that each team is responsible for the same group of children for all three years they are in the middle school. This arrangement is believed to increase opportunities for individualization and guidance. The school day is organized according to a very flexible format with variable time segments that can be tailored to meet the needs and objectives of each group. Del Mar School is organized to facilitate the goals of intellectual training of and development of student self-dependence in learning.

Upper St. Clair, Pennsylvania

The Boyce and Fort Couch schools in Upper St. Clair, Pennsylvania feature interesting grouping arrangements for middle school students. Based on multiage grouping, students move into different teams as they experience maturational or intellectual advancement, or a combination of both factors. The groupings are built on the findings of a local study performed by the Pittsburgh Children's Hospital (Eichhorn, 1973) and on the five classifications of development by Tanner (1962).

The grouping processes are based on medical and psychological data. They allow varied possibilities for grouping, such as combining sixth- and eighth-grade students, advancing students on the basis of maturity and the acquisition of intellectual skills to high school in as few as two years, or retaining socially mature students in the eighth grade for an additional semester of enrichment.

Decatur, Alabama

The Oak Park and Brookhaven Schools in Decatur, Alabama have the significant feature of mainstreaming students with learning disabilities into the regular middle school program (Bumpus, 1974). Sixth- through eighth-grade students with learning disabilities are grouped with regular students in "pod" arrangements with interdisciplinary teams being serviced by special education teachers.

Individualized experiences for these youngsters are also provided through learning resource centers and instructional media centers. The Decatur Middle Schools provide an excellent example of effective ways to integrate students with disabilities into the general school population.

League of Middle Schools

A very promising trend in middle school education is the development of a League of Middle Schools in various states. The membership of these state organizations is usually composed of institutions or agencies serving students aged ten to fourteen. Each League becomes an affiliate of the National Middle School Association and develops an Article of Association and Bylaws and a plan of action involving objectives, activities, conferences, and dissemination services. A Board of Directors is also set up, and a League Expediter is appointed by the Board. Some typical goals of a League of Middle Schools are:

1. To serve as a clearinghouse for exchange of ideas and materials
2. To facilitate continuing curricular improvement
3. To assist in developing plans for evaluating middle schools
4. To secure and maintain support of groups interested in educational improvement
5. To represent middle school youth in professional and public discussion of programs and problems

Leaders in the development and refinement of the League concept are the states of Florida, Texas, North Carolina, Georgia, Missouri, and Maryland. The League has proven to be most effective as a vehicle for facilitating continuing improvement in curriculum planning, in-service education, school planning, and middle school education in general. Information concerning the development of a League of Middle Schools may be obtained by writing National Middle School Association, P.O. Box 968, Fairborn, Ohio 45324.

Summary

Curriculum is what happens when people, ideas, and things are brought together in a dynamic relationship within a school setting. A middle school curriculum is made up of those learning experiences actually experienced by emerging adolescent learners under the responsibility of the middle school. It should be well planned, based on the best of middle school research, and it should be flexible and responsive to the continuously changing needs of middle school students.

A valid needs assessment at the local level is critical as a frame of reference for use in local curriculum planning and evaluation. Since the middle school occupies a strategic position between the elementary and high school, significant attention should be given to the articulation of students from kindergarten through high school.

Curriculum planners should synthesize the implications of significant middle school research that has been conducted over the past decade. They should use this synthesis as a guide to curriculum development in order to avoid some of the "pitfalls" of the past. A process of values clarification should undergird the middle school curriculum. Greater emphasis should be given to interdisciplinary curricular designs that interrelate the conceptual threads and processes of the various disciplines along with presenting instruction in life-long learning skills and opportunities for career exploration.

REFERENCES

Brodinsky, Ben. "Back to the Basics: The Movement and Its Meaning." *Phi Delta Kappan* 58(1977):522–27.

Bumpus, Robert, and Vann, Margaret. "An Innovative Approach to Special Education in the Middle School." *Educational Leadership Institute* 6(1974):2.

Coffland, Jack A. "Reexamining the Middle School." *Clearing House* 49(1975):154–57.

Eichhorn, Donald. "The Boyce Medical Study." *The Emerging Adolescent Learner in the Middle Grades.* Multimedia kit. Springfield, Mass.: Association for Supervision and Curriculum Development and Educational Leadership Institute, 1973.

Gross, Bernard M. "An Analysis of the Present and Perceived Purposes, Functions, and Characteristics of the Middle School." Ph.D. dissertation, Temple University, 1972.

Howe, Leland W., and Howe, Mary Martha. *Personalizing Education: Values Clarification and Beyond.* New York: Hart Publishing Co., 1975.

Kindred, Leslie W.; Wolotkiewicz, Rita J.; Mickelson, John M.; Coplein, Leonard E.; and Dyson, Ernest. *The Middle School Curriculum.* Boston, Mass.: Allyn and Bacon, 1976.

McCarthy, Robert J. *The Ungraded Middle School.* West Nyack, N.Y.: Parker Publishing Co., 1972.

Raths, Louis; Harmin, Merrill; and Simon, Sidney. *Values and Teaching.* Columbus, Ohio: Charles E. Merrill Publishing Co., 1966.

Raymer, Joe T. "A Study to Identify Middle Schools and to Determine the Current Level of Implementation of Eighteen Basic Middle School Characteristics in Selected United States and Michigan Schools." Ph.D. dissertation, Michigan State University, 1974.

Simon, Sidney B.; Howe, Leland W.; and Kirschenbaum, Howard. *Values Clarification: A Handbook of Practical Strategies for Teachers and Students.* New York: Hart Publishing Co., 1972.

Tanner, J. M. *Growth at Adolescence*. Second Edition. Oxford: Blackwell Scientific Publications, 1962.

Tyler, Ralph W. *Basic Principles of Curriculum and Instruction*. Chicago: The University of Chicago, 1950.

Learning Module

Middle School Curriculum

Directions

This learning module is designed to help you learn about middle school curriculum. Begin by taking the pretest. Review your pretest results with your instructor, who will assist you in selecting the appropriate objectives. Complete the required and optional activities that will assist you in reaching your objectives. Take the posttest to see what you have learned.

Pretest

1. Briefly discuss the programs of study included within a middle school curriculum.
2. List the advantages and disadvantages of the middle school curriculum compared with the junior high school curriculum.
3. List the ways the middle school curriculum meets the varying needs of the students.
4. Name the ingredients of a good middle school learning center.
5. Relate the guidance services of a middle school to student needs and the curriculum.
6. Identify the Lighthouse Programs and National Curriculum Projects and their contributions to middle school curriculum development.

Check

Review your pretest performance with your instructor.

Behavioral Objectives

Select appropriate objectives.

1. List the programs of study stressed in the middle school. Include the four-areas approach to the middle school curriculum.
2. Compare and contrast junior high school curriculum with middle school curriculum.
3. Make a list of the ways the core of the middle school curriculum meets the needs of the student and the demands of the community.
4. List the ingredients that constitute a good learning center for the middle school. Describe the part it plays in the curriculum.

5. Discuss the role guidance services play in determining the middle school curriculum.
6. Describe the Lighthouse Programs and the National Curriculum Projects and list their contributions to middle school curriculum development.

Required Activities

(Numbers in parentheses correlate with corresponding objectives.)

1. Read *The Middle School: A Bridge between Elementary and Secondary Schools* by Sylvester Kohut, Jr., (Washington, D.C.: National Education Association, 1976). (1) (2) (3)
2. Write your state Department of Education to obtain information dealing with middle school curriculum. (1) (2) (6)
3. Read "Musts for a Middle School," *Clearing House,* April 1976, pp. 377–79. (1) (2) (5)
4. Go to a nearby college or university and interview several education professors about what they believe are the "musts" for a middle school curriculum. (1) (2)
5. Read Samuel R. Porter's "The School in the Middle," pp. 248–58, in *The Middle School* by Louis G. Romano, Nicholas P. Georgiady, and James E. Heald (Chicago: Nelson-Hall Co., 1973). (1)
6. Read Chapters 2 and 3 in *Middle School* by Theodore C. Moss (New York: Houghton Mifflin Co., 1969). (1)
7. Visit two middle schools. Observe their curriculum programs and evaluate them according to what a middle school curriculum should include. To obtain information regarding the curriculum of each school, talk to the principal, guidance counselor, teachers, and students. (1) (2) (3)
8. Read about one of the original middle schools, St. Paul Middle School in *The American Middle School* by Samuel H. Popper (Waltham, Mass.: Blaisdell Publishing Co., 1967, pp. 242–45). Write to this school to obtain more information on its curriculum and how it has been determined. (1) (2) (3)
9. Read the article, "The Middle School Trend: Another Look in the Upper Midwest," by Thomas A. Sinks, John McLure, Max Bough, Robert Malinka, and Dorothy J. T. Terman, pp. 52–56 in *Clearing House,* October 1975. (1)
10. Read the article, "Toward a Student-Centered Learning Focus Inventory for Junior High and Middle School Teachers," by Robert E. Clasen, p. 9011 in *The Journal of Educational Research,* September 1974. (2) (3)
11. Visit two junior high schools to find out about their curriculum programs. Obtain relevant information by talking to principals, teachers,

counselors, and students. Then compare a junior high school curriculum to a middle school curriculum about which you have obtained information. (1) (2)

12. Read pages 335–39 in *The American Middle School* by Samuel H. Popper (Waltham, Mass.: Blaisdell Publishing Co., 1967). (1) (2)
13. Talk to a school superintendent in a junior high school area and then talk to one in a middle school area. Find out about the curriculum of each one as well as what each superintendent believes are the advantages and disadvantages of her or his type. Find out if both believe their types of programs are meeting the needs of students and the community. (1) (2) (3)
14. Read "Today's Junior High Students," pp. 68–71 in *Middle School in the Making* by Robert R. Leeper (Washington, D.C.: Association for Supervision and Curriculum Development, 1974). (2)
15. Read "Part 1 of Middle School's Report," pp. 104–5 in *Middle School in the Making* by Robert R. Leeper (1974). (2)
16. Conduct a survey of middle school students, asking them if they feel the school curriculum is meeting their needs. Calculate and evaluate the results. (3)
17. Read Edward A. McHugh's "The Middle School That Evolved," pp. 259–65 in *The Middle School,* edited by Louis G. Romano, Nicholas P. Georgiady, and James E. Heald (Chicago: Nelson-Hall Co., 1973).
18. Read pages 100–103 in *Middle School in the Making* by Robert R. Leeper (1974). Visit a middle school and conduct the "I Love to Do" survey that you just read about. Conduct it in two middle school classrooms. Evaluate the survey and determine if the curriculum used in each classroom is child-centered. (3)
19. Read Jack A. Coffland's "Reexamining the Middle School: A Student Survey," pp. 154–57 in *Clearing House,* December 1975. (1) (2) (3)
20. Read "What Our Son Needs in a Middle School . . ." by Lynn Oberlin and Mary Jean Oberlin, pp. 323–24 in *Clearing House,* March 1976. (3)
21. Conduct a survey of the parents of children attending a particular middle school. This can be done by sending questionnaires home with the students for the parents to return. Ask parents if they believe the middle school curriculum is meeting the needs of their children and the community. (3)
22. Interview several middle school teachers and principals to see if they believe their middle school curriculum is meeting the needs of the students and the community. (2) (3)
23. Read "Learning and the Learning Center," pp. 276–82 in *The Middle School* by Louis G. Romano, Nicholas P. Georgiady, and James E. Heald (1973). (1) (4)

24. Go to a middle school and look at some learning centers. Ask the teachers how they constructed them, used them, and evaluated them. (4)
25. Read pages 96–97 in *Middle School in the Making* by Robert R. Leeper (1974). (1) (2) (3) (4) (5)
26. Go to a classroom that you visited earlier and observe its learning centers. Find out what type of learning center the teacher still needs for that classroom. Make the learning center needed, try it out in the classroom, do a self-evaluation of it, and then let the classroom teacher evaluate it. (3) (4)
27. Read "The Middle School and Implications for the Guidance Program," pp. 292–301 in *The Middle School* by Louis G. Romano, Nicholas P. Georgiady, and James E. Heald (1973). (1) (2) (3) (5)
28. Read "Guidance in the Middle School," pp. 188–207 in *The Middle School* by Louis G. Romano, Nicholas P. Georgiady, and James E. Heald (1973). (5)
29. Visit a middle school and interview the guidance counselor. Find out about the guidance program and how it relates to the curriculum and how it meets the needs of the students. (1) (3) (5)
30. Read pages 76–85 in *Middle School in the Making* by Robert R. Leeper (1974). (1) (6)
31. Write to obtain information pertaining to the Lighthouse Programs and the National Curriculum Projects. Review the material you receive carefully and prepare a brief presentation for a middle school PTA meeting. (6)
32. Make a survey of all available middle school materials in your community in local middle schools, local libraries, and local colleges and universities. Put a listing of this information in logical order and distribute it to local middle school principals, teachers, counselors, and any other interested persons. (1) (2) (3) (4) (5) (6)

Optional Activities

Select activities from the Required Activities list that you have not completed.

Posttest

Design a model for a middle school curriculum based on what you have learned through completing this module. Present your model to your instructor for evaluation.

Chapter 9

Instructional Objectives: Keys to Learning

Imagine that you are seated aboard an airliner and you overhear the pilot instructing the stewardess, "Dispose of the flight plan and maps. Today the sky is the limit!" You would probably make your exit in record time.

Suppose you have employed a builder and given him a blueprint to follow in building your house. The builder decides to destroy the blueprint and "do his own thing." Upset?

Obviously an accurate flight plan is essential to a successful flight just as an architectural drawing is essential to building a successful house. Objectives are the blueprint of a successful curriculum; the quality of the objectives dictates the quality of the curriculum.

Too often teachers either fail to set meaningful goals for learners, or the goals they do set are stated in such a broad generalized manner that they prove to be almost worthless. Psychologists have long agreed that learning is greatly enhanced when the learner knows where he is going or expected to go. An instructional objective is a specific statement of the behavioral change expected to take place in a learner as a result of instruction. It is the key around which the teacher and learner focus their energies. In other words, it is a statement of what the teacher is trying to help the student learn from instruction—the ways of thinking, feeling, or acting that the teacher wants the student to develop. You will want to become competent in the effective use of instructional objectives. Let's see what we can learn about them.

There are two major types of objectives: (1) general objectives, broad statements of what an educational program is trying to achieve, and (2) instructional objectives, specific statements of a behavioral change expected to take place in a learner as a result of instruction. You will want to develop competency in the use of both general and specific instructional objectives. Let's first treat the subject of general objectives.

Function of General Educational Objectives

General objectives may range from statements of educational goals for a nation, region, or state to statements of educational goals for an individual school or a particular subject area of its curriculum. A general objective serves the function of providing a target toward which the school may direct curricular efforts. An example of a general objective could be stated as follows: Each student should be knowledgeable concerning the Civil War in American history. Obviously this is a broad, generalized target that would be almost impossible to measure at the teacher-pupil interaction level. To measure students' progress toward reaching this target at the classroom level, the teacher would want to employ an instructional objective, a specific statement of measurable change in the learner. An example may prove helpful: The student shall be able to contrast the battle tactics employed by General Lee and General Grant. This is a specific behavior that the student could master on the way toward reaching the general objective of becoming "knowledgeable concerning the Civil War in American history." General objectives serve several major functions:

1. They define the direction of educational development.
2. They help select desirable learning experiences.
3. They help define the scope of an educational program.
4. They help define the emphasis to be made in an educational program.
5. They form one of the major bases for evaluation.

Objectives serve as a statement of the values that help distinguish among the desirable and undesirable behaviors of students. In this sense, objectives define the nature of the educational maturities that children, parents, teachers, and society are striving to achieve.

Objectives also serve as the major basis for selecting learning experiences. Without setting the objectives first, teachers and students would spend enormous energies in a haphazard pursuit of experiences that lack direction and productivity.

One of the most important factors to consider in developing any educational program is scope—the number or range of elements to be included. Objectives aid in deciding which elements are essential or nonessential to an educational program. Objectives also assist in determining which of the essential components should receive the greatest emphasis.

Probably one of the most important functions of objectives, particularly in an age of accountability on the part of educators, is to provide a basis for the appraisal of the educational development of students. Without objectives it would be impossible to effectively evaluate a school program or evaluate and report pupil progress.

Significant Statements of General Objectives

One of the most widely distributed and influential statements of educational objectives published in America during the past century was the statement made by the Educational Policies Commission of the National Education Association in 1938. The Commission identified four aspects of educational objectives in detail: (1) a description of the educated person, (2) a description of the educated member of the family and community group, (3) a description of the educated producer or consumer, and (4) a description of the educated citizen (Ragen and Shephard 1971). This document has served extensively as a guide for educational program development at all levels of education.

A statement of educational objectives that has made a major impact on the evolution of the elementary school was made by the Mid-Century Committee on Outcomes in Elementary Education (Kearney 1953). Objectives appropriate for children at the third-, sixth-, and ninth-grade levels in each of nine curricular areas were listed in terms of knowledge and understanding; skills and competencies; attitudes and interests; and action patterns.

A very significant statement that has greatly influenced thinking regarding the central purpose of education was the report of the President's Science Advisory Committee published in 1964. The report emphasized the following: (1) stimulation of the will to learn—giving students a sense of pleasure and accomplishment in intellectual work and (2) development of general intellectual skills that transcend any subject matter, that is, teaching students how to learn using viable modes of thinking in varied situations. Translated into actual programs, several new curricular developments emphasizing mastery of process as well as mastery of content have emerged in the various subject areas. In fact, the curricular revolution of the 1960s was characterized by programs that emphasized "thinking and working like a scientist" and "thinking and working like a mathematician" in addition to mastering facts and concepts. Noteworthy were the SMSG (School Mathematics Study Group) math and the SCIS

(Science Curriculum Improvement Study) science program.

These are only a few of the major statements of educational objectives that have had an extensive influence on curriculum development at the national, state, and local level. They should serve as resources, guides to stimulate creative thought and planning at the local school level.

The school is charged by society with the responsibility of developing the "whole child". This involves the planning of educational objectives in a variety of areas or domains. Let's look briefly at how an educational objectives classification system can help us do this.

Classifying Educational Objectives

Bloom (1956) developed a taxonomy, or system, of classifying educational objectives. The taxonomy is divided into three domains or categories of objectives: cognitive, affective, and psychomotor. The cognitive domain includes objectives having to do with thinking, knowing, and problem solving (intellectual behaviors). The affective includes objectives dealing with attitudes, values, and interests (emotional behaviors). The psychomotor domain treats objectives having to do with manual and motor skills (skills). Each domain is divided into subcategories. (For a condensed version of the cognitive domain, see Figure 9.1.)

Affective objectives are more difficult to measure than cognitive objectives. For example, a teacher can measure how well a student can solve a math problem in a very short time; measuring his interest in math or how he values math, however, may require more time. Also, teachers sometimes sense an urgency to "get the facts across" or "cover the books," both of which are essentially cognitive tasks. Some teachers have indicated that cognitive objectives are easier to state and more specific in nature. Regardless of these and related concerns, however, we must give careful attention to providing the appropriate emphasis to the often-neglected affective domain. Careful application of a taxonomy of objectives will enable the teacher to provide a balance among the domains and to give meaning to the "whole child" concept.

Surveys of courses of study and instructional lesson plans reveal that teachers tend to give heavy emphasis to the cognitive domain and very little emphasis to the affective domain. It is very important that a student possess knowledge; however, if he doesn't value that knowledge enough to use it in a positive, productive manner, it will not benefit the student or others. (For a taxonomy of educational objectives in the affective domain, see Figure 9.2.)

Figure 9.1

Condensed Version of the Taxonomy of Educational Objectives in the Cognitive Domain

Description	*Category*
LOW LEVEL	1. KNOWLEDGE. (Remembering facts, terms, and principles in the form they were learned.) (a) Knowledge of specifics. (i) Knowledge of terminology. (ii) Knowledge of specific facts. (b) Knowledge of ways and means of dealing with specifics. (i) Knowledge of conventions. (ii) Knowledge of trends and sequences. (iii) Knowledge of classifications and categories. (iv) Knowledge of criteria. (v) Knowledge of methodology. (c) Knowledge of universals and abstractions in a field. (i) Knowledge of principles and generalizations. (ii) Knowledge of theories and structures.
	2. COMPREHENSION. (Understanding material studied without necessarily relating it to other material.) (a) Translation. (b) Interpretation. (c) Extrapolation.
	3. APPLICATION. (Using generalizations or other abstractions appropriately in conrete situations.)
	4. ANALYSIS. (Breakdown of material into constituent parts.) (a) Analysis of elements. (b) Analysis of relationships. (c) Analysis of organizational principles.
	5. SYNTHESIS. (Combining elements into a new structure.) (a) Production of unique communication. (b) Production of a plan or proposed set of operations. (c) Derivation of a set of abstract relations.
	6. EVALUATION. (Judging the value of material for a specified purpose.) (a) Judgements in terms of internal evidence. (b) Judgements in terms of external criteria.

SOURCE: From *Taxonomy of Educational Objectives: The Classification of Educational Goals: Handbook: Cognitive Domain*, by Benjamin S. Bloom et al. Copyright © 1956 by Longman Inc. Previously published by David McKay Company, Inc. Reprinted by permission of Longman Inc.

How can the taxonomy help you? Of what value is the taxonomy to a prospective teacher? The taxonomy can help you in the following ways:

1. Describe student behavior in precise terms.
2. Focus on the change to be made in the student.

Figure 9.2

Condensed Version of the Taxonomy of Educational Objectives in the Affective Domain

Direction	*Category*
LOW LEVEL	1. RECEIVING. (Paying attention.)
	(a) Awareness.
	(b) Willingness to receive.
	(c) Controlled or selected attention.
	2. RESPONDING. (Committed and actively attending.)
	(a) Acquiescence in responding.
	(b) Willingness to respond.
	(c) Satisfaction in response.
	3. VALUING. (Concepts are seen to have worth.)
	(a) Acceptance of a value.
	(b) Preference for a value.
	(c) Commitment (conviction).
	4. ORGANIZATION. (Construction of a system of values.)
	(a) Conceptualization of a value.
	(b) Organization of a value system.
	5. CHARACTERIZATION OF A VALUE COMPLEX. (Acceptance of value system.)
HIGH LEVEL	(a) Generalized set.
	(b) Characterization.

SOURCE: From *Taxonomy of Educational Objectives: The Classification of Educational Goals: Handbook 2: Affective Domain,* by David R. Krathwohl et al. Copyright © 1964 by Longman Inc. Previously published by David McKay Company, Inc. Reprinted by permission of Longman Inc.

3. Design the kinds of learning experiences that are appropriate to developing the desired behavior.
4. Aid you in test construction and varied facets of evaluation.
5. Provide a framework for providing a better-balanced curriculum among the cognitive, affective, and psychomotor objectives.

Lawrence Kohlberg and Rochelle Mayer have provided valuable assistance in the defining of educational objectives, with particular emphasis on the affective domain.[1] There are three fundamental strategies, according to Kohlberg and Mayer, for defining educational objectives in early education: the "bag of virtues," or "desirable trait," strategy, the "industrial psychology," or "prediction of success," strategy, and the "developmental-philosophic" strategy.

1. Adapted from Lawrence Kohlberg and Rochelle Mayer, "Development as the Aim of Education," *Harvard Educational Review* 42(1972):449–96. Copyright © 1972 by President and Fellows of Harvard College. Used with permission.

The bag of virtues strategy includes a set of traits characterizing an ideal, healthy, or fully functioning, personality. This approach involves the use of such trait words as *honesty, self-confidence, curiosity,* and *self-discipline.* One problem associated with this approach is that the traits identified as goals for behavior are psychologically vague. For example, what one person might regard as honesty, another person might perceive as something else. In fact, Hartshorne and May (1928–1930) were surprised to discover that they could locate no such stable personality trait as honesty in school children. A student who cheated in one situation might not cheat in another, thus leading to the conclusion that cheating was, for the most part, situationally determined. The listing of traits is therefore suspect on the basis of definition; one person's "integrity" may be another person's "stubbornness," or one person's "honesty in expressing your true feelings" may be another's "insensitivity to the feelings of others."

The industrial psychology strategy involves the identification and measurement of intellectual skills and achievements judged to be predictors of success in meeting the task demands of a job in society. The major application of this strategy in education has been in the development and use of achievement tests, especially in the development of test items or minimal competencies judged to be predictors of success in a particular vocation.

The development-philosophic strategy emphasizes a standard of adequacy internal to and governing the developmental process itself. It suggests that development is not just any behavior change, but instead a change toward greater differentiation, integration, and adaptation. Based on extensive research, Kohlberg has developed a six-stage moral development model that could be of great assistance in developing objectives in the affective domain. A brief description of each stage is presented here.

Stage 1. A punishment and obedience orientation in which one responds to a moral conflict in terms of a superior power, possible physical consequences of an action, especially the avoidance of punishment.
Stage 2. An egoist, relativistic orientation in which the guiding principle is "you scratch my back and I'll scratch yours."
Stage 3. The "good boy-nice girl" orientation in which action springs from a need for the approval of others.
Stage 4. A "law and order" stance in which right behavior consists of doing one's duty toward authority, rules, maintaining social order.
Stage 5. The social-contract legalistic orientation in which right action is defined in terms of maintaining the social order and guaranteeing

individual rights on the basis of using legal channels and socially agreed upon vehicles in changing a law, for example.
Stage 6. Here, the right is defined in terms of self-adopted ethical principles, especially the principle of justice, which respects the dignity of the individual as well as going beyond personal needs or whims and the opinions of others. (Beck, Crittenden, and Sullivan 1971)

Kohlberg has emphasized that the sequence of the stages is culturally universal and cannot be linked to age levels, sex, or socioeconomic status. His moral development model emphasizes a commitment to justice as the core of morality.

Surveys of curriculum guides and actual teaching practices in the American classroom reveal that the affective domain has been neglected in recent years. A careful examination of Krathwold's affective domain research and Kohlberg's moral development research should serve as a tremendous source of assistance in the development of affective objectives. Application of this and related research should result in a more personalized curriculum in the middle school.

As we have seen, general educational objectives serve many useful functions. They tend to reflect a theme or a concern that applies to education in general or to an abstract treatment of a course of study. Some valid general objectives are (1) to help each child become more rational, more creative, and more humane; (2) to develop within all children a sense of personal worth; (3) to understand the basic causes of social unrest. In order for these general objectives to become productive in the lives of students, however, they need to be translated into specific objectives at the classroom teacher-pupil contact level.

Specific objectives direct student activity toward acquiring clearly described traits, skills, attitudes, and knowledge. The following are examples of specific objectives:

1. At the end of the course, the student will be able to list ten rights of an American citizen.
2. The student will document with five references the contributions of English poets to American literary criticism.
3. The student will be able to calculate how far he is from a thunderstorm when he hears thunder three seconds after he sees a flash of lightning.
4. The student will be able to read and write accurately any number from 1 to 10,000.

In essence, there is a significant difference between general course descriptions (what a course is about) and specific course objectives (what students should be able to do after completing a course).

Using Instructional Objectives

In order to develop a productive change in a learner's behavior, the teacher needs to identify the desired behavior in specific language that both he and the learner can understand. An effectively stated instructional objective should have three specific ingredients:

1. **Specific behavior**—a behavior that the learner must demonstrate. Examples: contrast, compute, differentiate, jump, write.
2. **Conditions**—the circumstances in which the learner is to demonstrate the behavior. Examples: when given x and y, while standing on one foot, by using the slide projector.
3. **Performance criterion**—the minimally acceptable level of performance (a standard of measurement). Examples: 70%, 6 out of 10, within 30 minutes, to your satisfaction.

A well-stated instructional objective should communicate three things: (1) what it is that a student who has mastered the objective will be able to do, (2) under what conditions he will be able to do it, and (3) to what extent he will be able to do it.

Instructional objectives provide a rational and valid basis for directing and assessing the performance of individual students. Mager has emphasized that "an instructor will function in a fog of his own making until he knows just what he wants his students to be able to do at the end of the instruction" (1962, p. 3).

Gagné states, "It is natural that one should attempt to identify the outcome of learning as something the student is able to do following instruction which he was unable to do before instruction" (1972, p. 395).

In developing instructional objectives, it is extremely important to use precise language and define the desired behavior clearly. You should generally avoid terms that are subject to a variety of interpretations such as *to know, to understand, to be familiar with, to appreciate*. We should use specific terms such as *record, write, contrast, solve, construct,* and so forth.

Conditions need to be stated clearly, and variety should be employed. Examples of stating conditions are *with the aid of a microscope, without the aid of a map, given a hammer and saw, under the following circumstances*, and so on. The performance criteria may include time allotted for the behavior, quantity or production, quality of product, or degree of skill.

Vargas (1972) emphasizes that for an objective to be behavioral, it must point to observable behavior on the part of the student—an act that can be seen or heard. Contrast the following:[2]

2. Adapted from Julie S. Vargas, *Writing Worthwhile Behavioral Objectives* (New York: Harper and Row, 1972). Used with permission.

Unobservable behavior	Observable behavior
know	list
understand	identify
have mastery of	state
acquire skills in	contrast

Words in the first list refer to states of the individual that are not directly observable. In contrast, the words in the second list refer to behaviors that the individual obviously can or cannot do.

Directions: Next to each of the following, write "O" if the behavior is directly observable and "N" if it is not directly observable.

______ 1. To have learned about history.
______ 2. To construct a square.
______ 3. To give examples of language dialects.
______ 4. To know about the Civil War.
______ 5. To check the errors in a typewritten paragraph.
______ 6. To grasp the significance of the battle.
______ 7. To sing.
______ 8. To achieve satisfaction.
______ 9. To appreciate.
______ 10. To identify the significant characteristics.

Answers: 1—N, 2—O, 3—O, 4—N, 5—O, 6—N, 7—O, 8—N, 9—N, 10—O

Instructional objectives should focus on the student's behavior, not on the teacher's; it is the change in the student's behavior that shows learning. In order for an objective to be behavioral, it must indicate what the student will be able to do as a result of instruction. There are four major purposes of stating objectives in behavioral terms:

1. To describe the behavior a teacher wants a student to exhibit in his learning experience
2. To provide a meaningful function for the learning experiences in the classroom
3. To provide a guide for teachers and students in the total learning experience
4. To provide a means by which teacher and student can measure a student's progress toward his long-range goals

Plowman (1971) has developed a very helpful coding system for coding and framing behavioral objectives.[3] It consists of a simple analytic

3. From *Behavioral Objectives* by Paul D. Plowman. © 1971, Science Research Associates, Inc. Used by permission of the publisher.

method for identifying the key components of written behavioral objectives—behavior, mediating conditions, level of proficiency, and methods of assessing it. The designations are:

B—a clear description of *Behavior*
C—mediating *Conditions*
P—level of *Proficiency*
M—*Methods* for ascertaining that the proficiency level has been reached.

Using the code designations, B, C, P, and M, indicate which elements are present in the following statements:

_____ 1. After listening to a recording of the inaugural address of John F. Kennedy, the student lists three things that the late President said.
_____ 2. Students are to appreciate poetry.
_____ 3. Skills of oral presentation are to be perfected by the student until he wins a debate sponsored by the National Forensic League.
_____ 4. Pupils are to learn the significance of the Declaration of Independence by observing and discussing a play on colonial America.
_____ 5. Without the aid of a dictionary, the pupil is to write correctly the spelling of five words indicated by the teacher.

Keys to questions:	*Elements Present*	*Elements Not Present*
	1. B, C, P	M
	2.	B, P, C, M
	3. P	B, C, M
	4. C	B, P, M
	5. B, C, P, M	

It would be helpful for you, as a prospective teacher, to practice writing some behavioral objectives. You may choose the areas of science, math, social science, or language arts for practice, or you may desire to choose another subject area. Also, you may want to review some of the material on the preceding pages. As you practice, concentrate on what you want the learner to be able to do and not on what you are going to do.

Check Yourself with BOWST

Lapp (1972) has designed the Behavioral Objectives Writing Skills Test (BOWST) to provide an estimate of the elementary teacher's ability to write behavioral objectives. The instrument requires the teacher to develop three behavioral objectives for each of four hypothetical classroom settings. It may be administered in either preservice or in-service programs.

The BOWST has several positive characteristics: (1) extensive preparation is not needed for administration or scoring, (2) it is not a speed test, (3) no oral response is required, and (4) alternate forms of the test are provided. The test uses a total of four hypothetical class settings, one in each of the curricular areas of reading, arithmetic, science, and social studies. Successful completion of a behavioral objective in each setting is dependent on the inclusion of the following specified criteria: (1) a description of the type of behavior that is to occur as a result of planned instruction, (2) a description of the external conditions, or the setting, in which a specific behavior will occur, and (3) a description of the performance level that will be considered acceptable.

Administration of the BOWST is simple. After the examinee receives the kit, which includes forms A and B, a scoring key, and a scoring sheet, he administers the test to himself. He reads the directions and proceeds at his own pace until he has completed the test. The highest possible score he can achieve on this test is thirty-six points. One point is given for each of the three criteria the examinee includes in an objective, and one point is given for each statement he makes correctly describing the exact setting or conditions that will be present when the learner exhibits a terminal behavior. Some examples of phrases describing external conditions include:

1. Given a set of criteria . . .
2. Given a list of . . .
3. Given a specific . . .
4. Without the aid of . . .

One point is also given for each correct statement of terminal behavior that describes the type of behavior that will be accepted as evidence that the learner has achieved the stated objective. Some examples of these are:

1. The learner is able to identify. . .
2. The learner is able to list. . .
3. The learner is able to recite. . .

In addition, one point is given for the statement of acceptable performance. Examples of these are:

1. . . . 50% of the basic sight words
2. . . . all of the division problems
3. . . . at least 6 of the problems

To arrive at the maximum number of thirty-six points, multiply the number of behavioral objectives to be written for each setting (3) times the number of curriculum areas (4), then multiply this product times the number of criteria included in each developed behavioral objective (3). Result: $3 \times 4 \times 3 = 36$ points.

Goal Setting: Dimensions of Schooling

Ragan, Wilson, and Ragan have provided a descriptive treatment of eight dimensions of schooling that relate to personalized instruction: purposes, rules, learning styles, content, time, space, participation, and evaluation.[4]

1. *The purpose of school.* We may argue about what purpose is being served in a given school situation, but we will probably agree that some purpose is being served. In the past, an excessive number of school activities have been directed toward the purpose of developing learners who are dependent on the teacher or various structures of the school. As a result, learners have become concerned with carrying out the orders of the teacher, doing the "class" assignment, and meeting group standards, regardless of the personal relevance of a particular experience.

   If the school desires to develop self-dependent learners using independent thought and action, then increasing attention must be given to personalized instruction, reducing to a minimum the times when all children are expected to complete the same activity.
2. *Rules.* It is important that all schools have rules to guide human interaction; the absence of such guidance usually results in chaos. Rules have two major aspects: quantitative and qualitative. From a quantitative standpoint, an excessive number of rules can result in unproductive group behavior. A few, carefully developed, meaningful rules are usually more productive. From a qualitative standpoint, rules should be relevant and clearly understood, and students should have a voice in their creation.
3. *Learning styles.* Every individual possesses a unique learning style. A school that provides a great variety of teaching/learning methods, varied environments, multimethod teachers, and multimedia is moving in the direction of personalized instruction.
4. *Content.* Many subject areas and topics are broad enough to allow learners to choose what it is they wish to study in those areas. This

---

4. Adapted from *Teaching in the Elementary School* by William B. Ragan, John H. Wilson, and Tillman J. Ragan. Copyright ©1972 by Holt, Rinehart and Winston, Inc. Reprinted by permission of Holt, Rinehart and Winston.

type of content selection process, when guided constructively by the teacher, can result in the student's realizing that the teacher respects his integrity as a person.

5. *Time.* Daily time schedules characterized by fragmentation, frequent interruptions and distractions, and regimented time segments are a barrier to personalized learning. A more flexible, less uniform time schedule is needed, with attention being given to how much time is necessary for an individual learner to complete an activity.
6. *Space.* Where can't learning take place? Greater attention should be given to capitalizing on learning opportunities in varied settings: classroom, media center, field settings, home, and en route to and from school.
7. *Participation.* The teacher must utilize diagnostic data effectively, particularly interest and attitude data, to design learning experiences in which students will participate.
8. *Evaluation.* Historically, evaluation has been thought of as a process that the *teacher* uses *after* a student supposedly has learned something. To better personalize instruction, however, we need to give greater attention to the *student's* evaluating before, during, and after he learns something (self-evaluation). Both teacher and student need to give greater attention to diagnostic and summative evaluation processes.

A behavioral analysis of education requires an examination of the entire instructional system. The teacher should ask himself some penetrating questions regarding learning objectives. What evidence do I have to support the assertion that everyone should master this objective? Is this objective essential? Should this objective be optional or required? Have students had a role in determining the objective? Are the same objectives required for all the students? Are provisions made for different rates of attainment? Are varied teaching strategies employed to achieve different objectives?

If a learner fails to master an objective, the problem may lie in an inappropriate selection of objectives or ineffective teaching strategy. To use instructional objectives effectively, the teacher should carefully examine each component of the instructional model (instructional objectives, pretest, teaching strategies, and assessment procedures) for effectiveness.

Summary

An instructional objective is a specific statement regarding the behavioral change expected to take place in a learner as a result of instruction. There are two major types of objectives: (1) general objectives, broad statements of what the educational program is trying to achieve, and (2) instructional objectives, specific statements of a learner's anticipated behavior as a result of instruction. At the classroom level of teacher-pupil interaction, specific instructional objectives give direction to the learning process and serve as a rational and valid basis for assessing learner performance.

As a prospective teacher, you will want to develop competence in stating objectives in behavioral terms, categorizing objectives into cognitive, affective, and psychomotor domains, and using objectives effectively with different learners in varied subject areas. The Behavioral Objectives Writing Skills Test (BOWST) is an excellent instrument to assist you in developing competence and confidence in the effective use of instructional objectives.

REFERENCES

Beck, C. M.; Crittenden, B. S.; Sullivan, E. V., eds. *Moral Education: Interdisciplinary Approaches.* New York: Newman Press, 1971.

Bloom, Benjamin S. *Taxonomy of Educational Objectives, Handbook I: Cognitive Domain.* New York: McKay, 1956.

Gagné, Robert M. "Behavioral Objectives? Yes!" *Educational Leadership* 29(1972):394–96.

Hartshorne, H., and May, M. A. *Studies in the Nature of Character.* Studies in Deceit, Vol. 1; Studies in Service and Self-Control, Vol. 2; Studies in Organization of Character, Vol. 3. New York: Macmillan Co., 1928–1930.

Kearney, Nolan C. *Elementary School Objectives.* New York: Russell Sage Foundation, 1953.

Kohlberg, Lawrence, and Mayer, Rochelle. "Development as the Aim of Education." *Harvard Educational Review* 42(1972):449–96.

Krathwold, D. R.; Bloom, B. S., and Masia, B. B. *Taxonomy of Educational Objectives, Handbook II: Affective Domain.* New York: McKay, 1964.

Lapp, Diane. "Behavioral Objectives Writing Skills Test." *Journal of Education* 154(1972):13–24.

Mager, Robert F. *Preparing Instructional Objectives.* Palo Alto, Calif.: Fearon, 1962.

Plowman, Paul. *Behavioral Objectives.* Chicago: Science Research Associates, 1971.

President's Science Advisory Committee. *Innovations and Experiment in Education.* Washington, D.C.: U.S. Government Printing Office, 1964.

Ragan, William B.; Wilson, John H.; and Ragan, Tillman J. *Teaching in the Elementary School.* New York: Holt, Rinehart and Winston, 1972.

Vargas, Julie S. *Writing Worthwhile Behavioral Objectives.* New York: Harper and Row, 1972.

Learning Module

Behavioral Objectives

Directions

This learning module is designed to help you learn how to use behavioral objectives. Begin by taking the pretest. Review your pretest results with your instructor who will assist you in selecting the appropriate objectives. Complete the required and optional activities that will assist you in reaching your objectives. Then take the posttest to see what you have learned.

Pretest

1. List three major ingredients of a behavioral objective.
2. Contrast cognitive, affective, and psychomotor objectives.
3. Write an example of a cognitive, affective, and psychomotor behavioral objective for your subject specialty.

Check

Review your pretest performance with your instructor.

Behavioral Objectives

Select appropriate objectives.

1. Write examples of cognitive, affective, and psychomotor objectives.
2. Compare the ideas of Paul Plowman and Robert Mager regarding the use of behavioral objectives to improve instruction.
3. Describe the specific ingredients of a behaviorally stated objective.
4. Explain the value of stating behavioral objectives in behavioral terms.
5. State behavioral objectives for a unit of instruction in a middle school subject area.

Required Activities

(Numbers in parentheses correlate with corresponding objectives.)

1. Read Chapters 1, 2, and 3 in Robert F. Mager's *Preparing Instructional Objectives* (Palo Alto: Fearon, 1962). (2) (4)
2. Read Chapters 1 and 2 in Paul Plowman's *Behavioral Objectives* (Chicago: Science Research Associates, 1971). (2) (4) (5)

3. Practice writing behavioral objectives that illustrate your understanding of the three specific ingredients, behavioral term, content, and performance criterion. (3)
4. Interview a middle school classroom teacher on the topic, "Using Behavioral Objectives." (4) (5)
5. Interview an educational psychologist on specific ways of stating performance criteria. (3)
6. Visit a middle school classroom and develop three behavioral objectives appropriate to the needs of an individual student whom you have selected. (3)
7. Read Chapters 1, 3, and 5 in *Behavioral Objectives and Instruction* by Robert J. Kibler and others (Boston: Allyn and Bacon, 1972). (1) (3)
8. Read *Using Behavioral Objectives in the Classroom* by Daniel Tanner (New York: Macmillan Co., 1972). This book contains an excellent condensed version of Bloom's Taxonomy with explanation. (1)
9. Read Chapter 2 in *Individualizing Instruction* by Helen Davis Dell (Chicago: Science Research Associates, 1972). Practice writing instructional objectives. (1) (5)
10. Visit a local middle school and compare the instructional results of an instructor who uses behavioral objectives with those of an instructor who does not. (4)
11. Evaluate Mager's statement that teachers who teach without stated behavioral objectives "operate in a fog of their own making." (4)

Optional activities

Select activities from the Required Activities list that you have not completed.

Posttest

Prepare for your instructor's evaluation a written report presenting what you have learned from the activities that you have completed. The report should not exceed five double-spaced, typewritten pages.

Chapter 10

Guiding the Emerging Adolescent

Guidance in the middle school derives its purpose from the basic philosophy of the school program, which should be based on the belief that each student has the innate capacity for educational, personal, emotional, and social growth. The program should reflect faith in the individual student's potential for growth and in his ability to shape the future. It is the responsibility of the school, through its guidance services, and parents, teachers, and members of the community, to help individual students develop the unique skills they will need in their search for responsible freedom and a productive life.

Basic Objectives of the Middle School Guidance Program

The guidance program should provide opportunities for the emerging adolescent to mature in the following ways (Hill and Luckey, 1969):

1. Understanding himself and others
2. Understanding the world of education and the world of work
3. His ability to make decisions
4. His ability to understand and attempt to solve his own problems and to help others cope with their problems
5. Understanding human behavior, especially in regard to his relations with others
6. His ability to adjust to the demands of life
7. His sense of value in the achievement of high ideals.

What is counseling? Counseling is an encounter in which a counselor helps a student begin to work out the problems or concerns that he brings with him to the encounter. The goal of the encounter is to help the student arrive at solutions, answers, plans, decisions, and understandings that are satisfactory to him and that help him grow toward becoming an independent, self-directing person, able to function optimally in the society in which he lives.

Different people counsel differently. The approach a counselor uses is very personal and, in order to be genuine, must be developed individually within the framework of his own values and beliefs. Regardless of the approach he uses, however, the relationship a counselor establishes with a student is important. Qualities that are essential to the counseling relationship are sensitivity, caring, love, compassion, nonjudgment, respect, and dignity. In addition, it is imperative that confidentiality be maintained in this relationship. If school staff members do not understand the need for confidentiality in counseling, the counselor must endeavor to communicate this to them.

Counseling in a school setting presents problems not commonly found in clinic or mental health center settings. For instance, the counselor in a school must work with the significant others in the counselee's life. Effective communication between the counselor and parents, teachers, and others is therefore very important.

The major purpose of the middle school guidance program should be to provide services that will enable each emerging adolescent to successfully encounter the developmental tasks he faces during the middle school years. The following set of representative guidelines for the middle school counselor are used by the Armstrong Middle School, Flint, Michigan. According to these guidelines, the middle school counselor:

1. Shall closely follow an elementary counseling role
2. Shall work extensively with teachers and parents as well as with students
3. Shall have a complete and thorough understanding of the middle school philosophy and curriculum and must be supportive of these concepts
4. Shall initiate contacts with teachers, programs, and students
5. Shall work about the school—in clusters, learning center, and community—not just in his office
6. Should be experienced in group work
7. Should participate in each cluster team as an advisor for special problems

Functions of the Middle School Counselor

The role of the middle school counselor may be described in terms of six functions: counseling, consultation, coordination, communication, curricular development, and child growth and development (Keat 1974).

1. Counseling role assumes that the middle school counselor will counsel individual children and groups of children. The focus of these counseling relationships will be determined largely by individual and group needs, the availability and system of referral, and the degree to which consultant efforts with teachers and parents are effective.
2. Consultation or collaboration role assumes that the knowledge of individual behavior possessed by counselors will be primarily used to complement teacher efforts in implementing positive classroom climates, individualizing experiences for particular students, creating constructive behavioral models and reinforcement schedules, developing experiences which emphasize self-understanding attuned to the needs of educational and vocational development, and identifying student needs through the use of available objective and subjective information. Consultant relationships will also be focused on helping teachers, parents, and administrators to work more effectively with students.
3. Coordination role utilizes psychological services, social work, and health services in the school system and community which can be activated for specific purposes and to meet particular needs.
4. Communication involves contact with community groups to disseminate information as to the services offered by the middle school counseling staff. Counselors should communicate effectively with elementary and senior high personnel relative to articulation among the various levels of schooling.
5. Curriculum development involves the counselor in collaboration with administrators, curriculum specialists, and teachers to integrate the thinking and feeling aspects of the educational process.
6. Child growth and development expertise is essential to the work of the middle school counselor.

Bohlinger (1976) has presented five components of a middle school guidance program: the counselor component, the advisor component, the teacher-student interaction component, the peer counseling component, and the exploratory component. The counselor component involves the coordination of numerous services such as testing, referral, and parent education services. The advisor component provides each student with assistance in solving personal problems and in enhancing his developing self-concept. The teacher-student interaction component emphasizes the opportunity each teacher has to help students improve their self-concepts and to assess individual student progress. Peer counseling assists students in talking over problems with peers and encourages them to rely on peers for support and advice. The exploratory program component provides opportunities for students to explore and develop new interests through mini-courses and to improve their decision making skills.

The degree to which these components may be implemented at the local school level is dependent on various factors including how well informed the school faculty, administration, and parents are. These components, however, serve as a valid model to follow in the development of a productive guidance program for emerging adolescents.

How May the Teacher and Counselor Work Together?

Counselors and teachers must work together as a team, sharing ideas related to the learning process and student behavior. How may the counselor help the teacher to reach each child? The counselor may demonstrate specific counseling techniques that help the teacher view each child as a unique individual. Counselors can best help teachers by being supportive, by making practical suggestions for promoting humaneness, by encouraging the consideration of human relations in teaching, and by facilitating the teacher's efforts to use productive guidance functions in the classroom setting.

Teachers help the counselor in many ways. Five important ones are as follows:

1. Because teachers study students daily, they become aware of differences in their behavior patterns as well as unusual behavior. The teacher may therefore serve as a resource person for the counselor, providing insight into students' daily patterns.
2. Teachers identify and refer students with special needs to counselors for observation and testing. Without the sensitive identification skills of teachers, counselors might overlook some of the students who need help.
3. Teachers and counselors work together in the administration of tests and in the interpretation of test data.
4. Teachers and counselors cooperatively reinforce each student's efforts to develop effective study habits and problem-solving skills.

5. Teachers and counselors work with students, administrators, and parents to develop student conduct codes that are fair and productive to all concerned.

Counselors do not have all the answers for teachers in dealing with students, nor is it their role to tell teachers how to teach or what to teach. Instead, their role is to help teachers better understand students and student behavior. When teachers and counselors work together, the student is the winner.

Developmental Group Counseling

A developmental group counseling approach, with all students participating, has been suggested as the best method of assisting the emerging adolescent to give systematic consideration to his or her developing personal self. Lewis (1976) has described a program used in two middle schools in North Carolina that includes a scheduled daily class or program of human development. The program involves the use of developmental counseling, which is a change from crisis counseling to a preventive, positive approach, involving the counselor in an acting rather than reacting role. The three-pronged program includes:

1. *Parent groups.* Each small group of parents comes weekly to one of six sessions, each lasting approximately one and one-half hours. Parents' discussions in these sessions focus on problems affecting their children. An active parent volunteer organization has emerged from this process.
2. *Teacher groups.* While parent volunteers direct the regular classes, teachers of the same grade or with similar problems get together in sessions once or twice each month. The counselor assists the teachers in clarifying problems and exploring solutions.
3. *Student groups.* All students are scheduled to attend once a week by classroom groups a counseling-learning session in the counseling center. Some of the objectives for the group sessions are identifying the purposes for school rules, identifying important qualities of friendship, and exploring student interests and aptitudes as they relate to the world of work.

One year after the implementation of the group counseling program, a significant decrease in unacceptable behaviors and referrals to social agencies was noted. The developmental counseling approach had a positive impact on students, teachers, and parents. It became evident through group counseling that the counselor's major commitment should not be to getting to know the student but instead to getting the student to learn how to know the ever-changing self.

Principals' Perceptions of Their Counselors

Counselors and administrators have not always agreed on what the significant functions of the counselor should be. What does the counselor do? What should the counselor do? Pappas and Miller (1976) reported the results of a Michigan survey involving the principals of 120 middle schools. The principal in each school was requested to rate specific counselor functions in relation to their existing programs. The ten highest-ranking counselor functions, as reported by principals with organized guidance programs, are presented in Figure 10.1.

Role of the Principal

The principal establishes the climate, sets the pace, and assumes leadership for the organization and administration of guidance services as an integral part of the total school program. As the administrator of the school, he should assume leadership in establishing a policy that provides

Figure 10.1

Highest Ranking Counselor Functions as Viewed by Middle School Principals

Ranking	*Percentage*	*Functions*
1	98	Providing individual counseling for students with personal concerns.
2	96	Communicating the guidance program and its services to students.
3	89	Organizing and administering the guidance program.
4	86	Identifying students in need of special services.
5	84	Communicating the guidance program to school personnel.
7	80	Interpreting standardized test results to students and parents.
7	80	Communicating the guidance program to parents.
7	80	Identifying and making referrals to other school personnel.
9	77	Consulting with teachers on developmental needs and concerns.
10	75	Conducting small groups counseling for selected student population.

SOURCE: Reprinted from John G. Pappas and Gary M. Miller, "Middle School Principals' Perceptions of Their Counselors," *Middle School Journal,* December 1976, p. 6. Used with permission.

for the development of an effective guidance program. Specifically, the principal should:

1. Provide time in the school's daily schedule for students to take advantage of both group guidance processes and individual counseling
2. Clarify the roles of the professional staff as they relate to guidance
3. Help keep the superintendent, school board, and the community informed of the progress and needs of the guidance program
4. Provide appropriate physical facilities, equipment, and materials for guidance services
5. Provide all professional personnel with an opportunity to participate in guidance activities through in-service education

In cooperation with teachers and guidance personnel, the principal may insure that each student benefits from a well-designed guidance program. It is the "principal" of the thing that makes the difference!

Summary

The middle school guidance program should provide essential services designed to facilitate the maximum growth and development of each student. The major functions of the middle school counselor include counseling, consultation, coordination, communication, curricular development, and child growth and development.

An effective middle school guidance program should focus on three major programs: preventive, remedial, and developmental. The preventive program emphasizes early identification and treatment of adjustment and learning problems. The remedial program is designed to identify and remedy problems through an intensive counseling approach. The developmental program is a guidance service that helps all students to understand the growth and development factors that accompany their age and to develop abilities to cope with their world.

REFERENCES

Bohlinger, Tom. "Middle School Guidance: Problems in Comprehensiveness and Implementation." *Middle School Journal*, December 1976, p. 7.

Hill, George E., and Luckey, Eleanore Braun. *Guidance for Children in Elementary Schools*. New York: Appleton-Century-Crofts, 1969.

Keat, Donald B. *Fundamentals of Child Counseling.* Boston: Houghton Mifflin, 1974.

Lewis, Katheryn Coor. "Developmental Group Counseling for Transteens." *Middle School Journal,* 16 December 1976, pp. 4–5.

Pappas, John G., and Miller, Gary M. "Middle School Principals' Perceptions of Their Counselors." *Middle School Journal,* 22 December 1976, p. 6.

Learning Module

Values Clarification in the Middle School

Directions

This learning module is designed to help you learn how to use values clarification in your classroom. Start by completing the pretest. Review your pretest performance with your instructor who will aid you in the selection of appropriate objectives. Complete those activities, both required and optional, that will assist you in obtaining your objectives. Upon completion of this module, take the posttest in order to measure what you have learned.

Pretest

1. Define values clarification and discuss its role in the classroom.
2. Compare and contrast the use of values clarification with the use of moralizing as ways of teaching values.
3. Write an example of a values-clarification lesson or strategy that could be used in the classroom.

Check

Review your pretest results with your instructor who will guide you in selecting the proper objectives.

Behavioral Objectives

Select only those objectives that are appropriate for you.

1. List and discuss four specific aims of values clarification.
2. Explain the value of implementing values clarification methods in the classroom and in the total education process.
3. Discuss several current methods and/or approaches that are frequently used in teaching values clarification in the schools.
4. List the seven subprocesses of valuing set forth by Raths and give an example of each.
5. Plan and implement a values clarification lesson with a group of middle school students.

6. Compare and contrast five different instruments that may be used in the evaluation of a values education program.

Required Activities

1. Interview a middle school classroom teacher on the topic, "Using Values Clarification in the Classroom." (2) (3)
2. Read Chapters 2, 7, 8, and 9 in *Personalizing Education—Values Clarification and Beyond* by Leland W. Howe and Mary Martha Howe (New York: Hart Publishing Co., 1975). (2)
3. Visit the middle school classroom of a teacher identified by the principal or your supervisor as one who makes excellent use of values clarification. Discuss your observations with the teacher. (1) (2)
4. Read Chapter 1 in *Values Clarification—A Handbook of Practical Strategies for Teachers and Students* by Sidney B. Simon, Leland W. Howe and Howard Kirschenbaum (New York: Hart Publishing Co., 1972). (2) (3) (4)
5. Practice planning various types of values clarification strategies and indicate how you would integrate them into a total educational program. (5)
6. Review examples of values clarification strategies and lessons. See *Personalizing Education—Values Clarification and Beyond* (Howe and Howe 1975). This book contains over 100 strategies and worksheets. Also see *Values Clarification—A Handbook of Practical Strategies for Teachers and Students* (Simon, Howe, and Kirschenbaum 1972). This book contains seventy-nine strategies. (5)
7. Plan, implement, and evaluate a values clarification strategy in an actual classroom setting. (5) (6)
8. Read the article by Sally J. Allen and Dale I. Foreman, "Can Values Be Evaluated?" in *Today's Education* 66 (1977):66–67. (6)
9. Read the article by Sidney B. Simon and Polly de Sherbinin, "Values Clarification: It Can Start Gently and Grow Deep," in *Phi Delta Kappan* 56 (1975):679–83. (1) (3)
10. Plan and implement a lesson for a middle school classroom using as a basis the filmstrip *Values for Teenagers—The Choice Is Yours* (Part 2, "Decisions", Guidance Association, Harcourt, Brace and World.) (5)

Optional Activities

Select activities from the Required Activities list that you have not already completed.

Posttest

Prepare a written report in which you discuss the importance of a good value education program, including in the report those things you have learned in relation to the objectives that you completed. Design a sample lesson or strategy that may be used in a middle school classroom.

Chapter 11

Teaching Exceptional Learners

The history of education for exceptional children, told from their point of view, is a story of neglect, denial, and rejection. For centuries it was believed that handicapped children could not be taught and were not able to learn at all. Beginning in the early nineteenth century, however, special education programs were started by such pioneers as Maria Montessori (1870–1952), who began the study and training of mentally deficient children; Samuel G. Howe (1801–1876), who started the first school for the blind in the United States and worked with a blind and deaf student named Laura Bridgeman to prove that the blind could be educated; Thomas H. Gallaudet (1787–1851), who organized the first school for the deaf in this country; and Louis Braille (1809–1852), who invented the Braille system of writing.

The first institutions designed for blind, deaf, and retarded children were residential. Residential schools are still in use today, primarily for the most significantly handicapped children.

Prior to 1940, formal programs designed to train teachers for the handicapped were instituted in a few universities, including Wayne University and the Teachers College of Columbia University. Most programs, however, were developed after 1940 with the education of exceptional learners receiving significant attention after World War II. In 1948, 442,000 children were enrolled in special education programs, and in 1963, 1,666,000 were enrolled. According to Bureau of Education for the Handicapped data, 2,857,551 handicapped children were receiving special education services by 1972. In addition, from 1948 to 1973, the number of training programs for teachers of the handicapped in the United States increased from 77 to more than 400.

In recent years, schools and other institutions have been urged by organized groups of parents to provide services for exceptional children, and these groups have turned to the courts as a means of promoting public action. Based on recent court decisions, the concepts of "right of education," "right to treatment," "due process," and "least restricted environment," have become influential in guiding program development for exceptional learners. The PARC (Pennsylvania Association for Retarded Children) case (1971) and related cases have established the principle that all children, no matter how seriously handicapped they may be, have the *right to education*. Stated differently, the public schools have the obligation to provide appropriate education for all children. The term *least restricted environment* refers to the view by the court that handicapped children should be placed in regular classroom settings whenever possible.

The Council for Exceptional Children, in a policy statement made in 1971, defined the principle of education for all children as

> the philosophical premise of democracy that every person is valuable in his own right and should be afforded equal opportunities to develop his full potential. Thus, no democratic society should deny educational opportunities to any child, regardless of his potentialities for making a contribution to society.

The education of exceptional children is currently receiving significant emphasis, especially in the area of mainstreaming. Let's look at this concept in detail.

Mainstreaming: Help for Exceptional Learners

For many years, public school programs for exceptional children were organized separately from regular education. An effort toward linking special education and regular education, however, emerged during the 1970's. This effort is based on the concept of mainstreaming. The following statement, which was presented by the Council for Exceptional Children in 1973, describes the concept of mainstreaming:

> Special education must provide an administrative organization that facilitates, for exceptional children, achievement of the same educational goals as those that are pursued by other children. This purpose can be achieved through structures that are sufficiently compatible with those employed by regular education to insure easy, unbroken passage of children across regular-special education administrative lines for

whatever periods of time may be necessary, and sufficiently flexible to adjust quickly to changing task demands and child-growth needs....

Under suitable conditions, education within the mainstream can provide the optimal opportunity for many exceptional children. Consequently, the system for the delivery of special education must enable the incorporation of special help and opportunities for them in mainstream settings whenever such an approach is feasible. Children should spend only as much time outside regular classroom settings as is necessary to control learning variables that are critical to the achievement of specified learning goals.

As a prospective middle school teacher, you will want to explore the changing patterns in the education of exceptional learners. Some of the implications of mainstreaming are:

1. Regular classroom teachers need to become more highly trained and more resourceful in meeting the needs of exceptional learners.
2. Special education personnel need to change roles, moving from functioning in an isolated, restrictive environment to working more closely with regular teachers in the classroom setting.
3. Teachers need to develop a diagnostic capacity in the classroom, placing less emphasis on traditional methods of referring children to specialists.
4. Teachers need to employ less simple categorization of and prediction for children, using instead more explicit planning and evaluation of instruction.

The concept of mainstreaming has varied interpretations and applications. Caster (1975) has presented a workable definition of what mainstreaming is as well as what it is not.

Mainstreaming is:

Providing the most appropriate education for each child in the least restrictive setting,

Looking at the educational needs of children instead of clinical or diagnostic labels such as mentally handicapped, learning disabled, physically handicapped, hearing impaired, or gifted,

Looking for and creating alternatives that will help general educators serve children with learning or adjustment problems in the regular setting. Some approaches being used to achieve this are consulting teachers, methods and materials specialists, itinerant teachers, and resource room teachers,

Uniting the skills of general education and special education so that all children may have equal educational opportunity.

> Mainstreaming is not:
> Wholesale return of all exceptional children in special classes to regular class,
> Permitting children with special needs to remain in regular classrooms without the support services they need,
> Ignoring the need of some children for a more specialized program than can be provided in the general educational setting,
> Less costly than serving children in special self-contained classrooms. (p. 174)

Helping Exceptional Learners in the Regular Classroom

Who is the exceptional child? How does the regular classroom teacher help the exceptional child? What are learning disabilities? There has been considerable research directed toward the identification of exceptionalities. There has also been considerable confusion concerning which students are truly learning disabled and therefore should receive specialized instruction in specialized settings. Ames (1977) emphasizes that we should differentiate the underachievers who, with an adopted curriculum, could remain in the mainstream of education from the *specific* learning disabled who need special education. The specific learning disabled require special education beyond the scope of the regular classroom teacher.

We must avoid the tendency of many educators to quickly label a child who is demonstrating academic difficulties as having a learning disability. Kirk and Elkins (1975) reviewed 3,000 children who were enrolled in twenty-one states in Child Service Demonstration Centers for Learning Disabilities. The researchers found that most of the children were moderate underachievers in reading, spelling, and arithmetic. Kirk and Elkins concluded that the 3,000 children they studied needed help, but help in the form of a curriculum better adapted to their needs. Many children who are supposedly learning disabled children are simply academically overplaced, potentially good students who are suffering because their academic diet does not fit their maturity level. Children who have IQs in the 80 to 90 range also suffer when they are pressured to perform at a level far above their own. In addition, there is a tremendous number of children suffering from minor physical difficulties such as allergies, poor hearing, poor vision, or overweight who could be helped if the true cause of their difficulties were not hidden under the deceptive label of learning disability. It is possible that perhaps half the children classified as LD and taught and treated accordingly actually suffer from one of these correctable medical difficulties. What then are "learning disabilities?" Hallahan and Kauffman (1976) state that this term is of utmost use if it is treated as a concept rather than as a category. Learning disabilities are learning problems in one or more areas of development or ability. We must utilize better diagnostic procedures before placing any child in a special learning disability class.

As a prospective middle school teacher, you must be able to work with exceptional children in the regular classroom. The treatment of children who have specialized learning problems of development or ability lies beyond the scope of the regular classroom teacher's expertise. Therefore, the emphasis here is to concentrate on those students you are likely to encounter in regular classroom settings.

In order to clarify what is meant by the expression *exceptional child,* we need to examine some major categories that can be used in describing exceptional children. Shuster and Ploghoft (1977) have presented the following three categories:

1. Mentally exceptional children
2. Physically handicapped children
3. Maladjusted children

The *mentally exceptional* category includes the retarded, the gifted, and children with special abilities or disabilities. The intelligence ratings of retarded children may range from very low to somewhat below average. Children with IQs of less than 60 are generally not included in school rosters; attention in the regular classroom is given instead to slow learners and borderline cases. An IQ of 130 or more is generally indicative of a gifted child. There are also children who have special abilities in selected areas. For example, an average child with an IQ of 100 may possess outstanding ability in music but rather average ability in reading or mathematics. In contrast, a child who is described as "normal" or "average" may have a mental disability in one specific category such as numerical reasoning. *Physically handicapped* children may be described in terms of sensory defects that may be auditory or visual in nature, motor defects that are orthopedically crippling, or a combination of physical defects. (One of the most prevalent types of physical defects are speech defects.) *Maladjusted* children are those that have social adjustment problems or emotional difficulties.

Let's now look at some different types of exceptionalities and ways in which the teacher may help learners with these exceptionalities.

Teaching the Gifted Learner

There are various ways of defining or describing a gifted learner. Essentially, the gifted child is one whose measured intelligence exceeds an intelligence quotient of 130, but often a gifted child may have an IQ of 150, 170, or above. Gifted children have one characteristic in common—superior cognitive abilities. These include outstanding ability in academic attainment, in creative performance, and in the generation of original ideas. Gifted children constitute about 5 to 7 percent of the average population, a much larger group than is usually realized. There are variations and degrees of giftedness, but, according to Shuster and Ploghoft, each gifted child possesses some of the following characteristics:

—usually a high academic status that is substantiated by results of standardized tests
—high verbal comprehension; superior vocabulary
—personality ratings are superior or above average
—stability in school attendance and punctuality
—physical and emotional maturity and stability are marked
—social maturity is generally advanced and good
—the ability for objective self-analysis is present
—a high production rate is evidenced with a corresponding quality in the productions
—the mind is active, inquiring, curious, and alert, original, imaginative
—powers of observation are keen, coupled with an ability to make critical analysis
—creativity is evident in many, varied ways
—a longer attention span, deeper insights, and powers of discrimination mean abilities to generalize and come to conclusions
—adjustment to change is readily, easily made
—the ability to preserve and accept responsibility is present
—a sense of humor is noticeable
—reading is a pleasure and occupies 2 to 3 hours average a day in history, folk tales, biographies, science, poetry and drama[1]

Schoolwork in general is commonly geared to students of average or just-above average ability, and the school setting often fails to take into account the personal qualities that accompany high intelligence and frequently result in unique requirements. Gifted children of all racial, economic, social, and cultural backgrounds have unusual needs, not as much because they are highly intelligent as because they are different from their contemporaries for whom most school and community programs are planned. Unless their schoolwork is stimulating and challenging, gifted children may attempt to retain a kind of self-respect by rejecting it.

Teachers should be as much concerned with youngsters who have

1. From Albert H. Shuster and Milton E. Ploghoft, *The Emerging Elementary Curriculum* (Columbus, Ohio: Charles E. Merrill Publishing Co., 1977), pp. 368–69. Used with permission.

leadership ability, creativity, and artistic talent as they are with youngsters with high IQs. A survey conducted by the recent White House Task Force on The Gifted asked some of the country's most successful citizens what factor had made the biggest difference in their lives. Almost every one of them gave the same answer to that question: Somewhere along the line, a teacher, a coach, or some respected adult had built an intimate one-to-one relationship with them, encouraging them to believe in themselves as human beings and to try new things. This one-to-one relationship is critically important in the development of the gifted or talented child!

One of the major difficulties in planning programs for the gifted is that the term *program* suggests an administrative arrangement for a group with similar attributes. Gifted children, however, tend to be intensely individualistic and versatile. Their interests, knowledge, and abilities are wide-ranging; they constitute a heterogeneous population of learners. The need for flexible planning and innovation in dealing with these learners is acute. According to authorities in the field of education for the gifted, the neglect of gifted students in the United States has been appalling. Approximately two million gifted students receive little attention beyond that which they receive in the regular school program.

Varied organizational arrangements should be used in working with gifted learners. Payne (1974) has identified three major administrative approaches that can be used for educationally placing and serving the gifted: enrichment, ability grouping, and acceleration. Enrichment involves increasing the quality and/or quantity of gifted children's experiences while they remain in the same class with their peers. Ability grouping separates the gifted into special classes and/or ability tracks. Acceleration refers to moving gifted learners through school programs faster or beginning their educational experience earlier. Research studies indicate that acceleration may be the most effective administrative approach.

There are a number of ways that a teacher may help the gifted learner in a regular classroom setting.

1. *Laboratory method of inquiry.* The gifted learner needs opportunities to engage in in-depth problem solving and experimentation. Flexible time should be provided for inquiry related to specific interests.
2. *Release time.* The learner may be allowed a certain portion of the day to engage in activities that are relevant to her particular educational program.
3. *Subgroup formation.* Selected gifted learners may form a subgroup within the regular class in order to explore a particular interest or topic.

4. *Special assignment.* The gifted child may be assigned special projects and reports that require in-depth study and exploration.
5. *Pupil-team learning.* Two or more students may be assigned to work together and to evaluate one another on established criteria.
6. *Extracurricular or extraschool activities.* Students may participate in a variety of activities including school clubs, special classes, field experiences, and community action projects.
7. *Tutoring opportunities.* The gifted child may gain valuable learning experience through tutoring another child in a specific subject or skill area.
8. *Special lecturers.* Scientists, artists, authors, and related resource personnel may provide gifted students with guest lectures on a variety of topics of special interest.
9. *Special subject matter units.* Special units for brighter children, reflecting higher level mental processes and advanced methodologies, can be introduced into the regular classroom.
10. *Supplemental learning kits.* Science kits, programmed learning materials, and a variety of media may be used to provide a more enriched educational diet for gifted students.
11. *Classroom theatre and related cultural experiences.* Many opportunities should be provided for students to experiment with live performances of their own and to observe the performance of others.
12. *Musical experiences.* The gifted child should be given varied opportunities to share and develop musical talent within the regular classroom setting.

Gifted students also require specialized guidance services. The unique characteristics of gifted students may result in the development of emotional, social, and motivational problems. Figure 11.1 presents some of these characteristics and related problems.

Teachers and counselors should work cooperatively in designing counseling strategies appropriate for gifted learners. Since your own way of teaching must be your own invention, no one can present you with a prescription for working with gifted learners. It is possible, however, for you to derive from research and experience some principles and approaches that have considerable potential for success with gifted learners. It is your task to weave them into successful learning experiences for individual students.

Teaching the Learning Disabled Child

The term *learning disabilities* came into existence in the late 1950's when material regarding exceptionalities began appearing in professional jour-

Figure 11.1

Characteristics of the Gifted and Concomitant Problems

Characteristic of Gifted	*Possible Concomitant Problems*
Critically observes, analyzes; skepticism	Teachers feel threatened; peers censure, try to silence discussion; argumentative
Emphatic response to people; leadership capabilities	Rejection causes intense reaction (e.g., depression or hostility); may seek to dominate rather than understand others
Independent perception of self and world	Egotism; alienation; odd interpretations of reality
Individuality; search for freedom	Isolation; loneliness; combativeness; lack of socially acceptable identities
Intellectual interests; intellectuality	Snobbishness; limited recreational outlets; boring to others; intolerance for lesser capabilities
Intense application of energies; persistence	Obsession with problem tasks; compulsivity; obstinacy; overwork toward physical exhaustion
Large vocabulary; verbal facility; high retention	Inappropriate level of communication; dominates class discussion; unnecessary elaboration
Originality	Perceived as "off the subject" by others; impracticality; frequent breaks with tradition; radicalism
Scholarliness	Anti-intellectual reaction by peers; stuffiness; pedantry
Theoretical-aesthetic mixture of interests	Simulated masculinity in girls, effeminacy in boys; overemphasis of importance of science; escape into art forms
Thinks with logical systems; objective, rational problem solving	Disregard for intuitive, retrospective or subjective solutions; rejection of belief, revelation as methods
Unusual, esoteric subjects appealing	Eccentricity; gullibility; mysticism; attraction to untried avant-garde causes

SOURCE: From Joseph Rice, *The Gifted: Developing Total Talent,* 1970. Courtesy of Charles C. Thomas, Publisher, Springfield, Illinois.

nals. Historically, the "slow learner," or the "learning disabled child," has been viewed as an imposition placed on teachers as a result of the philosophy that literacy and education should be universal. In recent years, however, significant effort has been directed toward identification and remediation of learning disabilities. A national organization, the Association for Children with Learning Disabilities (ACLD), has played a significant role in promoting legislation at the state and federal levels to provide professional training and research in the field of learning disabilities. Public Law 91–230, which became law in 1970, set forth a definition of the term *learning disability* and authorized grants for research and training for professional personnel in learning disabilities, model programs, and promotion of new methods and technologies for working with the learning disabled child. Public Law 91–230 defines learning disabilities as meaning

> those children who have a disorder in one or more of the basic psychological processes involved with understanding or in using language, spoken or written, which may manifest itself in imperfect ability to listen, think, speak, read, write, spell, or do mathematical calculations. Such disorders include such conditions as perceptual handicaps, brain injury, minimal brain damage, dyslexia, and developmental aphasia. Such a term does not include children who have learning problems which are primarily a result of visual, hearing, or motor handicaps, of mental retardation, of emotional disturbance, or of environmental disadvantage.

This definition is acceptable for administrative use; however, it is not directly applicable to the classroom situation. Gleason and Haring (1974) have provided a flexible, practical definition of learning disability as a behavioral deficit almost always associated with academic performance that can be remedied by precise, individualized instructional programming.

This definition can serve as a guide for positive action in a classroom situation. It focuses on students' observable behavior but does not rule out their having possible dysfunctions or disorders in perceptual or underlying psychological processes.

Diagnosing Learning Disabilities

The diagnosis of learning disabilities has been primarily divided into two types of procedures: (1) those used for determining if a specific disability exists or will be likely to develop, and (2) those used for planning remedial strategies to help the child overcome a disability. Diagnosis of learning disabilities is usually done by a specialist in a child development center or special resource setting. The specialist prepares an educational prescription that is to be implemented by the classroom teacher. One of the problems with this process is that in many cases the regular classroom teacher is unprepared to apply the prescription effectively. Another problem is that many teachers believe that formal testing is less reliable than sophisticated teacher observation in finding potential problems.

A coverage of all the various diagnostic-assessment procedures that have been developed for use with students having learning disabilities is far beyond the scope of this section. Attention to one experimental approach that has had a significant impact in the field, however, should prove helpful. Lovitt (1967) reported a four-phase assessment program that includes (1) baseline assessment, (2) assessment of behavioral components, (3) assessment based on referral, and (4) generalization of assessment.

In phase one, baseline assessment, the initial procedure is to analyze the behavior of the child upon entering the classroom situation. The technique used for this purpose involves the administration of a series of *probes,* short segments of academic skill materials that measure skill performance areas and reveal specific academic deficiencies. Probes are usually administered over a three- to five-day period, providing teachers with a continuous assessment of a child's behavior until a stable measure of performance can be obtained.

Phase two, assessment of behavioral components, involves a careful examination of the components that maintain and modify behavior. These components may include stimulus materials presented to children, the rate and duration of their response behaviors, the rate of teacher interaction with them, and the influence of environmental factors on their behavior. Phase three involves the referring agent, either the teacher or parent, as well as the child since the possibility exists that the managerial and programming skills of the adult may be as inadequate as the learning skills of the child. The teacher and the diagnostician should collaborate in the diagnostic-prescriptive process directed toward remediation of the child's learning difficulties. Phase four emphasizes the application of the diagnostic-prescriptive data to the teaching procedures used in the regular classroom environment. The diagnostician and classroom teacher must continue to work closely together, continuing to collect data and to make adjustments in procedure and materials as the child's behavior changes.

Application of Levitt's work and related approaches has greatly influenced the development of the concept that the resource room teacher functions as a bridge between the regular classroom teacher and the specialist. This involves training regular classroom teachers as special education resource teachers who manage the academic and social behavior problems of moderately handicapped children in the school but also act as resource teachers to regular classroom teachers.

Middle School Resource Room Model

There are many emerging models that can be used for organizing educational programs for exceptional learners in the regular school setting. Paroz, Siegenthaler, and Tatum (1977) have described a model for developing a resource room in a middle school setting.[2] The primary intent of this resource room program is to meet the special needs of children within the regular school setting. Children participating in this type of program receive individual instruction in the resource room for part of the day but spend the majority of their time in a regular classroom. It is critical that the resource room teacher build a climate of trust and implement straightforward diagnostic-prescriptive strategies. The focus of the resource room program should be on an instructional diet that is helpful, nonthreatening, and constructive.

The school faculty and administration should establish priorities for student placement in the program. A formal review committee should assist in the screening and placement process. The teacher operating a resource room should complete the following:

1. Arrange for vision and hearing testing for each student.
2. Develop a schedule for each child in conjunction with her classroom teachers.
3. Prepare a list for teachers and administrators of the students who are receiving resource room assistance.
4. Design a folder for each child. Included in the folder should be (*a*) written forms for referral, parent's permission to test, permission for placement, and permission for any involved special agency to release information to the school; (*b*) testing data; (*c*) dated classroom observations and dated conference information; (*d*) dated samples of the child's work; (*e*) objectives for the child; (*f*) other pertinent information.
5. Order any additional materials and supplies necessary for meeting student needs.
6. Discuss resource room placement with each child.
7. Establish and maintain a cooperative relationship with each regular classroom teacher. Cooperation is critical in helping the student reintegrate in the regular classroom. If possible, conduct joint parent-teacher conferences.

---

2. Adapted from JoAnne Paroz, Loy Sue Siegenthaler, and Verlene H. Tatum, "A Model for a Middle School Resource Room," *Journal of Learning Disabilities* 10 (1977): 1–9.

8. Continually reevaluate student progress. Keep the program flexible.
9. Develop in-service experiences that facilitate the regular faculty members' understanding and appreciation of the resource room concept.
10. If possible, arrange to visit the student at work in his regular classroom setting.

The resource room may serve as a bridge or transitional vehicle toward mainstreaming or as an adjunct to it. The actual model employed should be adapted to local needs.

Instructional Strategies for the Learning Disabled Child

Providing a positive, reinforcing experience for learning disabled or academically handicapped children in the regular classroom requires systematic planning and the application of learning principles that are based on the scientific analysis of behavior. The most effective instructional strategy for helping the learning disabled student in the middle school is one built on this seven-step approach outlined by Dunn (1973):

> 1. A general area of behavior is designated for attention;
> 2. the child is studied to find out what behaviors he has acquired along this dimension;
> 3. specific behavioral objectives which need to be acquired next are identified;
> 4. the relative effectiveness of different motivators and reinforcers are investigated;
> 5. the most effective modalities for reaching the child are identified;
> 6. the needed materials for implementing the instructional program are assembled; and
> 7. the best strategy is determined to teach the child the identified specific behaviors. (p. 163)

Several systematic instructional programs have been developed and tested both in laboratory classrooms and in regular classrooms. The primary focus of these programs is precise daily measurement, the underlying assumption being that an individual child functions best in a program that is tailored to his or her unique characteristics. There are basically four steps used in applying precise daily measurement to the classroom setting: (1) identifying those behaviors that promote or interfere with learning; (2) developing a lesson plan designed to structure teaching conditions; and (3) actual charting/recording of pupil performance data to determine student progress and effectiveness of the teaching plan.

Two particularly effective general procedures that can be used are *drill* and *practice*. Drill involves rote repetition, and practice refers to the actual performance of a task. In mastering skills through drill and practice, children are naturally reinforced by being able to apply skills either for fun or for obtaining new information.

No matter how good their elementary school program has been in helping learning disabled children, it is unrealistic to expect the majority of them to return to the educational mainstream at the middle school level and proceed satisfactorily. This presents a serious quandary for middle school educators. In terms of school organization, since segregated special classes are illegal, a flexible grouping plan within an ungraded setting would be feasible. Such a plan should give significant attention to life adjustment skills, home management, and career education in addition to remediation in specific skill areas.

Working with the Physically Handicapped Child

The teacher needs to help the physically handicapped child acquire a common-sense viewpoint in regard to himself or herself and to life itself. Let's look briefly at some specific physical exceptionalities and at some ways teachers can help students affected by them.

Hearing and Speech Impairments

It is almost impossible to determine the exact number of hearing- and speech-impaired children in the United States. Screening programs conducted by public schools indicate that approximately 5 percent of public school children may have mild to moderate hearing impairment, although many of these children may not recognize the nature of their problem. The classroom teacher should be aware of the following indications of possible hearing impairment:

1. Tilting the head at an angle
2. Listless or inattentive behavior
3. Poor oral reading ability
4. Failure to respond to questions
5. Peculiar voice quality, high-pitched or flat in nature
6. Tendency to watch the face of a speaker with considerably greater attention than is normal
7. Discharge from the ear
8. Excessive earaches
9. Undue muscular tension when listening
10. Louder speech than would be indicated by the situation (L'Abate, 1975)

The teacher should be familiar with some informal screening procedures. The "watch test" consists of holding a watch to either side of the student's head at increasing and decreasing distances. Without looking at the watch, the student should indicate when she first hears it. A "whisper test" may be administered in a similar manner. The teacher should stand at a distance from the student, whispering very quietly in an attempt to find out if the student has a hearing problem. A more sophisticated screening device is the audiometer, which is utilized by speech specialists in identifying hearing impairment. If a child has a hearing impairment, referral should be made to specialized professionals.

Integration into Regular Classes

Students with mild hearing loss may spend the majority of the day in regular classes, receiving additional help through speech therapy or tutoring. Students who have a more significant hearing impairment, however, may spend only part of the school day in a regular classroom setting. Lowenbraun and Scroggs (1974) have provided the following guidelines for facilitating the integration of the hearing-impaired child:[3]

1. Seat the child where he can see your lip movements easily. Avoid seating him facing bright lights or windows.
2. Speak naturally and particularly avoid speaking too loudly if the child has a hearing aid.
3. Avoid visual distractions such as excessive make-up and jewelry.
4. Do not stand with your back to a window or bright light source. This throws your face in shadow and makes speechreading difficult.
5. Try not to move around the room while speaking or talk while writing on the board. If possible, use an overhead projector, which allows you to speak and write while maintaining eye contact with the children.
6. During class discussions encourage the hearing-impaired child to face the speaker. Allow him to move around the room if necessary to obtain a better view.
7. In some cases, a manual interpreter will be assigned to the child. Allow the interpreter and child to select the most favorable seating arrangements. Manual interpreters should interpret to the child everything said in the classroom as precisely as possible. They may be asked to interpret the child's oral or signed responses to the teacher and class. Interpreters are not tutors or classroom aides, but rather professional personnel who are facilitators of classroom communication.

---

3. From Sheila Lowenbraun and Carolyn Scroggs, *Behavior of Exceptional Children: An Introduction to Special Education* (Columbus, Ohio: Charles E. Merrill Publishing Co., 1974), pp. 516–17. Used with permission.

8. When possible, write assignments and directions on the blackboard or distribute mimeographed directions to the class. If assignments are given orally, a hearing student may be asked to take notes for the hearing-impaired child.
9. Ask the handicapped child to repeat or explain class material to make sure he has understood it. Embarrassed by their handicap, many hearing-impaired children learn to nod affirmatively when asked if they understand, even though they may not have assimilated the instructions at all.
10. If the child has a hearing aid, familiarize yourself with its operation and ask the child or his special teacher to demonstrate it to the class. The child should assume responsibility for the care of his aid.
11. Maintain close contact with the other professional personnel who have responsibility for the child's education. If possible, exchange visits with the special class teacher or therapist on a regular visit to observe the child in his other educational settings.

To help you learn more about the hearing-impaired child, you may seek assistance from the following organizations and agencies:

The Alexander Graham Bell Association for the Deaf, Inc., founded in 1890 by Bell himself, maintains its headquarters at 1537 35th Street, N.W., Washington, D.C. 20007. Its official publication is *The Volta Review,* an important source of information to teachers, parents, and the hearing-impaired.

The American Speech and Hearing Association is a professional organization whose membership is confined to speech and language pathologists, audiologists, and educators of the deaf. Its headquarters are at 9030 Old Georgetown Road, Washington, D.C. 20014, and its journals include *The Journal of Speech and Hearing Disorders, The Journal of Speech and Research,* and *ASHA.*

The Conference of Executives of American Schools for the Deaf, founded in 1868, is an organization for administrative heads of schools for the deaf. The Conference publishes a monthly periodical, *American Annals of the Deaf,* which is edited at Gallaudet College, Washington, D.C. 20002. *The Convention of American Instructors of the Deaf* is an affiliate organization of the Conference and represents the one professional organization that is comprised solely of teachers of the deaf.

The National Association of Hearing and Speech Agencies (NAHSA), formerly the American Hearing Society, is a voluntary health agency that has been in existence since 1919. Its headquarters are at 919 18th Street, N.W., Washington, D.C. 20006. Hearing and speech conservation and distribution to the public of information regarding the needs of the communicatively handicapped are its primary objectives. A monthly publication, *Hearing and Speech News,* is published by NAHSA.

Major Speech Impairments

The primary speech impairments may be grouped into three categories: articulatory disorders, voice problems, and stuttering. An articulation problem could be either a speech problem or a language problem or a combination of the two. Articulation errors involve substitutions, omissions, and distortions within the sound system of the language. Some of the minor, or *functional,* articulation problems, such as omissions or substitutions, may be treated by the classroom teacher. The more severe, or *organic,* articulation problems, including structural deficiencies in the mouth and palate, cerebral palsy, and disrupted sensory systems, are very complex and require treatment by specialists in medicine, dentistry, speech pathology, and physical therapy (McLean 1974).

The human voice production mechanism is vulnerable to all types of abuse. Common voice disorders include inappropriate intensity, pitch, and/or quality of the vocal tone produced. These more common voice disorders should be treated by a specialist, because medical treatment and voice therapy are most often required.

Stuttering is one of the most frustrating speech impairments. Speech pathologists generally classify stuttering using two categories. *Primary* stuttering involves simple repetitions of syllables and related mechanical mistakes in speech reproduction. *Secondary* stuttering includes additional nonspeech behaviors such as gasping, eye blinking, and facial contortions. Although there is considerable difference of opinion among researchers regarding the causes of stuttering, it is generally considered to be learned or acquired behavior. The following are suggestions for helping the stuttering student in the middle school setting:

1. Give the student time to say what she has to say.
2. Create a warm, accepting, noncritical classroom climate.
3. Find out whether the stutterer enjoys singing since many stutterers can sing without stuttering.
4. Many stutterers can read aloud fluently. Encourage the student who has this ability to utilize it in class.
5. Avoid any kind of "label" or other possible cause of embarrassment for the stutterer.
6. Work closely with both the stutterer and the speech clinician.

Helping children with hearing or speech impairments requires tremendous patience and understanding. Experiencing success, however, can be extremely rewarding for both teacher and child.

Helping Children with Visual Impairment

Although almost every person can anticipate having some degree of visual impairment during his or her lifetime, the visually impaired represent one of the smallest groups of handicapped children. The age group under twenty accounts for only approximately 10 percent of the legally blind persons in the United States.

The identification of children with some type of visual impairment, however, often depends on careful observation by the classroom teacher. The National Society for the Prevention of Blindness (1972) lists these signs of eye trouble in children:

Behavior:
- — Rubs eyes excessively
- — Shuts or covers one eye, tilts head or thrusts head forward
- — Has difficulty in reading or in other work requiring close use of the eyes
- — Blinks more than usual or is irritable when doing close work
- — Holds books close to eyes
- — Is unable to see distant things clearly
- — Squints eyelids together or frowns

Appearance:
- — Crossed eyes
- — Red-rimmed, encrusted, or swollen eyelids
- — Inflamed or watery eyes
- — Recurring styes

Complaints:
- — Eyes itch, burn, or feel scratchy
- — Cannot see well
- — Dizziness, headaches, or nausea following close eye work
- — Blurred or double vision

Severe visual impairment is usually identified in preschool or elementary school years; however, mild or moderate impairment may not be identified until sometime during the middle school years. In the school-age population, an estimated 1 in 500 has a visual impairment of sufficient severity to require some remedial measures.

Visually impaired children include those with no useful vision who must be educated through sensory modalities other than vision, those who have some useful vision but whose major avenue of learning may still be through senses other than vision, and those who can learn through visual media even though their vision is severely impaired. Visually impaired children may be educated in residential or local public school programs. In recent years, the number of public school programs has accelerated at such a rapid rate that more visually handicapped children are in public school classes than in residential schools.

To help you learn more about the visually impaired, please consult the following:

The American Printing House for the Blind, 1839 Frankfort Avenue, Louisville, Kentucky 40206, assists in the education of the visually impaired through the production and dissemination of educational materials. It has received federal assistance in financing its operation.

The American Foundation for the Blind, 44 East 23rd Street, New York, New York 10010, is a privately supported service and research agency that provides consultant services, library loan services, and publications. It also sponsors institutes, workshops, and conferences related to teacher training and research and provides support to the National Accreditation Council for Agencies Serving the Blind and Visually Handicapped.

The National Society for the Prevention of Blindness, Inc., 79 Madison Avenue, New York, New York 10016, is a privately supported agency that concentrates on public education and research. Its publications include *Sightsaving Review,* the *Wise Owl,* and a variety of pamphlets, films, and related materials.

Recording for the Blind, 205 East 58th Street, New York, New York 10022, is a national voluntary organization that provides recorded educational material to visually impaired students. Its national library service provides books in all major fields of study.

The Association for Education of the Visually Handicapped, 711 14th Street, N.W., Washington, D.C. 20005, is a professional organization of educators of children with visual impairment. The organization publishes a journal, *Education of the Visually Handicapped,* and a newsletter, "Fountainhead."

Abused or "Battered" Children

The abuse and neglect of children in the United States is a serious national health problem. Although there are no accurate statistics on the incidence of child abuse and neglect, conservative estimates range anywhere between 60,000 and 500,000 cases a year. Schmitt (1975) emphasized that teachers are in a strategic position for detecting the abused child and reporting the case to the local child protective agency for evaluation and treatment. The Child Abuse Prevention and Treatment Act (P.L. 93-247) was signed into law on January 31, 1974, providing a national focus for all children in the United States needing protection. The law created a National Center on Child Abuse and Neglect for the purpose of administering grants to the states and to public and private agencies for programs concerned with child abuse. The Act defined child abuse and neglect as "physical or mental injury, sexual abuse, negligent treatment or maltreatment of a child under the age of eighteen by a person who is responsible for the child's welfare under circumstances which indicate that the child's health or welfare is harmed or threatened."

Schmitt (1975) has presented several important ideas concerning what teachers need to know about child abuse and neglect. According to Schmitt, the major types of abuse and neglect are (1) nutritional deprivation or deliberate underfeeding by parents, (2) drug abuse, (3) medical care neglect, (4) sexual abuse, (5) emotional abuse, (6) severe hygiene neglect, and (7) educational neglect. If a teacher suspects the presence of child abuse, the teacher and/or counselor should talk with the child in a private setting. The consultation of a school nurse and school physician can also be extremely helpful. Once a diagnosis of child abuse is certain, the child's case should be reported to the child protective agency in the child's county of residence. (In all fifty states, the person making this report is protected against any type of liability suit.)

There is a significant need for all schools to have a standard operating policy regarding child abuse. Proper intervention is critical because it can break the vicious cycle of children growing up to become tomorrow's child batterers or violent society members. It may also save a child's life. For a comprehensive treatment of this problem see the November/December 1975 issue of *Childhood Education*. Extensive bibliographic material is provided in that issue.

Some educators are reluctant to report suspected abuse or neglect for a number of reasons, such as fear of having to deal with hostile parents, no assurance of support within the school, or fear of legal entanglement. Each school should provide in-service education experiences for school personnel, in order to help them understand the dynamics of abuse and neglect and the medical, legal, and therapeutic interventions and to decrease their hesitancy to report suspected abuse and neglect.

School-Age Pregnancies—School-Age Parents

Even though the number of births in the United States has been declining overall since 1960, the number of births to women under the age of twenty has steadily risen (Braen and Forbush 1975). Further, the number of out-of-wedlock births in the under-twenty group has shown a steady increase in recent years. It is therefore especially important for the school to meet its obligation to provide effective family life education to help each student better understand the responsibilities of parenthood. In the past, many schools have contributed to the problem (1) by not providing information that could have helped students prevent pregnancy; (2) by refusing the pregnant student the right to an education through practices and policies that often had no foundation in law; (3) by discouraging the young mother from returning to school; or (4) by imposing unreasonable waiting periods between delivery and the time of her return.

Fortunately, as a result of an increased national awareness of the problem, family life education has emerged as an integral part of the school curriculum. The home, the church, the community, and the schools all have important roles to play if quality family life programs are to be made available to the youth. Program planning must be a cooperative venture that utilizes all appropriate community agencies and resources. Hopefully, quality programs in parenting and family life education will help to significantly reduce the number of school-age parents. Nonetheless, there will always be some youngsters who will become parents either by purpose or by indifference or ignorance. These individuals need help through infant care and parenting skills training and appropriate medical services. Young mothers should be encouraged to continue their education and to develop a productive and meaningful life-style that can provide them with opportunities for self-fulfillment.

Helping Maladjusted Children

Middle school learners are products of our contemporary society, which is characterized by excessive stress, the decay of the work ethic, the revelation of corruption and deceit in high and low places, the breakdown of the family unit, and the emergence of varied life styles. It is not surprising that many of these learners are maladjusted or disturbed. Morse (1975) has described the maladjusted or disturbed pupil as follows:

> From the educational stance, a disturbed pupil is one who is persistently unable to cope with reasonable school environment even though expectations are geared to his age and potential. His behavior may be (1) so disrupting as to violate the rights and educational growth of his peers, or he may (2) manifest social withdrawal, and/or (3) require an inordinate amount and depth of teacher involvement for control and emotional support. (p. 556)

For regular classroom teaching purposes, the maladjusted child can be considered to be one who has difficulty relating to the classroom group or has some emotional, social, or personal problem that interferes with total adjustment. Any excess display of the following may be symptomatic: nervousness, crying, fighting, daydreaming, withdrawing, or truancy. The varied anxieties and fears of different individuals are difficult to identify and interpret. In each case, the teacher should seek professional assistance.

Vacc and Kirst (1977) reported research findings regarding three major questions: Do emotionally disturbed children placed in a special program show greater benefit than emotionally disturbed children remaining in regular classes? What effect have emotionally disturbed children had on nonhandicapped children in the same classroom? How have teachers in regular classrooms provided for and managed emotionally disturbed children? The research reported lends support to the conclusion that special classes have not produced results significantly better than regular classes. Very little experimental research has been conducted on the implications of mainstreaming emotionally disturbed children into the regular classroom and the effect on children who are not handicapped. Research studies indicate, however, that exposure does influence a child's attitude toward handicapped children. A generalization may therefore be made that the more contact a nonhandicapped child has with an emotionally disturbed child, the more positive the attitude will be toward the emotionally disturbed child. Finally, with regard to the effect of mainstreaming on regular classroom teachers and their programs, the research is too limited to be conclusive. It does appear, however, that the more training the teacher has regarding exceptional children, the more positive her attitudes toward the exceptional child will become.

Summary

In recent years, education of exceptional children has begun to receive significant emphasis. The movement toward teaching the exceptional child in the regular classroom setting has raised a number of significant questions that have implications for middle school teaching. Does the exceptional child receive better instruction in a regular classroom setting or in a special classroom setting? What are the skills and attitudes that a regular classroom teacher must possess in order to teach the exceptional child? What effect do handicapped children have on nonhandicapped children in the same classroom? What are the pros and cons of mainstreaming? What teaching techniques and materials are most productive in helping specific exceptional learners? How can the middle school best serve the needs of all learners, exceptional and nonexceptional? The answers to these and related questions should be an objective of inquiry for you as you continue your preparation for middle school teaching.

The exceptional child deserves the best education possible. You should look forward to the challenge and the joy of becoming a part of the enterprise of providing that education.

REFERENCES

Ames, Louise Bates. "Learning Disabilities: Time to Check Our Roadmaps?" *Journal of Learning Disabilities* 10(1977):328–30.

Braen, Bernard B., and Forbush, Janet Bell. "School-Age Parenthood, A National Overview." *Journal of School Health* 45(1975):256–62.

Caster, Jerry. "Share Our Specialty: What Is Mainstreaming?" *Exceptional Children* 42(1975):174.

The Council for Exceptional Children. *Basic Commitments and Responsibilities to Exceptional Children.* Reston, Va.: Council for Exceptional Children, 1971.

"The Organization and Administration of Special Education—ACEC Policy Statement." Arlington, Va.: The Council for Exceptional Children, 1973.

Dunn, Lloyd M. "Children with Mild General Learning Disabilities." In *Exceptional Children in the Schools,* edited by Lloyd M. Dunn. New York: Holt, Rinehart and Winston. 1973.

Ferro, Frank. "Protecting Children: The National Center on Child Abuse and Neglect." *Childhood Education* 52(1975):63–66.

Gleason, George, and Haring, Norris. "Learning Disabilities." In *Behavior of Exceptional Children: An Introduction to Special Education,* edited by Norris G. Haring. Columbus, Ohio: Charles E. Merrill Publishing Co., 1974.

Hallahan, D., and Kauffman, J. *Introduction to Learning Disabilities.* Englewood Cliffs, N.J.: Prentice-Hall, 1976.

Kirk, S. A., and Elkins, J. "Learning Disabilities: Characteristics of Children Enrolled in the Child Service Demonstration Centers." *Journal of Learning Disabilities* 8(1975):630–47.

L'Abate, Luciano, and Curtis, Leonard T. *Teaching the Exceptional Child.* Philadelphia: W. B. Saunders Co., 1975.

Lovitt, T. C. "Assessment of Children with Learning Disabilities." *Exceptional Children* 34(1967):223–42.

Lowenbraun, Sheila, and Scroggs, Carolyn. "Hearing Impaired." In *Behavior of Exceptional Children: An Introduction to Special Education,* edited by Norris G. Haring. Columbus, Ohio: Charles E. Merrill Publishing Co., 1974.

McLean, James. "Language Development and Communication Disorders." In *Behavior of Exceptional Children: An Introduction to Special Education,* edited by Norris G. Haring. Columbus, Ohio: Charles E. Merrill Publishing Co., 1974.

Morse, William C. "The Education of Socially Maladjusted and Emotionally Disturbed Children." In *Education of Exceptional Children and Youth,* edited by William M. Cruickshank and G. Orville Johnson. Third Edition. Englewood Cliffs, N.J.: Prentice-Hall, 1975.

Paroz, JoAnne; Siegenthaler, Loy Sue; and Tatum, Verlene H. "A Model for a Middle School Resource Room." *Journal of Learning Disabilities* 10(1977):1–9.

Payne, James. "The Gifted." In *Behavior of Exceptional Children: An Introduction to Special Education,* edited by Norris G. Haring. Columbus, Ohio: Charles E. Merrill Publishing Co., 1974.

Rice, Joseph. *The Gifted: Developing Total Talent.* Springfield, Ill.: Charles C. Thomas, 1970.

Schmitt, Barton D. "What Teachers Need to Know About Child Abuse and Neglect." *Childhood Education,* November/December 1975, pp. 58–62.

Shuster, Albert H., and Ploghoft, Milton E. *The Emerging Elementary Curriculum.* Third Edition. Columbus, Ohio: Charles E. Merrill Publishing Co., 1977.

"Teaching About Vision." New York: National Society for the Prevention of Blindness, 1972.

Vacc, Nicholas A., and Kirst, Nancy. "Emotionally Disturbed Children and Regular Classroom Teachers." *The Elementary School Journal* 77(1977):309–17.

Learning Module

Mainstreaming: Helping the Exceptional Learner

Directions

This learning module is designed to help you learn more about mainstreaming and how you can help exceptional learners. Begin by taking the pretest. Review your pretest with your instructor who will assist you in selecting the appropriate objectives. Complete the required and selected optional activities that will assist you in reaching your objectives. Take the posttest to see what you have learned.

Pretest

1. Briefly summarize the concept of mainstreaming.
2. List some of the advantages of mainstreaming.
3. List some of the disadvantages of mainstreaming.

Check

Review your pretest performance with your instructor.

Behavioral Objectives

1. List the steps you would take upon learning that you are to have an exceptional learner in your class.
2. Discuss the advantages of including exceptional learners in regular classes.
3. Discuss the disadvantages of including exceptional learners in regular classes.
4. Explain the law concerning placing exceptional learners in regular classes.
5. List individuals, groups, and services who can aid the teacher of exceptional learners.

Required Activities

(The numbers in parentheses correlate with corresponding objectives.)

1. Read Chapter 1, "Perspectives on Teaching Special Children," in

Teaching Special Children by Norris Haring and Richard Schiefelbusch (New York: McGraw-Hill, 1976). (1)

2. Interview a special resource teacher who works with exceptional children and their classroom teachers. (5)
3. Read "Mainstreaming, Who?" by Theresa Monaco in *Science and Children,* March 1976, p. 11. (2)
4. Read "Confrontation: Special Education Placement and the Law" in *Special Education in Transition* by Reginald Jones and Donald MacMillan (Boston: Allyn and Bacon, 1974). (4)
5. Visit a classroom in which the teacher has worked effectively with exceptional learners and observe her teaching procedures. Discuss the pros and cons of mainstreaming. (1) (2) (3)
6. Read "Preventive Mainstreaming: Impact of a Supportive Services Program on Pupils" by Robert P. Cantrell and Mary L. Cantrell in *Exceptional Children* 42(1976):381–85. (5)
7. Read Mary Brown's "Is Mainstreaming Fair to Kids?" in *Instructor,* March 1976, pp. 38–40. (3)
8. Interview the parent of an exceptional learner who has been in the mainstream situation. (2) (3)
9. Read Chapter 3, "The Teacher's Role," in *Special Education in the Regular Classroom* by Ernest Siegel (New York: The John Day Co., 1969). (1)
10. Interview a school psychologist and discuss the effects of mainstreaming she has observed. (5)
11. Read "Law and the Handicapped" by Larry Molloy in *Science and Children,* March 1976, pp. 7–10. (4)

Optional Activities

Select activities from the Required Activities list that you have not completed.

Posttest

Prepare a written report presenting what you have learned in relation to the objectives that you have completed. Your report should not exceed five double-spaced, typewritten pages. It should be evaluated by your instructor.

Chapter 12

Career Exploration

Career exploration is a process for helping students relate educational experiences to the world of work. An effective career exploration program in the middle school should allow each student to:

1. Focus on better understanding of self and on the process of self-concept development.
2. Better understand the great variety of occupations in society.
3. Appreciate the dignity of work and develop positive attitudes toward work.
4. Receive informed guidance, counseling, and instruction regarding occupational choice.
5. Interrelate academic preparation with career application.

Career education is not specific job training. Specific job training, or vocational education, may be pursued at the secondary or postsecondary school level. It is instead a normal part of the educational process, which provides middle school students with activities and programs designed to help them develop a greater awareness of the knowledge and skills required for living, learning, and working. These activities and programs should provide students with opportunities for expanding their occupational horizons, developing positive attitudes and appropriate work habits, and exploring the world of work, and they should provide them with information on which they can act in making career choices. The relationship between reading and employment, arithmetic and income, and writing and self-respect should be reinforced. The student should also learn to become a better interpreter of technology and a more discriminating consumer. A fundamental concept of career education is that all educational experiences including curriculum, instruction, and counseling should be geared to students' preparation for economic independence and their gaining an appreciation for the dignity of work.

Middle school students are interested in and acquire a large amount of information about work, including differences in occupations, their own personal preferences regarding occupations, and social rankings of occupations. In fact, many students are formulating concepts about the world of work without the assistance of accurate or systematic experiences in career exploration. Ginzberg et al. (1951) have asserted that occupational choice is a developmental process; it is not a single decision but a series of decisions made over a period of time. They have labeled the developmental stages of the choice process as *fantasy* (ages 1–11), *tentative* (11–17), and *realistic* (beyond 17). The fantasy stage is the "I want to be" stage. During the tentative stage, the child begins to assess her personal strengths and weaknesses in relation to a career. During the realistic stage, the individual decides what she can realistically become on the basis of her personal strengths and weaknesses. The rate at which young people move through these stages varies.

Super et al. (1963) have emphasized the significance of the exploratory period of preadolescence and adolescence for helping the student formulate ideas regarding different fields and levels of work, for developing concepts relating to career choices, and for making commitments to a type of education or training leading toward some partially specified occupation. Super's extensive research documented the fact that boys in the ninth grade and later who were able to make the best career choices in regard to their personal abilities and opportunities were those who had earlier received the greatest exposure to valid experiences about the world of work (1969).

Bugg (1969) states the function of career exploration in the elementary and middle school years as follows:

> The job of the grade school is to focus the attention of children on the general meaning of work in our society and to assist them in gaining information about the total range of occupational opportunities. Considerable attention should be given to the individual differences of both workers and jobs and to the varying rewards (intrinsic and extrinsic), social and physical characteristics, and general training requirements of different occupational fields. The elementary school program should attempt to communicate to children why people work; why all honest work is important; the fact that someday they, too, will work; and the impact that a job is likely to have on them personally. (p. 180)

Career Exploration Models

The Wisconsin Model for Integrating Career Development into Local Curriculum described by Drier (1971) includes the following fourteen concepts that are developed during grades K–9:

1. An understanding and acceptance of self is important throughout life.
2. Persons need to be recognized as having dignity and worth.
3. Occupations exist for a purpose.
4. There is a wide variety of careers that may be classified in several ways.
5. Work means different things to different people.
6. Education and work are interrelated.
7. Individuals differ in their interests, abilities, attitudes and values.
8. Occupational supply and demand have an impact on career planning.
9. Job specialization creates interdependency.
10. Environment and individual potential interact to influence career development.
11. Occupations and life styles are interrelated.
12. Individuals can learn to perform adequately in a variety of occupations.
13. Career development requires a continuous and sequential series of choices.
14. Various groups and institutions influence the nature and structure of work.

Bottoms (1972) has reviewed the Career Development Education Program in Georgia and has found it to be composed of eight elements:

1. Orientation—assisting individuals to learn about their own characteristics and environment in relation to a career
2. Exploration—providing opportunities for students to test themselves regarding their career self-concept through "hands-on experiences" in simulated or direct work settings
3. Interdisciplinary Education—"unifying the natural relationship between the academic and career curriculum so that selected concepts and skills of general and academic courses are required through career oriented activities, problems and tasks" (p. 24)
4. Career Curriculum—focusing on job preparation skills related to specific career areas as well as on math, science, communication skills, and social science in the context of these career areas
5. Intensive Short-term Specialized Courses—preparing students for employment in a single skilled occupation through specialized training lasting less than a year
6. Outreach—reaching, through personal contact, unemployed youth and adults for the purpose of returning them to an appropriate learning situation or to part-time training and related employment

7. Job Placement and Follow-through—assisting youth and adults to enter, adjust to, and satisfactorily progress in a job
8. Guidance and Counseling—helping students personalize the meaning of career-related experiences at each educational level, assisting them at key decision-making points, and helping prescribe their educational treatment

Guidance and counseling, interdisciplinary education, orientation, and exploration are particularly appropriate to the middle school.

Middle school learners need accurate information concerning occupations. Hoppock (1957) presented eight reasons why young people need this information:

1. To increase the child's feelings of security.
2. To encourage the natural curiosity of young children.
3. To extend the occupational horizons of the child.
4. To encourage wholesome attitudes toward all useful work.
5. To begin developing a desirable approach to the process of occupational choice.
6. To help students who are dropping out of school and going to work.
7. To help students who face a choice between different high schools or high school programs.
8. To show children who really need money how they can get it without stealing. (p. 344)

The World of Work

What is work? According to the U.S. Department of Labor, it's 23,000 different occupations. What work do people do and why do they do it? Let's listen as five different people talk about their jobs.[1]

> *Richard, Forester:* I'm a forest consultant. We're constantly concerned with natural beauty, with wildlife, with protecting the soil . . . producing the timber needs of the country . . . using the resource wisely and preserving it for the future. The main advantage to this particular job to me is working in the out-of-doors. I just really would feel very confined in a city environment where I had to report to an office every day and do paperwork and whatnot. The starting salary in this particular state is about $8,000 a year for a graduate forester with no experience, just a college education. (I could make more money working for private in-

1. Adapted from DISCOVERY: A CAREER EDUCATION PROGRAM. Copyright © 1973 Scholastic Magazines, Inc. Reprinted by permission.

dustry, but) I make my own schedule . . . and that is just as important as money.

Penny, Bank Teller: My job is to serve the people who come into checking—get their balances or, you know, help them with problems in their accounts and everything, but it's definitely routine, definitely. The only thing that adds any interest to the job is the people. . . . You get to meet quite a few. But the job itself, there's very little variation to it. There's no great responsibility to it. My pay . . . I get enough, but I would make a lot more as a secretary. As a teller you do have the chance of going to other departments in the bank and maybe you could become an officer, but most of the (bank) officers are men.

Sara, Marine Biologist: I am a marine biologist, and basically my job is culturing algae (growing algae in a laboratory, so it can be studied scientifically). It's the smallest part of the food chain in the open ocean. And it doesn't feed upon any other living creature. What it feeds upon is chemicals. . . . It's not pressured work at all. You can set your own pace, it's very flexible. It pays very little, but the freedom that you get with the job and being happy with your job means a lot to me also. So if it doesn't pay, you know, a lot, I don't mind if I enjoy what I'm doing. I like being independent of groups and doing special little projects on my own. . . . You get a lot of self-satisfaction, and you're able to publish (the results of your experiments), and you'll have other people reading your results and writing you. That's exciting also. You feel really important if someone calls you up and says they'd like your opinion on something else. It's the satisfaction that I want, otherwise I guess I'd go into something that would pay better.

George, Office Manager: As office manager, I am responsible for ordering office supplies such as pens, pencils, stationery, and the upkeep in maintenance which we provide, that is, my maintenance staff. . . . I make sure all the lights are working and things of that nature. The job with the money I get makes it possible that my wife and I can maybe have a baby, or have our own house, which we are planning, and we're able to make it on my salary . . . which is great. . . . I am interested in bettering myself. Since I've been working as an office manager—well, it's given me the type of lifestyle which is possible now, whereas before it was not. The reason I work is, because through the money I make, I can live the way I really want to live.

Maryanne, Social Worker: My job title is Social Case Worker with the Bureau of Children's Services; it's a state agency which handles a wide variety of services like driving people places, getting them to clinics, making clinic appointments, listening to people, helping them make decisions about their lives. I have people come in with problems, and essentially they just need someone to listen to their problems. They don't really need answers, because the answers are really somewhere within themselves. Often, we work with families who are having trouble with their teenagers, or teenagers who are having trouble with their parents. I get to be with a lot of different people during the day, which I like. Also, I am not confined indoors. I really like that . . . and this is a good way for me to earn money so I am able to do all the other things that I want to do. And I guess I just, I do it 'cause I like it. I guess it fulfills a need in myself, too. . . . I'm doing something for someone. . . . I get good feelings from it. And I think that every person has a responsibility—to do something.

Summary

The modern middle school should provide opportunities for students to develop a greater awareness of the world of work, assess their personal strengths and weaknesses, and receive informed guidance concerning occupational choices. Career education is not specific job training. Theoretically, career-based curriculum development is built on the principle that all areas of the curriculum should be taught with career implications.

There is a great need to help students interrelate schooling and nonschooling. Career exploration provides an excellent vehicle for accomplishing this purpose; it helps young people understand who they are and what they can become.

REFERENCES

Bottoms, G. "Career Development Education—Kindergarten through Post-Secondary and Adult Levels." Atlanta: Georgia Department of Education, Division of Adult and Vocational Education, 1972.

Bugg, C. A. "Implications of Some Major Theories of Career Choice for Elementary School Guidance Programs." *Elementary School Guidance and Counseling* 3(1969):180.

Drier, H. N., Jr., ed. "K—12 Guide for Integrating Career Development into Local Curriculum." Madison, Wis.: Wisconsin Department of Public Instruction, 1971.

Ginzberg, Eli; Ginzburg, S. W.; Axelrod, S.; and Herma, J. R. *Occupational Choice: An Approach to a General Theory*. New York: Columbia University Press, 1951.

Hoppock, R. W. *Occupational Information*. New York: McGraw-Hill, 1957.

Super, D. W. "The Natural History of a Study of Lives and Vocations." *Perspectives on Education* 2(1969):13–22.

Super, D. W.; Starishevsky, R.; Matlin, N.; and Jordoan, J. P. *Career Development: Self-Concept Theory*. New York: College Entrance Examination Board, 1963.

"What Is Work?" *Junior Scholastic*, 2 May 1974, pp. 4–5.

Learning Module

Career Education in the Middle School

Directions

This module is designed to help you become seriously involved in activities and/or programs that will expand, rather than limit, your knowledge of careers and career opportunities. It should help you to expand your occupational horizons, explore the world of work, and provide information you can use in helping students consider possible career choices. Begin by taking the pretest. Review your pretest with your instructor. Complete the required activities that will help you in reaching your objectives. You may choose to complete activities that were not required in order to broaden your understanding. After you have completed all activities, take the posttest to see what you have learned.

Pretest

1. Define career education and vocational education and contrast the two.
2. Why do you feel there is such a high level of emphasis on career education in the United States today?
3. Name the major goal of career education. What elements of career education should be most helpful in guiding an individual to make an appropriate career selection?
4. What is a "hands-on" activity?
5. According to Kenneth Hoyt, authority on career education, what are the five components of career education?
6. List some examples of strategies for interrelating career education and traditional academic subjects in a middle school classroom.
7. The scientific way for students to get to know themselves is to take vocational preference tests. Name two of the most commonly used tests.
8. List social factors that affect career education development.
9. Briefly discuss some selected career education programs at the national, regional, and local levels.

10. According to Sidney P. Marland, Commissioner of Education, what are five action steps for implementing career education?
11. Name five of the fifteen occupational clusters for career education.

Check

Discuss pretest results with your instructor.

Behavioral Objectives

Select those that are appropriate for you.
You should be able to:

1. Give reasons for including career education programs in the middle school.
2. Identify fifteen occupational clusters, the entry-level jobs in each cluster area, and the job skills required for each job.
3. Organize learning centers that can be used by individual students and groups of students to explore career interests.
4. Incorporate into classroom use career education ideas from the curriculum guide for teachers, *Bread and Butterflies* (Bloomington, Ind.: Agency for Instructional Television, 1974).
5. Recognizing the need for a differentiated curriculum for bright students, plan a hands-on middle school program.
6. Describe the hierarchy of jobs in the fifteen occupational clusters and identify educational and/or skill requirements for each level.
7. Name and discuss the elements of our private enterprise system as they relate to the occupational clusters.
8. Devise and/or locate materials designed to help students understand and appreciate the career implications of the subject matter they are studying.
9. Provide a wide variety of career education activities and experiences for middle school students.
10. Provide information on career clusters by inviting guest speakers who are professionals in these clusters to the classroom.
11. Convey an awareness and an appreciation for the importance of five different types of jobs that were unfamiliar to you at the beginning of this module.
12. Acquire experience with the concept of exchange programs between business, labor, and industry personnel and school personnel.
13. Become familiar with career development specialists and their role in helping the teacher.
14. Become aware of various programs the middle school has to offer students that relate to their interests, aptitudes, and possible occupational choices.

15. Recognize students who should consider career education and those who should not by becoming knowledgeable in the use of the different types of vocational tests.

Activities

Select those that correlate with your objectives (Required or Optional).

1. Interview a professional from any of the career clusters about which you need additional information. (1) (2) (5) (10) (12)
2. Write to the Awareness and Exploration Staff of the Department of Public Instruction, Room 551, Education Building, Raleigh, North Carolina, requesting a list of career education programs to be used in the middle school. (1)
3. Read "Why We Need Career Development" in *Bread and Butterflies* (Agency for Instructional Television, 1974). It describes societal changes in relation to career development concepts. (1) (4)
4. Visit the career awareness center at a local middle school. Then make a list of ten different items that would help you as a teacher in planning your own middle school career program. (1) (8) (9)
5. Study carefully pp. 7–12 in *Guide for Designing and Implementing a Career Exploration Program* (Raleigh: North Carolina Department of Public Instruction, 1972). (2) (6) (14)
6. Review pp. xiii-xv in *Hands on Career Exploration for Bright Students* (Raleigh: Division of Exceptional Children, North Carolina Department of Public Instruction, 1972). (2) (5) (8)
7. Select ten activities from *Bread and Butterflies* that you feel would be effective teaching tools.
8. Review the fifteen career clusters. If possible, visit several middle schools that have career awareness programs in operation. List media tools that could be used in learning centers to help students explore career interests. (2) (3) (6) (7) (8) (9) (14)
9. Make a bulletin board on *one* of the fifteen occupational clusters of career education. Include the entry-level jobs in your cluster and identify the job skills required for your job. (2)
10. Make a puppet that represents a specific career. Write a dialogue discussing the career to use with the puppet in a group presentation. (2) (6) (11)
11. Make a career collage using magazine pictures. (2) (6) (11)
12. Make clay models of people or objects related to five different careers. Have these fired in a kiln. (2) (6) (11)
13. Make a notebook containing information about the fifteen career clusters.
14. Write a career exploration unit for bright students on one of the fifteen clusters. Include some hands-on activities in your unit. (2) (5)

15. Design two instructional games that could be used in a learning center on career education. (3)
16. Plan a short-term activity and a long-term activity that could be used by middle school students to identify worthwhile career roles. Use *Bread and Butterflies* for a guide. (4) (9)
17. Study the "Agenda for the Television Utilization Workshop" in *Bread and Butterflies*. As a result of studying this workshop, you will know how to use the *Bread and Butterflies* materials and activities with children to achieve the learning goals of the program. In turn, you will be able to conduct workshops and other in-service activities for teachers in how to use *Bread and Butterflies* (4) (8) (9)
18. Research an occupation with which you are unfamiliar. Write a report on the education and training you would need for the job. (6)
19. Investigate the world of work: make a graph classifying ten different occupations according to projected demand by the year 1985. (6)
20. Complete the duplicating master, "Occupational Classification by Occupational Level," by filling in other hierarchy jobs under each reading. This duplicating master can be found in the back of the curriculum guide, *Career Education Program* (Boston: Houghton Mifflin Co., 1973). (6)
21. Make transparencies depicting the elements of our private enterprise system as they relate to the occupational system. (7)
22. Visit several places of employment, observing the employees at work. (7) (12) (14)
23. Interview a random sample of middle school pupils concerning their understanding and appreciation for the career awareness program in their school. Focus particularly on the career implications of the subject matter. (8) (9) (11) (14)
24. Prepare contrasting skits depicting both well done jobs and poorly done jobs. These should help students to develop an appreciation for the importance of all types of jobs. (9) (11)
25. Read p. 7 in "Internship Program for Individualizing Instruction," a pamphlet printed by the North Carolina Department of Public Instruction. It explains how teachers should set up activities in career education. (9)
26. In order to obtain commercially prepared material regarding career education, refer to p. 35 in "The Caldwell Experience, An Infusionary Approach to Career Information Program" (Lenoir, N.C.: Caldwell Career Education, 1974). (8) (9)
27. Make up a crossword puzzle using terms associated with different types of vocations. Duplicate this puzzle so that each teacher in the group will have a copy to use in the middle school. (9)
28. View one film from the series, "Career Development" (Imperial Film Co.), which contains interviews with actual workers. Education,

training, and responsibilities are stressed. Survey forms indicate areas of high career interest. (11) (13)

29. Get involved in working with industry on such things as BIE days or Junior Achievement Programs. School and industry personnel need to know each other better before they try to set up any ambitious exchange programs. (12)
30. Take two inventories: *a*) an inventory of persons with occupational skills who are willing and can be released for a time to teach in the schools; *b*) an inventory of school personnel possessing occupational skills (such as math skills or typing) that industry might need. Using both inventories, it should be possible to set up exchange programs benefiting both the school and local industry. (12)
31. Interview a career development specialist. Discuss and summarize information regarding the specialist's role in helping the classroom teacher. (13) (14)
32. Interview a middle school teacher. Discuss his or her approach to the teaching of career education. (14)
33. Survey a class of fourth, sixth, and eighth graders. Note the difference in the approaches to career education used by the teachers at the different grade levels. (14)
34. Read p. 3 in "The Function of the Career Development Specialist" in *Cobb County Occupational and Career Development Program,* published by the Cobb County District Schools, Marietta, Georgia. This explains what the specialist's function is in helping you as a teacher. (13)
35. Read pp. 75–77 in *Guide to Career Education* by Muriel Lederer (New York: Quadrangle—The New York Times Book Company, 1974). (15)
36. Visit a school psychologist, guidance counselor, or career awareness counselor for an interpretation of the different types of vocational tests used for advising students whether or not to consider career education. (15)
37. View the film, *Why People Have Special Jobs* (New York: Learning Corporation of America). This film could be used to introduce career education in the lower middle grades. It presents the basic economic concept of specialization of labor. Evaluate the film; decide whether or not you would use it in a middle school class.

Posttest

Prepare a written report on career education. The report should contain all you have learned from this unit of study. You should completely cover the objectives you have completed, summarizing your readings and research findings and stating your conclusions and their educational implications. The report should be typed and double-spaced. Each objective should be covered in approximately one page. The paper should be evaluated by your instructor.

Index

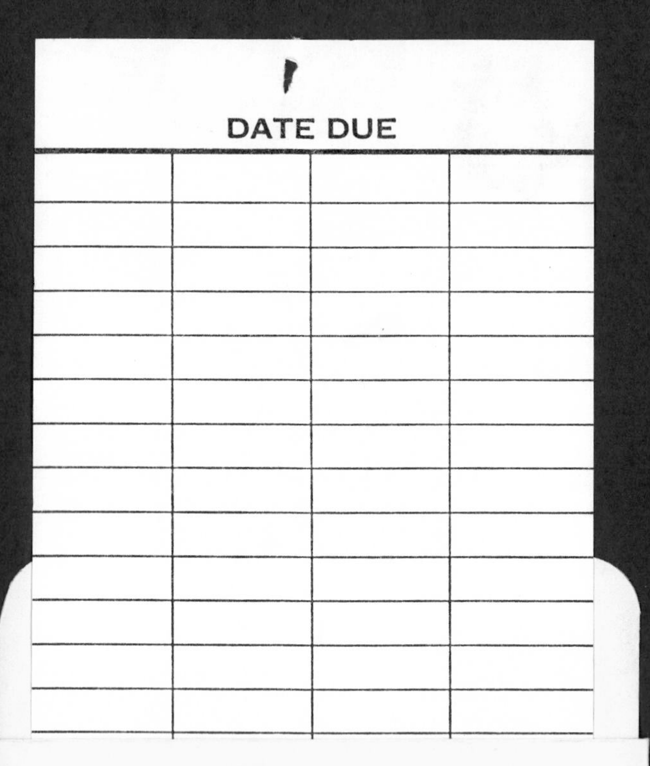
DATE DUE